THE BANK SHOT
AND OTHER GREAT ROBBERIES

The Bank Shot

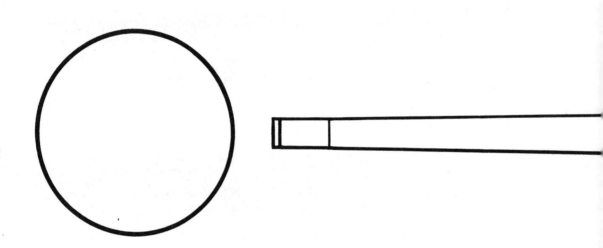

And Other Great Robberies

Minnesota Fats

WITH TOM FOX

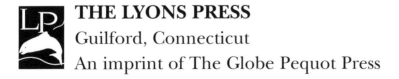

THE LYONS PRESS
Guilford, Connecticut
An imprint of The Globe Pequot Press

To The Dolls...
Eva-line and Karen

The Lyons Press is an imprint of The Globe Pequot Press.

10 9 8 7 6 5 4 3 2 1

Printed in the United States of America

ISBN 1-59228-701-8

Library of Congress Cataloging-in-Publication Data is available on file.

Introduction to the 2006 Edition

By R.A. Dyer

The drive between Evansville, Indiana, and Johnston City, Illinois runs approximately 120 miles. It is (or was) mostly two-lane flattop, mostly unlit; a roadway bordered on either side by farmland, mining pits, and empty spaces.

One might say that it was along this route, during a long drive in 1961, that Minnesota Fats was born. The literalists claim Fats's birth came in 1913, that he began competing in regional tournaments during the 1930s, and that he worked as a road player through the 1950s.

But that person was not yet Minnesota Fats.

I say America's most famous hustler was born during those frigid drives between Evansville and Johnston City—two hours there, two hours back—cooked up in the turns of phrase and imaginative lines of journalist Tom Fox. A long drive to be sure, and desolate, but one that gave Fox the pensive quiet he needed to conjure up one of the most iconic figures in American sport.

The Bank Shot and Other Great Robberies—written by Fox, but in an approximation of Fats' own words—emerged from the friendship of those two great storytellers. They met one night in Johnston City, became friends, and the eventual result was this book, a collection of tall tales that nonetheless stabs at the true nature of American pool.

The story of those drives goes like this: A phone tip came to Fox's desk at the *Evansville Courier and Journal*, where the journalist worked as a sports writer. The tipster told Fox there'd be pool played in Johnston City—pool like Fox had never seen. *Stacks of cash*, the tipster promised. *Giant wagers. High-rolling gamblers.* And remember, the call came in 1961, shortly after the Hollywood release of *The Hustler*—so interest in pool would have been high.

Tom loaded his station wagon with the following items: a notebook, at least two pens, a box of Viceroy cigarettes, four female co-workers, and maybe a six pack. As directed, Tom drove directly to the Cue Club, a cinder-box dive located not far from the edge of town. It had one pool table, no windows, a cement floor, and was the improbable headquarters for what was being billed as the first annual world one-pocket championship.

There, Fox discovered Rudolf Walter Wanderone, Jr.: fat, loud, and just then beginning to mount an outrageous claim to be the real-life model for Jackie Gleason's Minnesota Fats character. The crusty sportswriter immediately recognized the promise of the moment and so called an editor at *Sports Illustrated*. The result was "Hustler's Holiday in the Lion's Den," published on December 4, 1961.

During the entirety of the twentieth century, there was never a more important article written about American pocket billiards. As a result, a flood of network cameras, newspapermen and magazine writers all descended upon Johnston City. The piece rerouted Fox's newspaper career, forged his celebrity within the world of pocket billiards, and led to the writing of this book. But most importantly, it linked in the public's mind Rudolf Walter Wanderone (a hustler then going by the name New York Fats) with Gleason's character from the 20th Century Fox movie.

The Hustler had kick-started a pocket billiards craze in America. And thanks to the writer of this book, Rudolf Walter Wanderone would reside at its center.

Here's an excerpt from Fox's first *Sports Illustrated* article:

> The spokesman for the Loyal Fraternal Order of Pool Sharks was a roly-poly 250-pounder called New York Fats (Rudolf Wanderone) who thrives on high stakes and egotism but lives not in shadows nor speaks in whispers. Fat Man is short (5 feet 8), with a shock of brown hair, a 52-inch waist and a philosophy to fit all occasions. He announced that the Johnston City promotion drew 14 of the 'best one-pocket players in the world,' and added modestly that he was once the best of the best.
>
> "I was automatic champion one-pocket player of the world," Fat Man proclaimed. "They never had any tournaments. I always had to give great odds, most of the time two balls. The great champions would never play me. They dodged me at all times."
>
> The hustlers listened when the Fat Man talked. They laughed and poked fun at him. But when an outsider asked questions about the hustlers, they let the Fat Man do the talking. He's the shark's public relations man. . . . Fats is a hustler's hustler.

***

Fox claimed Algiers, Louisiana as his birthplace. He was one of ten children, all of whom grew up in a ten-room house located a block from the Mississippi River. As a kid, Tom took jobs acting and at the horse track. He spent World War II in the Coast Guard and then later went to work for the *New Orleans Item*, long considered a writer's paper.

As an adult, Fox stood 5'11" and had brown eyes and red hair, which he wore slicked back. He was a snappy dresser who wore tailored suits and white-tipped Florshein shoes—but no hat. Fox was also a well-known curmudgeon, although his was a crankiness mixed with rich humor. When Fox wrote that first article about Minnesota Fats, he would have been about forty years old.

Less than a year after "Hustler's Holiday" appeared in *Sports Illustrated*, Fox made the acquaintance of Mort Luby, Jr., the then-editor of the *National Bowling Journal and Billiards Revue*. Fox began writing articles for Luby— brash, colorful articles—that would change the course of the magazine. Because Fox's compelling storytelling typically muscled out the bowling pieces, in 1978 Mort Luby decided to spin off *Billiards Digest*, now considered by many to be the nation's premier cue sports magazine.

"I was the editor and publisher and one-man band," Luby recalled of those early days. "This was the early 1960s, and there was a tremendous slump in the bowling industry. The magazine wasn't doing too well, and so Tom Fox was a godsend to me. He wrote so well. Frequently, his stuff was the best stuff in the magazine. The man could really spin a tale. He was a terrific writer."

Amidst all this pool writing—and not long after his story appeared in *Sports Illustrated*—Fox left the Evansville paper for a gig at the much larger *Philadelphia Daily News*. It was after making that move that he wrote *The Bank Shot*, which World Publishing released in 1966. He sealed the deal by fortuitously bumping into the publishing firm's senior vice president outside a taxicab in New York City.

Research mostly consisted of Fox and his wife Karen holing up for weeks with Fatty and his then-wife, Evelyn. One can hardly imagine the impossibility of this situation: The pool hustler was so jarringly hyperactive, so prone to such terrifying attacks of ego, that he could rarely sit still long enough to finish his own sentences. "He would go into these rages," said Karen Fox. She said her husband compensated by also interviewing Evelyn Wanderone, Fats's wife. The result is this book, based on Fats's truncated tall tales of himself, but combined with his wife's more complete and truthful telling of events.

So make no mistake: confirmed lies and unverified boasts pile up one upon the other in *The Bank Shot*. One thing this book is not is Woodward and Bernstein journalism. But to quibble with the facts is to miss the point. Fats is important not despite these tall tales, but because of them. Above all, he was a storyteller.

Fox eventually went on to become a five-day-a-week columnist for the *Philadelphia Inquirer.* "During more than a quarter century in Philadelphia journalism, Mr. Fox had become a city institution, a writer whose observations and opinions were tracked by loyal readers who believed he talked straight and told it like it was," the newspaper noted in 1989.

Fox died in May of that year after suffering a stroke. He was sixty-four.

***

One more important note. To this day, the notion that Rudolf Wanderone was the real-life model for the Jackie Gleason character in *The Hustler* remains very much in dispute. Walter Tevis, the author of the book from which the movie was based, always denied it. "I made up Minnesota Fats as surely as Disney made up Donald Duck," he once wrote.

But it's also likely that Tevis would have come across Wanderone in the poolhalls that Tevis frequented before writing *The Hustler.* It's also true that pool legend Willie Mosconi at one point acknowledged the connection. The fictional Fats and the real-life Fats also resembled each other in some striking ways—look for details in the pages ahead.

But getting to the truth of this, the most famous and outrageous claim in the history of pocket billiards, is about as useful as trying to figure the riddle of the chicken and the egg. The important thing is what resulted from that claim. It helped usher in a resurgence of pool during the 1960s, it brought national attention to a sport then in decline, and it made the world a more magical place.

Without Tom Fox, without his note-taking and his interviews, none of this would ever have happened. Through the pages of *Sports Illustrated, Billiards Digest,* and this book, Fox pulled Fats from obscurity; he was the midwife to the legend. Thank goodness he acted on that late-night tip, loaded the station wagon, and brought his notebook.

Those were important drives indeed.

Foreword

As a pool player, I'm no threat. My typewriter-oriented fingers are incapable of forming a proper bridge. When I pretend to impart English to the cue ball, I more often scratch. My wife, Karen, frequently tops me in Nine Ball and I'm no match for my sure-shooting young nephews, Billy and David. My all-time high run is a robust six. Crouched over a table I have been compared (by the subject of this book) to a shoemaker. Yet, I'm fascinated by pool.

It wasn't always that way. Until five years ago, my experiences with cue stick in hand were limited to occasional Sunday-morning sessions of Rotation in the game room of a Knights of Columbus Home in New Orleans, where I grew up the third of ten children of a Little Theater director. I never put a foot in a poolroom as a boy. I was too busy taking elocution lessons. I thought a high run was 106 degrees of fever. I might have been totally deprived of the roguish charm of the poolroom, but one October evening in 1961 in Evansville, Indiana, where I was writing a sports column, I saw the movie *The Hustler,* starring Jackie Gleason and Paul Newman, and for me pool took on a new dimension. I was smitten with the rowdy patois of the poolroom and fascinated by the intrigue and charlatan-like psychology behind the making of a big money match. The social cell of the pool hall not only aroused my curiosity; the movie's power of suggestion affected me strongly for, like many other moviegoers, when I walked out of the theater I rushed for the nearest pool table.

Evansville is a gracious, slow-paced Ohio River town in southernmost Indiana, where the social mores dictate the shutting down of poolrooms by the witching hour. Fortunately, I remembered there was a coin-operated table at the Press Club and there I engaged another sportswriter, Michael

Lee Porter, from Terre Haute, Indiana, in a few beer games, which I promptly lost. As he ran balls with the consistency of a computer, Porter, soon to be dubbed "Terre Haute Squirrelly," informed me that something called the First Annual World's One Pocket Billiard Tournament with $5,000 in cash prizes was beginning that very week in Johnston City, Illinois, a gaunt little coal-mining center 90 miles west of Evansville. He said the tournament had attracted the leading pool hustlers in the country and perhaps there might be a good off-beat sports column there. The next evening a photographer named J. Bruce Baumann and I headed for Johnston City.

A fine, tantalizing drizzle was falling as Baumann and I drove cautiously down a lonely state road through a soupy fog rolling in from the abandoned strip mines outside of Johnston City. As the fog thickened, reducing visibility to almost naught, I wondered if we had made a wrong turn at the big highway intersection five miles back. Too, I gave some thought to the possibility that I might have been the victim of Porter's sometimes caustic humor, but suddenly from the mist there emerged a pink neon sign that spelled out: "Cue Club—Members Only." Baumann smiled and said, "This must be the place."

Johnston City (population 3900) seemed an unlikely place for an international competition of any kind; the tournament prize pot of $5,000 left something to be desired as world championship stakes go; and the Cue Club, a dimly lit, newly completed cinder-block building consisting of crudely constructed built-in bleachers surrounding a lone pool table, was hardly the atmosphere for championship pocket billiards traditionally contested by the ad man-ale man-club man type in black tie and tux. But inside the Cue Club, located on the rear of the parking lot of The Show Bar, a night club, my misgivings were arrested by the tournament sponsor, George Jansco.

Jansco, a short, square-shouldered, smiling man of Hungarian descent, said he was conducting his promotion "hustler style" and the only tuxedo in Johnston City would be found on the bandleader in The Show Bar. He blushed when he said, yes, it was true that he had played minor league baseball with Dizzy Dean and he blushed again when he confessed he had once operated a race-horse book in Evansville. "That," he said, "was all B.K.—Before Kefauver." Then, with the swift, gracious moves of a maitre d', he weaved through the crowded club, beckoning me to "come—I've got a surprise for you." At the far end of the room, he stopped, whispered to a roly-poly, thick-haired, fiftyish-looking man, turned to me and said, "Meet Minnesota Fats."

Rudolf Walter Wanderone, Jr., nee Minnesota Fats, nee New York Fats, was an impressive sight. His hands were clasped behind his back, his broad shoulders were propped against the wall and his ample waist, which he said measured 52 inches, projected outward, accentuating his massiveness. He said he wasn't playing a tournament match that night, but he was waiting, just waiting. As an appleknocker on a brand-new beat, I asked what I thought was a cautious question. "For Godot?" I suggested. "Godot?" he bellowed. "I never heard of no pool player named Godot. I'm waiting for some serious money action in the back room. In fact, I've been waiting in this very same spot for three days and three nights, but none of these mooches will play me for a grape. I'm eating myself broke. There's not a bum in the place who would play me for peanut brittle." There was a flowing meter to the monologue, a poetry I had never heard in the raw before. He was the outrageous overstatement in an era of the subtle understatement. He was brash. He was irreverent. He was verbose. And, he said, after 40 years of "dodging publicity like it was poison," he would hold still for a column.

I told him I knew nothing about pool. But as the self-appointed spokesman for the Loyal Order of Pool Sharks, he said he would "tell me the way it was." For a starter, he said he was the greatest pool hustler who ever lived and at one time he was the greatest pool player alive, adding that for money he was still the best there was. He explained that the tournament was "strictly a filage," a word I had not heard before, and that the 14 participants couldn't care less about the $5,000 in cash prizes. The tip off, he said, was the name of the game—One Pocket. He said he had "practically invented the game," a variant of simple pool calling for each player to sink his shots in one corner pocket. He said the game was the most difficult of all forms of pocket billiards to perfect, that it was played only by the masters and reminded me, again, that he was the master of them all. He cited the lack of action he was getting as proof of his claim.

He explained that money breeds money in the hustler's world and the high stakes players in the tournament had not come to Johnston City to play for trophies but to hustle one another at One Pocket. He said that Georgie Jansco and his brother, Paulie (sometimes called Joey), who had guaranteed the prize money, were "the biggist hustlers of them all—don't think Georgie built this $25,000 joint (the Cue Club) because he's philanthropic. By the time this is over, Georgie won't have to file income tax. He'll just call Washington and ask, 'What do you need, boys?' "

Later that night, Fat Man okayed me with the doorman guarding the entrance to the back room and there he introduced me to the nonpareils of the pool hustling art: Weenie Beanie of Baltimore, Boston Shorty, Knoxville Bear and Tugboat Whaley, not to mention Connecticut Johnny, Cowboy Jimmy, the Cincinnati Kid, Cornbread Red, Handsome Danny, Tuscaloosa Squirrelly and Daddy Warbucks. There were all for real and "as harmless as canaries," the Fat Man said.

He walked to the table, picked up a cue and, as he ran rack after rack of balls, shooting first with the right hand and then the left, battled his peers with quips and boasts. The dialogue made *The Hustler* sound like a morality play. It took the Fat Man more than an hour to proposition Handsome Danny Jones, of Atlanta, Georgia, onto the table (I later learned that the proposition preceding a high-stakes match sometimes lasts for days), where he promptly busted Mr. Jones, who is handsome enough to be in the movies, down to his alligator-skin shoes. Then he lured Cornbread Red (Bill Birge, of Detroit) from a corner stool, promising that when he was finished with him he would be known as "No Bread Red." He and Red were still on the table when Baumann and I called it a night at 5 A.M.

What I had heard and seen the night before seemed like a bizarre dream when I awoke the next morning. I telephoned *Sports Illustrated* in New York and queried Jack Olsen, a senior editor, on a story on the hustler's holiday in Little Egypt (as southern Illinois is called). "Little what?" Olsen screamed before commissioning me to do 5000 words.

For the next three weeks I drove to Johnston City almost nightly, frequently bringing along Evansville newspaper associates, particularly pretty girls with whom Fat Man, who *les dames* said was as light as a feather on his feet, danced all night. Soon the girls around the *Courier-Press* office were calling each other by such sobriquets as Kentucky Stella, The Duchess of Dubuque, Aunt Lavender, Princeton Red and St. Louie Mary. Of course, the male staffers got attention too. The news editor was Blue-Eyed Charley and there was Toronto Dave, Pittsburgh Roy and Small Man. I was dubbed Louisiana Lard, an unflattering but rather appropriate nom de plume at that. The situation got completely out of hand when the editor, a Yul Brynner type, learned that he was Bald Man. The appeal the colorful pool hustlers had to a cross-section of society was remarkable. Everybody had, or wanted, a nickname. Overnight it was *Camp* to be called, say, Market Street Fats or Scranton Slim or Newport Nate. By 1962 almost all sportswriters were calling the great Ohio golfer, Jack Nicklaus, Ohio Fats.

As my nightly trips to Johnston City for research continued, one by one my traveling companions dwindled. Loss of sleep was the widely professed reason. Yet, the society editor, Karen Ann Wessel, who was The Duchess of Dubuque (her home town), was stout of heart. She made almost every trip with me and by the time the tournament was over I was considering forsaking bachelorhood. Two years later I did. I tell her she hustled me and she says, "Quit trying to sound like the Fat Man." We are very happy. In addition to collecting antiques, Karen says we "collect pool hustlers." She loves to entertain them at our home in Philadelphia. We've had a dozen to our table, but the Fat Man remains the unchallenged champion of the calories.

When the story "Hustlers' Holiday in the Lions Den" was published in *Sports Illustrated,* the Fat Man was flooded with offers for exhibitions and personal appearances from all over the country. He loved the recognition. He delighted in being accepted. He frequently dropped into the *Courier-Press* office in Evansville unannounced and regaled the printers, pressmen and ad salesmen with stories. When I moved to Philadelphia he long-distanced me at least once a month. There was the night he called from Houston to report "some oil tycoon wants me to go into politics and campaign for (Senator) Goldwater. I told him I'm a 100 percent dyed-in-the-wool non-partisan." On another occasion he called to say he had "taken a job—I'm a vice president (of Rozel Industries, a billiard equipment manufacturing firm)." Most memorable was the call from Chicago two years ago when he announced: "Tom, I've got a Social Security card—you ever hear of a pool hustler with a Social Security card?" I have learned something new and exciting every day as a friend of the Fat Man. With him, a walk around the block is an adventure.

He has a quality of spirit that communicates itself not only to the hustlers and eyeballers in poolrooms from "here to Zanzibar," but also to corporate executives, society matrons, bellhops, waitresses and avant-garde writers whose paths he crosses in his endless travels about the Great Society. He is the reincarnation of a bygone period in American history when the Republic was young and still maturing and uninhibited characters dotted every walk of life. He is a free spirit, a one-man challenge to a society of Madison Avenue grays. He is a Man for all Seasons, as it were, for in the Fat Man, the Homo Saps of the Great Society see the epitome of dreams frustrated by the demands of an interdependent people. Nobody wants to work for a living, and although most of us find it necessary, the Fat Man was never bothered with such trivia. His calling was that of a pool hustler, the noblest of all the arts, he claims, and as a practitioner of his chosen profession for years his stick (in One Pocket) was feared in poolrooms from Bangor to Burbank, from Seattle to Sarasota. He was the best, he claims, and being the best in his particular field is a satisfaction that money couldn't buy.

In another 50 years, it will be difficult to visualize a man of Rudolf Walter Wanderone's wide swath having lived in the Great Society. He is the last of the high-rolling gamblers to wear $100 bills in his handkerchief pocket and play pool for outrageous stakes. He is a rollicking, rotund Runyonesque character on the loose who is part sinner and part saint, part poet and part philosopher, a gourmet, a raconteur and an animal lover without peer. He is also a rogue, which makes him lovable, for I have always felt that the rogue is by far the most interesting and intriguing of the many diffuse American personalities.

Rudolf Wanderone is also the greatest storyteller since Aesop, and when he spins his amusing folk tales of life in the poolrooms he employs his own, incomparable argot, which, though colorful and intriguing, demands definition. When we sat down to collaborate on *The Bank Shot and Other Great Robberies,* I insisted that Fat Man first define his terms so that I, not to mention the readers, might better undersand them.

Here is Minnesota Fats on Proper English at Tableside. It's not the type of English you might hear spoken in The Yard at Harvard. It's English, poolroom style, which is something the boys in The Yard might look into someday.

PROPER ENGLISH AT TABLESIDE

EYEBALLERS	Spectators in a poolroom, usually the ones with bets under the table.
BETS UNDER THE TABLE	No bets at all.
A MOOCH	A very undesirable person on account of he's always trying to put the bite on somebody else.
THE BITE	A so-called loan which is usually uncollectable.
A FILAGE	An out-and-out fraud. An imposter claiming he's a chef when he can't even fry an egg. (Note: The word, of French origin, is slang for cheating, as in palming a card, or faking, as in bluffing. Professor Minnesota Fats uses filage as both a noun and a verb.)
WHO SHOT JOHN?	Ridiculous conversation, ridiculous beyond compare.
A BROKE	A mooch without a quarter.
A TOMATO	A doll whose natural endowments are exquisite beyond belief.
A DOLL	A tomato whose natural endowments are exquisite beyond belief.
A SUCKER	A natural loser. A person with a weakness for taking on something he knows nothing about.

	Anybody who has anything to do with a doll is an automatic sucker.
A JOLT	Anything big.
A BEEF JOLT	A very serious disagreement.
HUNGARIAN CINCH	A proposition where there's no way to lose. A sure thing, a mortal lock. (Note: Professor Minnesota Fats also employs the terms "Hungarian lock" and "Hungarian combination." The meanings are the same.)
ACTION	A money game.
C NOTE	$100
A GRAND	$1000
A JILLION	A tremendous amount of money, more than you could ever count.
A ZILLION	A fantastic amount of money, even more than a jillion.
GELT	Money.
GOLD	Money.
SCRATCH	Money.
O.P. MONEY	Other People's Money.
A CARBUNCLE	A Gargantuan bankroll, like maybe the size of an eggplant.
A HIGH ROLLER	A gambler who will bet real high, maybe even as high as an astronaut's eye, or even higher.
A MULTI	A person who not only has millions, but lives like he has millions.
A GENERAL	A leader in his field. A real big operator who never gets hurt on account of he always takes the best of the proposition.
THE DOUBLE	Sweet talk.
THE DOUBLE-DOUBLE	Extra strong sweet talk, usually accompanied by a smile.

DOUBLE-DOOR	To get rid of somebody real quick, like walking in the front door of a joint and out a side door.
THE PROPOSITION	The hypothetical this-and-that necessary to discuss and finalize an agreement, such as a bet.
A BIG MAHAH	A very important person who moves like a very important person. (Note: Professor Minnesota Fats says "Mahah" is a short form of Maharajah.)
FUN PLAYERS	Pool players who would rather play for trophies than for cash.
AN OVERCOAT	The difference in skill between, say, a good player and an average player.
NOM-DE-PLUMMERS	Nicknames.
A STIFF	The deadest man in the poolroom, not only on account of he never has any cash, because even if he did have a roll, he wouldn't play for it, wouldn't bet it and wouldn't back anybody—not even in a sure thing.
TO STIFF	To beat real good, like in a money match, or to beat out of a sum of cash, like not paying the grocer or the tailor or sneaking out of a hotel without paying the bill.
THE CON	Very, very interesting conversation.
THE SOFT CON	Extremely smooth and painless conversation usually reserved for use on only very smart and knowledgeable persons.
HIGH-POWERED CON	An art practiced only by the past masters of conversation. Many practitioners of the art can be found in the legitimate business world.
HIGH-VOLTAGE CON	A superduper version of the High-Powered Con only with a little extra juice added.
THE CONVERSATION	The art of communicating, especially with a lamb.
A LAMB	A real pushover.

To Whack Out | To beat an opponent in a pool match real good. A no-seesaw conquest. An out-and-out annihilation.

To Belt Out | To put somebody, like an opponent in a pool match, completely and totally out of commission. (Note: Professor Minnesota Fats, a renowned gourmet, also uses the terms "belt out" and "whack out" in describing his personal assaults on food.)

Tapped Out | Flat busted.

Busted Out | A prisoner of The War On Poverty.

To Psyche Out | A brainwashing technique to arouse fear in your opponent. A very delicate art practiced only by extremely sensitive persons with keen and penetrating insight into the weaknesses of human nature.

An Ovation | A tribute that is fabulous beyond compare.

Get Position On | Moving somebody into a spot to use 'em real good.

Backer | A money man. In show business he's called an angel, but in most poolrooms he's known as a Fagin on account of when he backs a pool player in a cash proposition he always takes a small piece of the action, like maybe 90 per cent, for himself.

Hairy Leg | A man. (Note: Professor Minnesota Fats also employs the term "hairy leg" in referring to backers.)

Set 'Em Up | Preparing a lamb for a slaughter.

The Horns | When there's no way to win a bet on account of somebody has put a curse on you.

The Smarts | A very intelligent person who is always tuned to the situation.

Double Smart | A very, very intelligent person who is twice as smart as a very intelligent person.

TRIPLE SMART	An extremely intelligent person who is not only three or even more times more intelligent than a very intelligent person, but whose intellectual capabilities border on the phenomenal. A triple smart person is such a rare and extraordinary individual that only one comes along in a whole lifetime. (Note: In his long and illustrious career, Professor Minnesota Fats was widely known as both Double Smart Fats and Triple Smart Fats.)
A SQUARE	A person who conforms to the norm.
ON THE SQUARE	The absolute, brutal truth.
A SHARK	The pool hustler of the olden days. A man of consummate skill with cue in hand, but also a top-notch method actor, on account of he must play way below his speed until the cash is just right. Then he shoots out the lights. An expert at his chosen profession.
A BUSINESS SHARK	An executive with an Ivy League wardrobe, a desk full of telephones and tranquilizers, a permanent wrinkle of the brow and a talent for moaning and groaning about taxes. Also a capable practitioner of the art of executing the High-Powered and High-Voltage Cons.
JOINT	A business establishment, such as a poolroom, or even a taproom. Also a gimmick that's sure to win all the cash. (Note: The term "joint" is also favored by Professor Minnesota Fats to describe particular items or objects he feels merit special emphasis. Examples: "the lie detector joint"; and "the doctor put the joint (the stethoscope) on my chest.")
TUSH HOG	A very tough guy who is always looking to use the muscle on somebody.
TO MUSCLE	To take advantage of somebody by brute force or intimidation.

UNDER SPEED	Not shooting your best stick.
DODGE	Any means to skirt or avoid an issue. (Note: Professor Minnesota Fats also engages the term "dodge" as a noun in referring to "the working dodge" and "the hustling dodge.")
TAPIOCA	The never-never land of busted gamblers. A very, very lonely and hideous place, indeed.
THE JUICE	An invigorating beverage. Also the odds in a wagering proposition. (Note: In his colorful and inimitable patois, Professor Minnesota Fats frequently uses the term "juice" in recalling the critical moments of his many triumphs in crucial money matches. Example: "When all the money was up for grabs, I'd give 'em the juice real good.")
TO JUICE OFF	To apply English off a cushion.
SCRATCH HOUSE	A hotel that nobody could ever call The Conrad Hilton.

Philadelphia, Pennsylvania
July 1966

Tom Fox

Contents

Part Two

Part One

CHAPTER 1

Me and Methuselah

According to the Old Testament, Methuselah lived 969 years, which is as high a run as I've ever heard. Of course, Methuselah was a little before my time, although a lot of people think I'm older than even Methuselah. Those mooches and broken-down hustlers in the poolrooms know I've been whacking out every living human since the 20s, so they're always giving me a soft con about how old I am. Like one time this hustler Danny Jones, the ladies' man from down in Georgia who they call Handsome Danny, says to me, "Fatty, I heard you were a busboy at the Last Supper." I said, "Listen, sonny boy, if I had been at the Last Supper, I never would have been no busboy—I would have been eating."

I've been belting out the calories all my life. If there's one thing I love more than shooting pool for some cash, it would have to be eating good food. I'm 53 years old and 100 pounds overweight, but two years ago I had a physical examination in Chicago and the doctor said he couldn't understand it. He said when I walked in with all that weight (270 pounds) he knew 15 different things had to be wrong with me. But when he put the joint (the stethoscope) on my heart, he was amazed beyond compare. "My God," he said, "why, your heart purrs like a Rolls Royce." Then he called in a zillion doctors and they all listened and they all shook their heads.

I've been eating like a Sultan since I was two days old. I had a mother and three sisters who worshiped me and when I was two years old they used to plop me in a bed on a jillion satin pillows and spray me with exotic perfumes and lilac water and then they would shoot me the grapes. When my old man walked in, he would laugh and say, "Ah, my son, The

Sultan." He would tell my mother and the sisters, "More pillows—and more grapes." Then he would jump in the bed with me and we would wallow in those pillows and belt out the grapes until it was time for dinner. And when we got to the table, my mother and sisters fed us like we were kings.

My father's name was Rudolf Walter Wanderone and when I was born on January 19, 1913, in Washington Heights in New York City, they christened me Rudolf Walter Wanderone, Jr. I was the only boy.

My old man was a tremendous physical specimen. He was six feet two inches tall with shoulders like a longshoreman. He weighed in around 275 and he had fantastic blue eyes and a full head of reddish brown hair. Everybody said I was his double, although he had about four inches on me in height. He was born in Suhr, Switzerland, one of 16 children, and he came to America in the nineteenth century when the bottom dropped out of everything over there except the clock industry. "Who can eat clocks?" he used to say.

When he was a young man he was what they called a Soldier of Fortune. He fought in a half-dozen wars and revolutions but he wasn't what you would call a reactionary or a zealot or a fanatical partisan or anything like that. He always fought on whatever side offered the best proposition and the payoff always had to be in gold. He was a professional soldier, a gun for hire. He traveled all over, fighting in rebellions and uprisings in Mexico and South America, in the Far East and in some parts of Europe. My old man was one of the "Have Gun, Will Travel" originals. His last big jolt was the Russian-Japanese War of 1906. When he would return to Switzerland after one of those skirmishes, he would bring fabulous gifts for all his relatives. He had fantastic books from all of the countries, some in languages he couldn't even read, but he would look at the pictures and tell his Swiss friends how it was in those foreign lands.

That's how the gimmick with the grapes started. When I was a boy, my father would sit me on his knee and show me these fantastic color pictures in the books. Pictures of kings and sultans on gold beds with the most gorgeous tomatoes hitting them with the grapes and the kumquats and the lamb chops and 20-pound turkeys and hams the size of beer kegs. The old man always talked about what a great country America was for opportunity, so when he showed me the sultans with the beautiful dolls I would say, "Pop, if you ask me, this looks like the opportunity we've all been waiting for—I want to be a Sultan." So my mother and the sisters started shooting me the grapes. It was kid stuff with them but I was dead serious.

And it was all right with my old man because he said there's only one thing a man should be and that's happy.

He loved to tell the story about his first job in America. He was a blacksmith apprentice for $1.50 a week. He liked the job all right but he was hooked on the opportunity proposition, so after a few weeks he asked for a raise. He didn't want much—just another quarter a week—but the blacksmith said no. He thought my old man was out of his skull. So my old man said, "Vot about this I hear of opportunity in America? I am a good blacksmith, yah? I am strong like un ox, yah. I deserve more money." But the blacksmith told him if he wasn't happy with the buck and a half a week he could go find something else. Well, the old man went back to his anvil and considered the proposition. Five minutes later he picked up that anvil with one arm like it was a suitcase, carried it about 100 yards out into an open field and dropped it in a big hole. The old blacksmith screamed like he was getting deported but my old man walked off laughing. It took ten men to lift that anvil out of the hole.

My father was pretty particular about what kind of jobs he took after that. His Swiss cronies around Washington Heights began to worry about him being out of work and when they saw him in a saloon, they would ask, "Mr. Wanderone, vot are you doing now?" He would say, "I'm looking for opportunity." He finally found it in business for himself. He was in the heating and plumbing field and every nickel he made he lavished on my mother, Rosa, the three girls, Rosie, Julie and Jerry, and me.

Swiss people are hardworking people, especially the women. My mother came over from Basel, Switzerland and believe it or not, she was one of 18 children. She thought if you weren't working from sunrise to sunset that it was a mortal sin. She was a very devout Catholic and if a family man in the neighborhood happened not to be working, my mother would sic the priest on him. But my father always remembered his experience as a blacksmith and he figured being happy was more important than working.

"Never do anything that makes you unhappy, Roodle," he would tell me. "An unhappy man will not live long. Ah, but if you are happy, then already you are a rich man. If a man has health and a roof over his head and good food and good friends, what else does he need? What else? He is already wealthy beyond compare." So right then and there I knew what I would do in life: nothing. And that's all I've ever done.

When I was a little older, my mother wanted me to help out around the house. She would say, "Look, Roodle, your sister Rosie is cooking, your sister Julie is sewing and your sister Jerry is ironing. And what are you doing, Roodle? Nothing." I always gave my mother the same answer, nice and polite, of course. "Yes, ma'am," I'd say, "that's exactly what I'm doing—nothing. And that's all I'm ever going to do—absolutely nothing." She would tell my father and the old man would say, "But, Rosa, if Roodle does not wish to work, then he must not work. He must be a happy boy."

Then when I started hanging around the pool hall in Washington Heights, my mother worried more. She was afraid I would end up a ne'er-do-well or a gambler. But my father would tell her, "Rosa, we are all gamblers. Life is a gamble. Our Roodle is a good son. He will do nothing wrong." Then the old man would say, "Come, Roodle, let us eat—Rosa, my love, what is for dinner tonight?" He would chuckle as we ate and then he would retell the story about the blacksmith.

"Roodle, my son," he would say, "my experience as a blacksmith was a gamble. But I was quick to see that the odds were not in my favor. It was a bad proposition and not wishing to spend my life fighting such odds, I decided to do something else. But working as a blacksmith taught me a great lesson. It was simply this: never work for anyone else." Every time he told the story, I would say, "Pop, I can go you one better—never work. Never work, period." He would smile and say, "Well, Roodle, my son, if you do not care to work, then you must not work or you will be unhappy. But whatever you do, Roodle, I know you will be a success. Perhaps one day you will become President. I do not think that is a very difficult job."

Well, I never made it to the White House. But who wants that kind of action?

The old man is gone now but until the day he died in 1945, the one thing he was proudest of was my living like a king without doing a lick of work. "Ah," he would say, "my son, Roodle, he is a Big Mahah."

Back in the 30s and 40s when I was getting action all over the country and had so much money in my pocket that it looked like a carbuncle, I drove the biggest and finest cars, some of them even limousines. One time during World War II when they weren't making new cars, I bought this fantastic Packard limousine from the estate of the grand-mother of John Agar, the movie actor. It was a fabulous car, the kind bankers drove, and my wife Eva-line* fell in love with it. She called the car "Grandma Agar." It had a glass partition between the driver and the back seat and when I would go home to New York, the old man would

---

* Mrs. Wanderone's name is Evelyn Inez but the Fat Man prefers to call her Eva-line.

look at the big black limousine and say, "Roodle, let's go for a spin." I drove him all over New York and New Jersey and he would sit in the back seat and stretch out like he was Rockefeller or Vanderbilt and then he would start yodling. He was a tremendous yodler. He learned it as a boy in Switzerland and sometimes he would sing "Little Sir Echo" because he said it reminded him of the Alps. He would say, "Roodle, please, you be the echo." I was a tremendous yodler myself before my voice changed, only when I got older I couldn't get in the same key with the old man. But I'd do anything to make him happy so when he would sing "Little Sir Echo," my wife, Eva-line, would slide the glass partition back and forth and I would sing the echo part—"Hello— hello— hello." Sometimes we would be driving down Broadway or on Park Avenue and the old man would be yodling loud enough to wake up the tourists. He would stretch his arms across the back seat and say, "My son, Roodle, is the true success story—he does not work but he lives like a king. He has found opportunity. He is a happy man."

That's the way it was, that's the way it always was. My old man could lift an anvil and carry it for a block like it was a toy. But the heaviest thing I've ever picked up in my life was the cue stick, or maybe a knife and fork. For 53 years I've eaten anything I've felt like eating and any time I felt like eating it. I wouldn't know a calorie from a chrysanthemum. I mix my proteins and starches like fudge-ripple ice cream and I've never been on a diet in my life. The only time I think about losing weight is when I have trouble getting into my clothes. I've got a fantastic wardrobe, 39 tailor-made suits at $500 a pop, so when I reach the point where I can't button the pants, my wife says, "My God, Rudolf, you'll go bankrupt buying a new wardrobe." What I do then is lay off food—all food— for one day and I lose 12 pounds. The next day I start back in assaulting the calories all over again.

I've been shooting pool since I was four years old. No con. By the time I was six I was playing for stakes. My first sucker was a neighborhood kid in Washington Heights. I spotted him coming out of a candy store with an enormous bag of gumdrops. He was about five years older than me but I shot him straight pool and I won every last one of his gumdrops. He went home crying. When I was ten I started playing for cash.

When I was ten years old I was as big as I am now, in fact, about two inches taller, but the older I got the more weight I put on. The first six months after I got married I gained like 60 pounds. Finally, I began to get shorter. I never shrunk—I just sagged. What happened was my neck just disappeared down between my shoulders. That's on the square.

I've been haunting poolrooms from here to Zanzibar for almost 45 years. I've played every game in the book and some fantastic propositions you wouldn't imagine. I whacked out every top player in the game, including all those fun players who dress up in tuxedos and play in those big tournaments for trophies and $4 in prizes. The only trouble with those fun players is that they wouldn't bet fat meat is greasy if they had to put up their own cash. They wouldn't play for a grape if they owned a vineyard. But I've beaten them all. I won zillions and what I didn't give away, I lost shooting craps.

Craps was always my biggest vice. I played the horses when I was young but playing the horses is for suckers. You can't beat the odds. It's the same thing with craps. It's like my old man and the blacksmith proposition.

I would always gamble on anything that I could do myself. I figured if I could do it myself, I would have something to say about the outcome. But betting money on horses and just watching them run is ridiculous beyond compare. The same thing with craps.

Now, betting on a pool game makes sense. Shooting pool is something you have to do with your hands and that's why I never feared going to the table with anyone, including Methuselah if he had been around in my time. There's this pool hustler named Cornbread Red whose real name is Bill Birge and one night he cracked smart and asked if I had ever played Methuselah. I said, "No, Red, I never played Methuselah, which was lucky for him. That's why he never died broke."

But other than Methuselah, and maybe Napoleon and Josephine, I've played them all and I whacked 'em out like they were sawdust. I owned them all—the pool hustlers and those fun players who tell people they were born in the YMCA. Sure some of them beat me in matches, but the Fat Man never lost a session for cash in his life. Never. Right now I'm an old man 100 pounds overweight and 25 per cent below my best speed, but if the proposition is right I can still take care of myself on a pool table.

My game is and always was One Pocket. It's a tremendous game and the most difficult of all pool to play. You've got to know Three-Cushion billiards, Banks, Pocket Billiards, every game on the table. That's why only all-around masters can play it and that's why those fun players who are always screaming about 14.1 Continuous pocket billiards put it down and call it a hustlers' game. Very few of them can play One Pocket the way it's supposed to be played.

I played my best stick 15 years ago—say as late as 1948 to 1950. I was all over the country challenging any living soul to any game for any amount—money, marbles or chalk. Oh, they all wanted a piece of the Fat Man but after I whacked 'em out time after time, I became the loneliest man in the world. You couldn't get those tournament champions to play me for cash if you tied a rope around them.

That's how it always was. It got worse and worse until I couldn't get any action unless I gave tremendous odds, like a ball and the break, or two, even three balls. Some of them wanted me to shoot one-handed, or even left-handed. Giving those kind of odds, I'd be lucky to beat my wife. So what I did about 15 years ago was just retire to my home in Dowell, Illinois, a little town 100 miles southeast of St. Louis. I've lived there since 1941.

Every now and then I would go on the road looking for a little action but in those days poolrooms were like monasteries. It was unbelievable. Sometimes I caught a little action playing cards and once in awhile a high stakes pool player would build up a bankroll and come looking for me in DuQuoin, Illinois, which is about four miles from Dowell. But if I had depended on pool action to eat in those days, I would have starved to death. I whacked out so many of them I put myself out of business.

So I just settled down with my wife and my mother-in-law and my cats and dogs and began enjoying life. I've got 27 dogs and 14 cats at home and I spend more money feeding them than those pool hustlers spend for a car. I hustle for them because I know they can't hustle for themselves. I feed the dogs and my wife, Eva-line, feeds me. She's a beautiful doll and a fantastic cook and for almost 11 years I lived like one of those land barons in the olden days.

Then about five years ago, when the movie *The Hustler* came out, I began to get telephone calls from all over. Newspaper columnists and magazine writers began visiting me and I was invited to appear on television shows in St. Louis and all over southern Illinois. I heard a zillion propositions but I gave them all the same answer: "Work? You mean you want me to work?" I'd say, "You must take me for an imbecile."

Then one day about a year ago, I was feeding the dogs and cats in the backyard and my wife, Eva-line, called out of the back window of the kitchen.

"Rudolf," she yelled, "you've got another long distance call."

I told her to take the number. "Tell them I'm busy feeding my pets," I said. I really didn't want to hear any more propositions.

Eva-line took the number and later on I returned the call. It was from Chicago and it was to change my life.

It also was to give me my first grey hair.

CHAPTER 2

Me and Max Donovan

Eva-line said the call was from a fellow in Chicago by the name of Phil Zelkowitz.

"Zelkowitz?" I said, "Why, he sounds like some kind of revolutionary."

"He wants to offer you a job, Rudolf," Eva-line said.

"Well, then, you better believe he's a revolutionary, the worst kind of revolutionary," I said.

I told Eva-line I wasn't going to return this Zelkowitz's call because it would only be just more grief, just more of the same old con.

Until 20th Century Fox produced the movie *The Hustler,* with Jackie Gleason starring in a role fashioned after my life in the poolrooms, I lived as quietly as a cloistered monk. I mean I just moved around in my circles—the poolrooms. I never wanted any publicity; in fact, I always dodged it. Back in the olden days, a zillion magazine writers wanted to do stories about me and a couple of them wanted to write books. But I always double-doored them. Who needed publicity?

But after the movie hit the theaters I got this big ovation in *Sports Illustrated* and all of a sudden I was getting telephone calls from all over the country offering me the most ridiculous propositions you ever heard. So I figured this Zelkowitz was just another one of those business sharks out to give me the soft sell.

Some of the propositions were unbelievable beyond compare. A fellow from Memphis offered me $150 a week to manage a poolroom down there. He said business was falling off and an old-time player told him to hire me because I had filled every room I ever played. He said $150 a week and a percentage of the gross if business picked up. I told him, "Listen, I spend $150 a week on hors d'oeuvres." Who wants that kind of grief?

Then there was a call from a big man in the garment district in New York. He hit me with a proposition to push a line of fat man clothes, you know, the stout sizes. He was real cute. He said he would pay me $500 to endorse the line and fly me to New York to pose for a jillion pictures for advertising gimmicks. I said I might be interested if he threw in like a dozen suits on the side. I could hear him gulp on the phone. He said there was no way he could swing the suits but maybe he could get me a nice discount if I wanted to buy something. I told him he was as generous as Fagin.

But the most unbelievable proposition of all was the one I got in Houston, Texas in the fall of 1963. This big general who I met in a fabulous club I was playing down there wanted me to be a politician. He was a big multi, one of those big oil tycoons, and he and a couple of his multi friends stopped in at the joint every night to belt a few drinks and hear me make with the conversation. They would sit around moaning and groaning about dry holes and depletion allowances and how they were about to bust out. Then they would call me over and say, "Fat Man, you're the happiest person we know—tell us some stories so we can laugh and forget our business troubles." I told them their troubles were simple: they should all give up the working dodge.

Now this Big Mahah said he never heard anybody tell stories and make 'em sound as interesting as I did. In fact, he said I could take the most complicated problem and make the whole thing sound so simple that he figured I would make a tremendous politician. I thought the general was giving me the con until he told me he was a big Goldwater man and he would like me to campaign for the Senator in the presidential election.

I told him politics never was my jolt, only he said I should at least listen to his proposition. He claimed it was real urgent that Senator Goldwater be elected on account of Goldwater was a staunch conservative and what the country needed was a conservative in the White House. He said President Kennedy was entirely too liberal and that if something wasn't done about the deficit spending in Washington that we would all end up in the poor house.

I told this general when it came to politics I was what you call a real dyed-in-the-wool non-partisan but he said he would have one of his representatives explain everything to me. When I got home I mentioned the proposition to Eva-line and she said I should be nice about the whole thing and at least listen to what they had to say.

I thought about it for a few days and I even got to wondering if the conversation worked the same in politics as it did in the poolroom. But I never found out because the same week the general's man was supposed to see me in Dowell, everything happened down in Dallas.

I remember the day like it was yesterday—Friday, November 22, 1963. I was watching television at home when the program was interrupted to report that President Kennedy had been shot in Dallas. At first I thought it was one of those scare propositions, like the time Orson Welles had that radio program about the Martians invading the Earth and everybody went off their trolley. But a few minutes later Charlotte Peters, a friend of mine on KTVI-TV in St. Louis, came on and said: "The President is dead." I couldn't believe it.

I called to Eva-line out in the kitchen. "My God, Eva-line," I yelled, "Jack Kennedy's been belted out in Dallas. He's gone . . . he's dead."

Eva-line ran in and listened to the news for a few minutes and then she turned to me and said, "Why, Rudolf, you're crying."

I said, "You're goddamned right I'm crying, Eva-line, what the hell is happening in this country?" Then I saw that Eva-line was crying, too.

Of course, that was the end of the political proposition but I never would have touched it with a Geiger counter in the first place.

But Zelkowitz had a different approach. First of all, he was talking my line when he said he was a billiard equipment manufacturer. And the way he put it to me made me take it as a challenge. He didn't say, look, listen to what I'm going to do for you. He said, listen, how would you like to do this.

"How would you like to help me corner the billiards table home market?" he asked. "How would you like to bring billiards into the home —every home?"

"You mean like Hoover's proposition—a chicken in every pot?" I said.

Well, Zee, which is what I call him, said it wasn't exactly like the chicken in every pot con, but he said he wanted to bring the game of billiards to the masses. He said he figured there were a zillion dens and rumpus rooms and recreation rooms in homes that ought to have pool tables for the kids. He said he knew if I would join his firm and promote his products, his business would start popping out all over the place.

I'll say this for Zee, he sure knew how to approach me. Here I was past 50 years old and never had worked a day in my life but now I was listening to a business shark giving me the high-powered con and I was really interested.

I told him if I went to work for him I was going to be making a tremendous sacrifice getting up every morning just like the next sucker. But I said his idea of bringing the games to the masses appealed to me because I've always felt that pool was the most misunderstood game of all time.

Years ago you had to be a Manville or a Vanderbilt or a Harvey Firestone or an independent multi to afford a pool table for your home. Something else. Back then the tables were big—five feet by ten feet—and you had to have an enormous room to put one in. So the poor working man just didn't have the scratch or the space to own a pool table. Then there was the angle on the rooms. Back in the 20s and 30s, some of the rooms in New York and Chicago were like palaces. They were fantastic places with the most elegant furnishings and equipment. If they built those kind today they would have to call them the Conrad Hilton. That's how posh they were.

What happened was the bottom fell out of everything during the Depression and those fabulous rooms just went down and down until they looked like flea joints. The same thing happens in the big cities. A neighborhood starts sliding and first thing you know everybody says it's a ghetto. Well, that's exactly what happened to those tremendous rooms and a lot of people seeing those traps thought pool was always played in that kind of atmosphere. They never dreamed how fantastic the rooms were in the olden days. So I figured here was a chance to let the people know that pool wasn't always a skullduggery game.

"I'm interested in your proposition," I told Zelkowitz, "but what about the gelt?"

"You don't mean you let money worry you?" he said.

"Listen, Mr. Zelkowitz," I said, "let's me and you understand each other from the start. The way I see it, money is the root of all good."

So he said he would make me a vice president—an executive vice president—and take care of the food bills. I agreed to see him in Chicago.

"Vice President?" Eva-line said. "Well, you never would have done that well in politics, Rudolf."

Phil Zelkowitz and I hit it off real good from the start. He's a tremendous looking man. Zee is built like Johnny Weissmuller, except for the hair. He's as bald as Yul Brynner but he has shoulders like a line-backer and a neck the size of a wrestler. Zee developed himself carrying 10 and 20 gallon oil cans up four and five stories in the tenements in Chicago. He was born real poor and he had to hustle all his life just like every other sucker. But Zee finally got into business for himself and made zillions. He retired when he was 40 but couldn't stand it. He felt left out because nobody was sticking a telephone in his face and telling him he had tax problems. He missed all that ridiculous chaos so he went back into business. I told him he must have wanted to have the richest ulcer on Wall Street, but he said that wasn't it. "I just craved action," Zee said. I told him, "My God, you're a real hustler."

Now Zee is the president of Rozel Industries and he's getting up at six o'clock every morning and flying all over the country like he's a bird because he wants to corner the home table market. He's hooked, just like those hustlers in the poolrooms.

So now, after all those years of voluntary unemployment, Zee has made a general out of me. I've got this beautiful paneled office in Chicago and a secretary and a tax accountant and a dozen public relations sharks who put me on the "Johnny Carson Show," "What's My Line?" and some other TV jolts. They got me a big spread in *Life* and *Esquire* and those other big magazines and by the time they get finished exposing me I won't be able to get four cents of action. They're ruining me.

Now this accountant is real cute. He calls me on the phone and says, "Mr. Vice President, we don't have your Social Security number." It was unbelievable. I asked him if he ever heard of a pool player having a Social Security number and he said that didn't matter because I had to have one if I wanted to be a vice president. That touched off a real earthquake on account of I told Zee there was no way I was going to take out Social Security. So what happens? I got more of the high-powered con from Zee, me, an old master at the conversation, got the business from a business shark.

"Listen," Zee said, "I understand you love animals." I said that's absolutely right, I'm crazy about all animals. So he said I should hear the story of Max Donovan.

Then Zee told me the most unbelievable story I've ever heard. I thought I heard them all in the poolrooms, but this one was unbelievable beyond compare.

Max Donovan is a dog, only Max Donovan has a Social Security number. This is on the square. Now Cornbread Red doesn't have a Social Security card and neither does Tuscaloosa Squirrelly or the Knoxville Bear or Superstitious Aloysius and I know those old-timers like Pink Shirt Cassidy and Bicycle Charley and Drunken Floody would have gone to the chair before they took out Social Security. But here was Zee telling me about a dog with a Social Security number.

Zee said Max Donovan was a schnauzer and, although he had a Jewish first name and an Irish last name, his owner happened to be an Italian fellow from New York. This Italian found Max Donovan on a parking lot in New York and he figured it was the smartest dog he ever saw because Max Donovan could do all sorts of tricks. He really fell in love with Max Donovan, in fact, he enrolled him in the Book-of-the-Month Club and even took an insurance policy on Max Donovan's life. This fellow afforded Max Donovan such a tremendous life that his wife complained because she said Max Donovan got all the attention and she was leading the dog's life. Zee said the last time he heard anything about Max Donovan he was working as an actor in a traveling carnival. It's a true story. Zee showed me newspaper clippings on it.

So I figured if they were issuing Social Security cards to dogs, then it would be all right for a pool hustler. I gave Zee all the information and he sent it off to Washington. But when the card came back, instead of being in my regular name of Rudolf Walter Wanderone, Jr., it was issued to Minnesota Fats. It's number 322-42-2372. You can look it up.

When I told Eva-line about Max Donovan, she was very impressed. She said, "Rudolf, why don't we get Social Security for all the cats and dogs?" I said I would think about it, but we decided to wait until they passed Medicare.

I telephoned my mother in Sherman, New York, and told her I had a Social Security card and they had to put her to bed. She's 90 years old. My mother-in-law, Orbie, got all excited when I showed her the card. "That's wonderful, Rudolf," she said, "now if you would only join the church." But the Social Security number didn't go over too big with the hustlers and neither did my personal card, the one with my picture that says, Rudolf "Minnesota Fats" Wanderone, Executive Vice President. I showed it to Cornbread Red out in Detroit last year and he shook his head. "Fatty," he said, "I ain't never heard of a pool hustler having a calling card." I said, "Listen, Red, you don't understand. This means that I'm one of the generals of the Great Society." Sometimes Cornbread Red is slow to recognize progress.

Well, when the Social Security card arrives from Washington, Zee says, "Fatty, now you're a captain of industry." I said, "Is that so—well, in that case the captain is going out to eat." Zee said, "My God, Fatty, you're killing the budget." That's all those business sharks do, complain about budgets and taxes. I said, "Listen, Zee, you better get used to it because I've whacked out a lot of budgets in my time."

One day Zee had this public relations man come over to interview me about my life's story for some brochures. The first thing the guy asks is, "Mr. Vice President, just how did you get started playing pool?"

So I told him the way it was—it all started with Gans—Gans, the goose.

CHAPTER **3**

The Oversexed Goose

Gans was the most fantastic goose you ever saw. He was a family pet and we fed him like he was human and he got enormous, as big as a goose could get. But he had a couple problems. Like, one, he was a tremendous drunk; and two, he was oversexed. It was unbelievable because the more Gans drank the more excited he got about the dolls and Gans drank like he was brought up on the Bowery.

My old man won Gans in a raffle at a Swiss Verein outing in New Jersey. The Swiss Verein was a singing society made up of people who came over from the old country and 40, 50 years ago there were so many Swiss immigrants around New York that there were more singing societies than you've got Howard Johnson stops today. Every Sunday a different society would hold a picnic at the amusement parks around New York and New Jersey, and the old man would take the whole family to hear the singing and the yodling and to belt out the food.

Those outings were fabulous affairs. They would line up a jillion tables out in the open and spread the food and drinks like they were going to feed a whole army. Then they had had these Ferris wheels and carousel rides and potato sack races and the contests to show feats of strength. My old man won all the strong-man propositions. He had tremendous strength, like he could pick up a beer keg with just his fingers. Each society also had what they called a strong-man team and they competed with each other. One time an old Swiss hustler comes to my old man and says he's willing to bet any amount that his society's strong men could pull a boxcar further than my old man's Verein team. So everybody got down, you know, and I asked my old man if it looked like a good proposition and he said, "Roodle, we'll pull it like it was a tooth." Then they all got into these harnesses and hooked up to the boxcar. They looked like the galley slaves you see in those motion pictures about the days of the Roman Empire. When they were all set, my old man's crew gave a couple of grunts and they walked that big boxcar about a block like it was a baby carriage. The other society didn't even try to budge it. They were psyched out. Then my old man picked up all the gold. He was a tremendous proposition man for the cash.

When everybody was finished with the contests and the eating, the singing would begin and the old-timers would start to yodling like somebody was goosing them with a feather. My father was rated the top yodler in his Verein and my mother was a pretty good singer, too. All us little Wanderones yodled when we were kids but I had to give it up when my voice changed because I got to sounding more like a buffalo. My old man listened to me yodling one day and he said, "Roodle, you should stick to pool, maybe."

But where my gambling started was at those raffle wheels at the outings. An old fellow would spin the wheel and everybody got down with the nickels and dimes and the winner would get a ham or a salami. It was no gimmick because somebody won every time. I was real lucky and I always won. Always. It got so everybody was bringing me their money to bet for them like I was a numbers man but I would always win them a turkey or a liverwurst. I won so many I looked like a big wholesaler passing them out.

Now one day the big prize is this little goose, which was maybe a few weeks old at the time. So my old man says, "Roodle, you are lucky, here, you pick a number." So I'm down and my number comes up again so we win the goose. All the Swiss people said we should fatten up the goose and cook it but there was no chance of that because nobody in my family ever animal-killed or anything like that. "Roodle," my old man said, "we keep the goose for a pet. We will call it Gans." That's goose in German.

So we kept that goose a long, long time and it grew to a fantastic size and it was a tremendous attraction at the outings. Gans used to go from table to table hustling food and then when he got started drinking he liked the drinks better than the food. He would drink anything that could be poured—whiskey, beer, cognac, wine, anything. He would get blind drunk and stagger all over the place like a rummy. And when he got drunk he would do the most unbelievable things, like running up the ladies' dresses and sticking his beak down the dolls' bosoms.

The men would laugh but it used to embarrass my mother and she would ask my old man, "Why does Gans do such nasty things?" My old man would say, "Shh, Rosa, shh—Gans is oversexed."

Gans got so enormous that all the Swiss people at the outings would say, "When you going to cook the goose?" My old man would tell them, "This is mine and Roodle's goose and this goose won't ever make the oven." My old man told me never to let Gans out of my sight because somebody was sure to snatch him and then that goose really would be cooked. So I took care of Gans like he was a brother, except for the time he got away from me at the Verein's big masquerade dance.

The Swiss took the whole family to the dances and the kids played games while the old folks danced and drank. This night my old man was dressed as a clown. My mother sewed him this fantastic clown suit out of pure silk with big polka dots and the dunce cap and all. So the old man is dancing with all the dolls and not paying any attention to Gans and neither am I because I got an eye on a little doll of my own.

Well, Gans is going from table to table and his consumption was tremendous that night. Then he started attacking the tomatoes. One doll was dressed like Lillian Russell, you know, with the low-cut neckline. She had the most tremendous bosom you ever saw, like the size of bowling balls, and when Gans spotted her he was out of control. So Gans starts nipping at her and the tomato screams and screams and the men laughed until they couldn't see. Gans was always the life of the party when he had a load on.

Now the masquerade is over and my father says I should get Gans and we'll go home. But Gans is among the missing persons. He's nowhere to be found so my old man figures for certain that somebody has heisted Gans for Sunday dinner. We looked all over the place, under the tables, behind the bar, the rest rooms, the hatcheck booth, the big walk-in freezers, all over. But no Gans. So my father tipped the waiters and bartenders like a fin apiece and told them if Gans turned up to call him because he was offering a reward.

The next morning around eight o'clock we get the phone call. Gans was found in the big walk-in freezer behind a pile of beer kegs. So my old man and I drive over and Gans is stretched out on a table and he looked deader than a stiff. But when my old man petted him he opened his eyes like he knew us.

What happened was Gans walked in the icebox behind somebody when they opened the door and nobody saw him go in. He just got froze stiff and slept it off behind the beer barrels. If it hadn't been for all the booze he had in him, he would have croaked in that cooler. But Gans drank so much whiskey that night it was like he was full of Prestone.

We brought him home wrapped in a blanket and after awhile he was all right but my mother said she was embarrassed. She said she was going to talk to the priest to see if it was a sin to pour whiskey to a goose. But my old man said never mind on account of he had it on good authority that Gans wasn't a church goer in the first place.

Well, the way Gans introduces me to pool came about when I was four years old. We were at an outing and Gans took off on me and ran into a big pavilion at the amusement park and I ran inside after him. It was an enormous place with bowling lanes and card tables and a bar that looked like a distillery and right near the bar they had these pool tables. It was the first time I ever saw one. So I held Gans in my lap and watched the games. When I got to watching those balls rolling I was like in a trance and I would sit there for hours and hours. One day two fellows quit a table so I tied Gans to the table leg and started rolling the balls. At first I tried to shoot them like they were marbles but after awhile I started sneaking a cue stick and stroking off the balls. Kids my age weren't supposed to play pool in a bar but when I was five years old I was as big as a pony. I weighed over 100 pounds. Anyway, I had won the bartender a zillion hams and turkeys at the raffle wheels so he would let me play any time a table was open. And that's how it all started. I'll tell you what, when I was six years old I could already run a rack of balls. That's on the square.

I couldn't wait to go to those picnics after that because I knew I would play pool all day. Then pretty soon I discovered there was a Swiss Club in Washington Heights that had a pool table. It was a family club where the wives and children could go in and out all they wanted, so I started playing there every now and then. That's where I hustled the kid out of the gumdrops.

But it was in Europe that I really learned to play the game. My grandfather still lived in Suhr, Switzerland where he had a farm with a million storks, which might be why he had 16 children. My father used to visit him every year and we also visited my mother's relatives in Basel and sometimes we would go over for like six weeks and stay a whole year. When my old man decided to stay over like that, he would hire a tutor who instructed me every day. Then when I came back home to New York, I had to take tests at P.S. 132, but I belted them out without any trouble.

The big games in Europe in those days, which was just after World

War I, were Balkline and Three-Cushion billiards. They were tremendous games which required a lot of skill to play and that's all they were playing in France and Germany and Switzerland and England back then. There was a tremendous Balkline player over there by the name of Erich Hagenlocher who was the champion of Germany and a big favorite in Switzerland. Later on he won the world Balkline title. My father met him at a big club and told him about me and Mr. Hagenlocher said he would like to see me play. He really showed me how the game was supposed to be played, how to control a cue ball and know what you were doing. I think the reason I was such a tremendous One Pocket player was because I had this great foundation in Balkline and Three Cushions, which I learned from Mr. Hagenlocher. He was crazy about me. He called me "Little Pink Cheeks." Later on when I was ten I played him in an exhibition match at a men's club in Berlin and I beat him. On the square.

When I came back to New York that year, I really started taking the game seriously. I was ten but I weighed like 140 pounds and I was almost as tall as I am now. There were some real fine rooms in Washington Heights, only you had to wear long pants to get in—but I had been wearing long pants since I was eight on account of I was so enormous. Every day I would go there and play a fellow who lived in the neighborhood named Carl Schieder. He was a full-grown man, like maybe 20 years older than me, but he never dreamed I was just 11, almost 12 years old. He took me for a good 18 to 20. We played day after day and I kept improving all the time and first thing you know I asked him, "Carl, how would you like to play for some scratch?" So now we were going to the table for $5 and $10 a game and pretty soon I was beating Carl more than he could afford. I just kept getting better and better and by the time I was 13 I was shooting out the lights.

Back then in the 20s there weren't any talking pictures or radio or TV or anything worldly like that. So if a kid was 13 and he hadn't heard about the dolls yet, he was still playing Cowboys and Indians. I never played Cowboys and Indians in my whole life, which was a good thing because the first Cowboy I ever met I shot down in cold blood.

CHAPTER **4**

Shoot-out in Washington Heights

Back in the 20s, every living human was making what they called whoopee from morning to night. Whoopee meant a lot of different things in those days but mostly it meant doing exactly what the generals said you weren't supposed to do. Those whoopees broke more laws than Rudolph Valentino broke hearts. Captain Queeg never would have found his strawberries if someone had snatched them in the 20s.

The big proposition was the Volstead Act which said any sucker found belting the booze was a public enemy. So what happened was all the suckers wanted to be public enemies. They guzzled the bathtub gin like it was lemonade and cut up in those all-night speakeasy joints until the sun came up, even though that kind of action was against the law. The trouble was the generals never took human nature into consideration when they cranked out that kind of con. It was like telling a six-year-old boy he couldn't eat candy because it was bad for his teeth. Now that might have been all right. But if you were to put say a five-pound box of Marquetand's chocolates in front of the kid and then say, "Now, Junior, don't you dare touch that candy," that would be something else. Junior would start sneaking around and when nobody was looking, he would whack that candy real good. You could paddle him from morning till night but the more you said "don't," the more Junior would assault that candy until he ended up nutty as a Hershey bar. That's exactly how it was in the 20s. People went crazy doing ridiculous things that they never would have dreamed of doing if the generals in Washington hadn't put a contraband on the refreshments.

Now the reason pool thrived in that era was because of the same kind of thinking. Ever since Adam and the Apple Statute, the generals have been trying to tell people how to live, and in the 20s the poolroom got almost as much attention as the saloons. Back then it was against the law for a kid to be found anywhere near a poolroom and the word of warning in every home was "Junior, if I catch you around that poolroom again, I'll knock your damned block off." That started Junior thinking he sure must be missing out on something real interesting so he began sneaking in the poolroom just because his old man said it wasn't the right kind of place for a growing boy. You couldn't blame the kids because even the kids knew about the Volstead proposition. They knew it was against the law to drink but everywhere they went they saw people guzzling the juice and when they got home at night there was the old man sneaking in with a couple more pints. Junior knew the old man wasn't obeying the law, so when Papa told Junior the poolroom was out of bounds, the kid almost broke a leg getting there. Junior didn't want to miss out on any of the action either.

Back then people called poolrooms hangouts for ne'er-do-wells and rogues of the worst kind, which was partly true because some of the most hideous creatures I've ever known were bums I met in a poolroom. But I've also known some out-and-out hoodlums who wouldn't know a cue ball from a grapefruit. You just can't lump people into classes like that, there's no way. You might hear some outstanding thug is as ferocious as a man-eating barracuda and then you meet him and see he's as timid as a mockingbird. Now on the other hand, if you took the time to investigate some of history's outstanding leaders, men who were supposed to be righteous people, you might turn up some amazing facts. Some of those big generals would make Captain Kidd look like a pussycat.

My old man never was one to pigeonhole people and judge them by the acre on account of he saw so much skullduggery in those uprisings and revolts overseas. He knew more about people than those generals did. That's why the poolroom was never off limits to me. All I had to say was "Pops, I'm going over to The Heights," and he would say, "All right, Roodle, be on time for supper." He knew there was no chance of my missing out at the banquet boards.

The Heights was a fantastic room at 182nd Street and Broadway in my old neighborhood. It was called Heights Recreation and I could come and go there as I pleased, even though I was only 12 or 13 at the time. Back then they didn't have draft cards to prove your age so the way you got into a poolroom was if you were wearing long pants. You could be a midget but if you had on long pants, in you went. I started wearing long pants when I was eight because I was so enormous there wasn't a pair of knicker britches to fit me in all New York. So I had to buy my clothes in the men's department and once I got into those ankle satchels I was playing pool for cash in rooms all over Washington Heights.

Everytime a newspaper reporter interviews me he'll say, "Minnesota, where did you grow up?" They all ask the same question and I always give them the same answer. "I was born growed up," I say. And that's the way it was. I never was a kid.

There were some tremendous rooms around Washington Heights in the 20s and I was in every one looking for nickel-and-dime action. There was a beautiful room called Osborn's at 178th Street and St. Nicholas Avenue and another joint down in the subway stop at 181st and St. Nicholas. One time I hustled a kid out of a pair of ice skates down there. Cranfield's was another tremendous room at 181st and Bennett Avenue. Cranfield had another place at 146th Street and Broadway and I used to go there all the time to cut up jackpots with the owner's son who was a little blond-headed kid about five years younger than me. He was a little left-hander by the name of Babe Cranfield and when he was seven or eight he could shoot out the lights. In the 20s all the Yankee and Giant baseball stars hung around Cranfield's. I saw Babe Ruth there a hundred times. He would come walking down the street and the kids would mob him for autographs and balls and passes to the park, only when he got in the room, the Cranfield kid tried to get Babe Ruth to the table. I think the kid wanted to hustle The Babe out of his hot dog money.

The rooms were always jam-packed and sometimes you might have to wait in line for a table. But the places were *really* mobbed if one of the name stars played an exhibition in a neighborhood joint. When a fellow like Ralph Greenleaf, who was the world pocket billiard champion in the 20s, played a neighborhood the crowds would be so big they almost needed the militia to handle them. Greenleaf was the greatest tournament player who ever lived. He was my first idol and to tell you the truth, he's still my idol.

Usually when a name star came to a neighborhood room, the owner woud select one of his top players to represent the home territory. It was a gimmick to arouse neighborhood interest, but if you happened to be the young fellow selected it was a tremendous honor to play on the same table with one of the stars. I played Greenleaf years later down on Broadway but the first time I opened a rack with a top star was at Heights Recreation in 1926. His name was Cowboy Weston and he was a real genuine player and a tremendous old showman. He was in his 50s, and I was 13. It was one of those May and December propositions.

For three weeks there were big posters all over the neighborhood announcing "Cowboy Weston, The World Famous Cue Artist, Will Play Rudy Wanderone in an Exhibition Match at Heights Recreation." I never had a nom-de-plummer back then so I had to use my regular name. Everybody around the Heights asked me if I thought I could beat the old Cowboy and I told them, "Listen, I'll shoot that old rough rider right out of the saddle."

The day of the big shoot-out it looked like there was a coronation in Washington Heights. Cowboy Weston was sponsored by the old Auburn automobile people and when he made an appearance the local dealers put on a parade of cars that ran for blocks with the old cowpoke riding atop an open convertible at the head of the procession. He looked exactly like the President when he's out campaigning, only Cowboy Weston had on a fabulous Western outfit. They said it set his sponsor back $1000 and it looked every penny of it. He had on a big white cowboy hat that was like three feet wide and he wore chaps and boots, and had a beautiful pair of pearl-handled six-shooters on his hips. Tom Mix and Hoot Gibson in their balmiest days never had anything to touch it. He was fabulous and when he rode down the street up on the top of that old touring car he looked bigger than Primo Carnera.

When he finally got to the table and we were introduced I had to take a second look at the old Cowboy. He looked real glamorous in the parade but up close he was all grey and weatherbeaten looking. He looked so old I figured he came over on the Mayflower. We played 125 points straight pool, which was all I knew back then outside of a little Rotation, and once I got on the table it was brutal. I shot the old Cowboy clean off his horse and had the first notch in my gun. I mean I really whacked him out cold.

I was a big attraction around Washington Heights after that. Later on I played the Coca-Cola Masked Marvel in another gimmick promotion. Coca-Cola had to push its stuff real hard in those days because when somebody got thirsty in the 20s they belted down the alcohol and juniper berry juice, which was what they used to mix up a batch of bathtub gin. The Masked Marvel production was different than the Cowboy show because the Masked Marvel never paraded into town. He sort of sneaked in like he was a villain. There was always a lot of mystery and intrigue because nobody ever knew who the Masked Marvel was on account of he came to the table wearing a black hood over his head, just like the wrestlers. Sometimes they would have him come on like 15 minutes late just to keep the crowd buzzing and when he finally arrived the suckers thought he was an executioner from Sing Sing the way they eyeballed him. When it was all over, Coca-Cola would throw drinks on the house and the mooches would guzzle all they could hold. It was always a tremendous attraction and the fellow behind the mask would always be a top-notch player.

One time it might be Erwin Rudolph, who won the world title like five times, and the next trip you might catch Andrew St. Jean who was called The Lowell Kid because he came from Lowell, Massachusetts. Iron Joe Procita of New York City was another Masked Marvel. They had a zillion different players behind those hoods. Now if the local hope happened to beat the Masked Marvel, he got a beautiful two-piece cue stick. I won so many of them I had trouble giving them away, which is more than I could say later on after I won a cash proposition. In a poolroom if there's some cash up for grabs, you never have the slightest problem. Pool players are addicted to money, especially if it's OP money—Other People's money.

I won dozens of those exhibition matches when I was coming up but after I whacked out the old Cowboy I thought I was the greatest thing on earth. That's the day I decided I was going to be a pool player and leave the working dodge to other people. I knew I was pretty good at pool since I was ten years old, but after I beat Cowboy Weston I thought I was something real special.

When I finished the eighth grade, which was as far as most kids went in school back then, my old man wanted me to be a vaudeville strong man or a professional wrestler. He primed me pretty good on the strong-man proposition ever since I was a baby. He used to search out the big vaudeville houses where the muscle men were performing and if those Max Factor Ajaxes challenged anybody in the audience, the old man would run up on the stage and take over. He had forearms like old-time piano legs and he could take a spike and bend it like it was a pretzel. He made a lot of those vaudeville strong boys blush like a doll who got caught in the rumble seat.

One day we were watching a vaudeville strong man and he put an elephant on a platform and lifted the whole joint with his shoulders. "Anybody out there like to try it?" he asked. That was all my old man and his brother, Gottlieb, were waiting for. They rushed out on the stage and lifted that elephant without a grunt. Sometimes my old man would say, "This is easy, why I bet my little boy, Roodle, can do it." Then I'd go on stage and lift weights like they were basketballs. I always brought down the house because I was like six or eight years old with the most beautiful reddish blond curly hair you ever saw. I was 40 years ahead of The Beatles. One strong man team wanted me and my old man to go on the circuit. They said they would bill us as "Samson and Son" but the old man said there wasn't enough gold in the proposition.

I never went for the muscle dodge so the old man said I should consider the wrestling gimmick. One summer out on Long Island he wrestled the famous Stanislaus Zabisco, who was the leading grunt and groan attraction of the day, and they paid him a tremendous purse. "Look, Roodle," he said, "you are young and strong like a mule, you could make millions." But I never went that route because I had always avoided building up strength in the fingers and hands. I already knew I was going to be a pool player so the hands and fingers had to be real loose.

I had one other unbelievable proposition from a kid in the neighborhood who wanted me to be a 100 per cent genuine muscle man. The kid was about my age and he was named Saul and he was skinny and emaciated looking with pimples all over his face. He wasn't strong enough to swat a fly but he wanted to be a gang lord like Owney Madden, who lived up in the neighborhood. Saul used to read the papers about what a ruthless thug Madden was supposed to be and Saul got so he was trying to handle the kids in the neighborhood the way he figured the gangsters used the muscle. One day he tried to muscle this big kid we called The Kraut. The Kraut was enormous, even bigger than me, and he looked like he was in every battle since Bunker Hill. The Kraut belted little Saul pretty good and that's the day Saul asked me to be his bodyguard.

I talked to The Kraut and he said he wouldn't bother Saul so long as Saul didn't bother him so I told Saul it was all set and he was so happy he went beserk giving me presents. He belonged to the Boy Scouts so first he tried to give me his knapsack but I didn't know what to do with it because I never was a hiker or anything like that. Then he gave me his hunting knife. It was a tremendous looking thing with a carved handle and a hand-tooled sheath but I turned it down because even as a kid I never liked weapons or violence of any kind. So Saul said, "Let's go over to my house and see if we can find something you want."

Saul lived in a fantastic joint, I mean a real mansion, with fabulous velvet wallpaper and the most tremendous drapes and furniture you ever saw. His mother was a gorgeous doll and when we walked in she said, "I'm happy to meet you, Rudy—won't you sit down and have something to eat?" I went to Saul's house every day after that. "Listen," I told him, "if you want to pay me protection, all you have to do is invite me over to eat every day." So every day we would sit around belting out the marinated herring and smoked tongue and corned beef and then we whacked out the dried apricots by the hundreds. When the cupboard looked a little bare, Saul's mother would send us to the delicatessen for more. I guess that was the first budget I put out of business.

It was a tremendous proposition except that Saul really got caught up in the romance of the underworld. He was always talking about how we should muscle in on Owney Madden, so I would give him the con about what a tremendous idea that was while I was on the second helpings. But when I found out Saul was dead serious, I gave him the double and quit coming around.

A lot of remarkable things can happen when you're 13 years old but the one thing I remember most about being 13 was the day I whacked out old Cowboy Weston. Ambushing the old Cowboy the way I did was the real turning point in my life because after that all I ever did was shoot pool. I also graduated from P.S. 132 the same year. With no more school, I found myself with a whole lot of time on my hands and being dedicated to the advantages of unemployment, I used the time to polish my pool game.

Then one day when I figured I was ready to step up in class, I hopped a subway and rode downtown to Broadway—where the action was.

CHAPTER 5

A Sultan in Never-Never Land

Broadway in 1926 was the most exciting place on earth, especially for a 13-year-old man. I'm telling you, I never was a boy. Times Square in those days was fantastic. There were more poolrooms than hot dog stands and the tomatoes running on the loose were beautiful beyond compare. The first few days I forgot all about pool and just stood around belting out the hot dogs and eyeballing the dolls.

Everything about Broadway back then was like a Magic Carpet Ride. Just walking down the street I felt like a Sultan, especially when those gorgeous tomatoes were romping around. It was a different era, even the air was different. You could breathe it and get paralyzed with excitement. That's on the square. People spent money like it was confetti and the booze barons kept the playground open 24 hours a day so the suckers working on the night shift could get in on the action. I was afraid to go to sleep because I thought I might miss something.

Vaudeville and the musical comedies really had the action and the stars were real stars. There weren't any talking pictures yet and radio was just beginning and television was as far off then as the moon is today. So the Broadway actors were the legitimate attractions of the day. They all had an air of mystery about them and if you happened to see a star on the street, you just had to stop dead in your tracks and look. It was the way they carried themselves, the way they walked and dressed. They were fabulous to see, and everybody tried to copy their style because all the suckers were hoping to end up top bananas themselves.

It was the same way with the pool players. When I went down to Broadway I fashioned myself after Ralph Greenleaf. He was the all-time super star of billiards and a fabulous looking man. These fun players posing as luminaries today couldn't carry Greenleaf's cue case. Greenleaf had talent, which was an A Number One requisite for stardom in the 20s. Today you find the gimmick and you hire a press agent and in three weeks you're on television making serious money. But back then if you were a pool player, you had to know how to shoot pool and if you were a singer, you had sure better be able to sing. Listen, if The Beatles had come to New York in the 20s they would have ended up in the crapper.

One of the first shows I took in on Broadway was an afternoon bill at The Palace and it wasn't the dolls that attracted the crowd. It was Greenleaf. He played The Palace with his wife, Princess Nai Tai Tai, and the scalpers made zillions bootlegging tickets. The Princess was a headline singer in vaudeville pulling down $600 a week as The Oriental Thrush and when she married Greenleaf in 1925 the wedding made the front page all over the world, even in Hong Kong. She was half Chinese and half English, a tremendous looking tomato, and Greenleaf looked like a matinee idol. Together they pulled down like $2,000 a week for an act called "Ralph Greenleaf, The Aristocrat of Billiards, Assisted by Princess Nai Tai Tai." Greenleaf made with the fancy trick shots and The Princess just stood on the side of the stage and explained what was taking place.

The act opened with The Princess strutting out on the stage in a white ermine coat that went from her shoulders to her toes and when she walked on the whole place came apart. My God, she walked like a peacock. "Hello, out there," she said and The Palace got as quiet as the morgue. She was a tiny little woman but she had a deep, throaty voice that sounded like it was coming out of a megaphone. Listen, when she just whispered, you could hear her clean over in Hackensack. I'll tell you who she sounded like: Tallulah Bankhead, exactly like Bankhead. I already worshipped Greenleaf but after that matinee I had a terrific crush on his wife. She was exquisite beyond belief.

When the curtain opened, Greenleaf walked out in a tuxedo and he handled himself like a Barrymore. He looked so handsome in that high society get-up he would have made Rock Hudson look like Quasimodo. They had the pool table in the middle of the stage before a big black curtain and about a dozen mirrors were suspended from up top behind the table. Greenleaf did the tricks just like he would in a poolroom and the mirrors picked up every move of the balls and sent it out to the audience. When I hear about Telstar satellite, I always think of Greenleaf playing The Palace. It was the same principle when you think of it.

The Princess stood over on the side and put on that real thick actress accent. "Ladies and gentlemen," she would say, "Mr. Greenleaf, the greatest pocket billiard champion of all time, will now perform a series of intricate wing shots—your undivided attention, if you please." Then everyone got up on the edge of the seat and looked in the mirrors and Greenleaf would whack off a half-dozen wings like he was eating ice cream. He stepped up the trick shots as he went along and when the act was over he and The Princess had to take a hundred bows before the crowd would let them off the stage. Greenleaf and The Princess were 100 per cent star quality. No filage about it.

After the show a jillion people jammed the stage door hoping to get a glimpse of them when they came out. But I never went that sucker route because the guy with me happened to be a pool player and he said we could meet Greenleaf and his wife any time in the rooms around Times Square. I met them a few days later at Louie Kreuter's room, which was a walk-down establishment at 49th and Broadway. I told him, "Mr. Greenleaf, I want to warn you—I'm in love with your wife." He laughed and The Princess said to me, "Dah-ling," she said, "you're an adorable little fat boy." And then she kissed me on the cheek. "Princess Nai Tai Tai," I said, "you are the sweetest smelling woman I have ever known." I tell you, she smelled like a whole gallon of perfume. I got to know them both real well when I became a top player myself and every time I'd see The Princess she would say, "Fatty, Dah-ling, am I still your Cinderella? Do I still smell of lilac water and Cashmere Bouquet?" She was fabulous and she's still fabulous. She made 73 this year and she operates a high-fashion gown shop in Philadelphia where she creates fantastic ensembles for all those Main Line debutantes. I talked to her on the telephone a few months back and I asked her if she could knock out a fancy wardrobe for Eva-line and she said, "Come see me, Fatty, Dah-ling, and I'll give you a good price. I'll hustle you real good." She's remarkable.

I got to know Greenleaf real well a few years later when he was operating a room on Broadway and we played a couple of exhibition matches together but I never played him for cash. Greenleaf never gambled because he was hauling in $100,000 a year in exhibitions and vaudeville when $100,000 was like a million today. The world title really meant something back in those days.

Actually, I did hustle Greenleaf one time. It was in the early 30s when Three Cushions was still my best stick. It never was his game but we played for one dollar stakes and I beat him. He loved it. He told The Princess, "Nai," he said, "I've been busted clean by the Fat Boy," and the Princess said, "How could you let that happen, Ralph? Why, you know what Confucius said, 'Beware of Rudy Wanderone.'" They were tremendous people and they treated me like I was their son. They just don't make people like the Greenleafs any more.

The first room I went to on Broadway was Willie Hoppe's place, which was on top of a dance hall. It was on the fifth floor of the old Roseland Building at 51st and Broadway right where the City Squire Motel is today. I had read about Hoppe winning all those Balkline tournaments so I figured all the top action players would be looking for a little camaraderie in his room. But to tell you the brutal truth, it was a big letdown the first time I walked in. The room was packed with a hundred old men playing Balkline. It was unbelievable. The youngest kid in the place was like 70 and none of them would bet you they were alive. It was like going to the library. The only thing in the place that appealed to me was the lunch counter. I asked one of the younger players—a guy who was about 68—where the action was. "Down the block," he whispered, "at Louie Kreuter's." So I headed for Kreuter's.

I went back to Hoppe's joint many, many times. I loved Three Cushions in those days and me and Hoppe became good friends. I told him I hated straight pool and he wanted to know why. "Listen," I said, "you can get out of stroke, dead out of stroke, just sitting there while the other fellow is running balls." He was crazy about me and we played Three Cushions all the time. I beat him a few now and then and he told me I could become a tremendous cushion man if I worked at it. But I was always screwing out of his joint on account of you couldn't get a nickel's worth of action there. It was like a Sunday Night Prayer Meeting with all those elders creeping around the tables. Half of them didn't know the Spanish-American War was over.

I didn't get any serious action on Broadway for awhile because I was still an Appleknocker and I had to protect myself. But I met all the stars of the game at Kreuter's and I found out they were all timid, shy people who wouldn't harm a canary. The place looked like a Hall of Fame. You could look around and see the top billiard stars in the world—Jake Schaefer and Welker Cochran and R. L. Cannifaz and Joe Chamaco of Mexico and Kinrey Matsuyama of Japan and Jimmy Lee of China and Johnny Layton and Jack Forraker. Sometimes Hoppe would drop in at Kreuter's. Then all the top pockets men would hang there, too—Greenleaf and Andrew St. Jean and Andrew Ponzi and Jerome Keough, and old Cowboy Weston and Erwin Rudolph and Frank Taberski and Thomas Heuston and Arthur Woods and Chick Seaback. The place was always crawling with stars.

I met each and every one of them and they all helped me with my game. Like one might be fantastic on cutting a ball and the other would be an artist on drawing the cue ball back so what I learned was like going to a billiard college. Every one had a particular style and I watched them by the hour and I took a little bit from each one of them and put it all together in my game. That's exactly why I always excelled at One Pocket because it requires a tremendous knowledge of every game on the table and I learned them all from the masters. I not only learned all the games, but I remembered everything I saw and then I improved on it. Back then they used to chide Jack Dempsey because they said he was a braggart but it was like Dempsey said, "If you can do it, it ain't bragging." That's the way it was with me when I became a top player. I would say I would do it and then I would. So it wasn't bragging.

In those days I made my pocket money beating the suckers and mooches who came in looking for a mark and sometimes I'd play businessmen, like manufacturers and executives from the Garment District, or young song writers or actors. I played way under my speed, know what I mean, and let them beat me a few. Then I'd really stick 'em up.

Those old-timers would watch me and they would say, "Rudy, you ought to get yourself a backer," but I told them the Fat Boy would never need those hairy legs. "I'll be my own backer," I'd say. And I always was. The only backer I had in those days was my old man. He was a tremendous card player and he taught me how to play poker when I was two, three years old. When I was about eight I was playing clabbiash for cash. It was a tremendous game and when my old man saw how well I played it he backed me against other players, sometimes men as old as him. "Roodle," he would say, "this looks like a good match—see what you can do. If you lose, it will be a good experience and you can win next time." He let me keep everything I won. Those backers in the poolrooms chop you up like ground sirloin.

The first year I was romping around Broadway was the most tremendous time of my life. Thanks to my old man, I was already wise to the proposition angles and the card gimmicks when I went downtown but I got postgraduate training on Broadway. Since my old man and Owney Madden were friends, all I had to do was mention Owney's name anywhere on Broadway and I was accepted like a brother lodge member in good standing. Here I was like 13 or 14 and already I was running around with the smartest proposition men there was. I got to be tremendous friends with Titanic Thompson, who was the greatest proposition man who ever lived. He and I had a lot of action together later on in the Midwest and down around Norfolk, Virginia. Ty and I hit it off right from the overture, and since he was one of the highest rollers and top action men of all time, he introduced me to the important people on the street. I knew Nick The Greek and George The Greek real well and sometimes I used to swap the conversation with Arnold Rothstein and George McManus and Nate Raymond and Nickey Arnstein. Those were the faculty deans of my Alma Mater.

I would listen to those generals talk over a proposition and I'm telling you, they went over it with a fine-tooth comb. They never missed an angle. I had a fantastic memory and I never forgot a word I heard. I was what you call wise to the comings and the goings, like a good cop. If a cop is worth his night stick he has to be what they call street wise. He not only has to know the area but he has to know the situation. He has to know the people and know what they're going to do before they do it. It was the same thing in gambling. You have to know the situation, understand the proposition, so you will know what the other guy is going to do and then beat him to it. That's why I was always so cold-blooded when I took a proposition to the pool table. I had already studied the situation from every side and I knew I had a Hungarian cinch or I never would have gone for it in the first place. That's why you would hear some of my adversaries screaming murder a few minutes after I had put the show on the road. All of a sudden it would dawn on them that they had been had, and they would yelp like somebody was stretching their ears.

"Listen," I would tell them, "I know everything you know and nobody knows what I know," but none of those suckers ever understood what I meant.

Titanic was old enough to be my old man and he used to watch me operate, understand? He never let his eyes off me and he was always trying to steer me into a trap for one of his propositions. He had hundreds of 'em. He bet on some of the most fascinating things you ever heard. Like one time later on in Chicago he said he was willing to bet any amount that he could throw a walnut clear over a skyscraper in the business district. Now even a sucker knows something like that is impossible, but the difference is a sucker wouldn't be smart enough to figure out how Ty might pull it off at that.

He talked about the walnut proposition for weeks and finally some fellows who thought they were getting the best of the situation took Ty up on the offer. He got down for a zillion. So he says, "All right, gentlemen, now I'll go down to the Greek's fruit stand on the corner and I'll just select one nut—is it all right if I make it an English walnut?" Everybody said that would be fine. So Ty walks up to the Greek and flips him like a fin and says, "Sir, I'd like this English walnut." Then he took it and gave it a tremendous heave and that English walnut cleared that building like it was orbited at Cape Kennedy. Those suckers paid off but they all wanted to know how Ty was able to accomplish such a fantastic phenomenon that not only defied all known laws of science, but made Sir Isaac Newton look like a bellhop as well.

Ty kept them all guessing for weeks until the Greek who operated the fruit stand sang. Ty paid him like a C note to let him fill the English walnut with mercury and put it back in the box, understand. So when Ty picked out the walnut he really had the Hungarian lock going for him. Once that walnut started going up, you couldn't have held it down with the Queen Mary. Ty was always pulling cons like that. He handled a lot of serious money in his time but he lost most of it on a pool table to the past master of the proposition art.

He was always giving me the this-and-that about all sorts of unbelievable propositions but I always shortened him up. So he figured the Fat Boy from Washington Heights was real smart. In fact, one night he said, "Listen, Rudy, I'm beginning to believe you understand the situation. But," he said, "let me give you a word of warning, son. Don't you ever make the mistake of trying to outsmart Smart Henny because Smart Henny is the smartest man on Broadway." So right there I knew Ty was going to try and set me up for Smart Henny.

CHAPTER 6

A New Game
and a New Name

Smart Henny was a big-time Broadway bookmaker and if he liked a proposition real good he would go about as high as anybody ever dared to go. He would bet with both hands and when he won, which was like all the time, Smart Henny needed a sack to carry the cash.

He liked to drop in the poolrooms and back the hustlers if he thought he had a Hungarian combination going for him, but if Smart Henny didn't like the proposition, he wouldn't bet a match. He was always trapping those sucker-backers because half of those eggs didn't know their way to the Automat.

Smart Henny was always giving me the this-and-that about a zillion different propositions but I never went for any of his jolts because Smart Henny never gave odds any better than a shylock. He was real smart, I mean really cute, but what Smart Henny didn't know, and nobody else on Broadway knew, was that if Smart Henny ever tried to outsmart the Fat Boy, it would be like a teacher in a log cabin school in Kentucky trying to match wits with Einstein. I watched him operate for a long, long time and the more I saw of him, the more I knew it was going to take a tremendous proposition to prove that Smart Henny wasn't as smart as everybody on Broadway thought. I finally came up with a Hungarian lock-up to trap Smart Henny but I had to travel halfway around the country and back to New York City to find it.

Back in those days the pool players used to sit around Kreuter's cutting up jackpots, which is exactly the same thing as sitting around telling lies.

Like two of them would go to the lunch counter and one would say, "Yeah, I just got back from Detroit and I won enough money out there to retire. I ran 109 (balls) and out against Cross-Eyed Jesse and sent him to the poorhouse." So the other guy would say, "Listen, you ain't heard nothing yet. I'm in Chicago three months ago and I got Rotation Slim in the one-hole and I ran 79 and out for a real bundle." You always hear that kind of conversation in the poolrooms, even today, but I never pay any attention to it because it's right out of Aesop's Fables, except back when I was young and what you would call impressionable and I couldn't wait until I got out on the road myself.

I built up a bankroll of a couple C notes I had won from the manufacturers and doctors and lawyers and I told my mother I was going to take a trip to my uncle's farm out in Iowa. She thought it was a good idea because she said maybe my uncle would give me a job on his farm. My mother didn't know that the kind of action I was after didn't have anything to do with animal husbandry or soil cultivation. The only soil I was interested in cultivating was soiled, or unsoiled, cash.

My uncle Emil Schaub, who was the richest man in five counties, had this tremendous farm in Blairstown, Iowa. It was a hundred times the size of Central Park and he raised everything known to man, like corn and soybeans and alfalfa and oats—and milk cows and pigs and chickens on the side. He worked from morning till night like it was an obsession. It was ridiculous beyond compare, but what I really liked about farm life was they put tremendous meals on the boards. The calories were fantastic.

My Uncle Emil wanted me to get in the cattle raising dodge out there. He said, "Roodle, you love to eat—why don't you raise your own cattle?" But that never appealed to me because I thought killing those animals was a dreadful thing. "Well," Uncle Emil said, "if you're against killing the steers, how come you love to eat steaks the way you do?" I said, "Well, Uncle Emil, the way I see it, there's nothing you can do for those poor creatures once they're hanging on a hook in the A&P."

The country out in Iowa was beautiful beyond compare, especially in the northeast part of the state. A lot of Swiss people settled out there because it reminded them of the old country; in fact, a certain section around Dubuque is called "Little Switzerland." So I started moving around those little towns getting a little action here and there but the best action spot was around Dubuque, which was on the Mississippi River.

One day in a little settlement right outside Dubuque I asked a farmer where the poolroom was and he said it was at the feed store, which really sounded like a corny con to me. But when I got there I found out everything was at the feed store. In the front was a huge general store with a big potbellied stove smack in the middle of the joint and over in the corner they had a tremendous soda fountain, the kind they had in the old-time drug stores. The poolroom was right behind the general store and the feed store was behind the poolroom. It was a funny arrangement because the whole joint was under the same roof. The day I walked in they had just gotten a tremendous shipment of soybean meal, and it was so big they didn't have the space to store it. So they stacked the sacks one on top of the other all around the walls of the poolroom and the eyeballers climbed up on top of the sacks and watched the action on the tables. It looked like a Saturday Night Barn Dance except there wasn't a jew's-harp or a fiddle in the whole place.

I started playing a young farmer in his 20s and stuck him up for like $4 and he ran like a deer. He told me I was a pretty good pool player but he said there was no way I could beat a friend of his who he called Ole Sauerkraut. So I told him to go get Ole Sauerkraut and we'll really get the show on the road. About an hour later this old farmer comes rushing in and when I got a good look at him he was even more ancient than Cowboy Weston. He was in a pair of faded bib overalls and he had on a pair of plow shoes that looked like the kind the infantry wears. And suntanned? He was so suntanned he looked like a Polynesian. Ole Sauerkraut had a big gold watch, about the size the railroad men carry, and while we were getting together the proposition, he kept taking out that watch and looking at it every few minutes.

"Mr. Sauerkraut," I said, "let's get to the table. I'll try to take as little of your time as possible." He looked at me and said, "Fat Boy," he said, "when I come to play pool, time means nary a thing to me—I'll play you Rotation."

The eyeballers sitting up on the sacks started hee-hawing and giggling and one of them said, "Fat Boy, you'll never whup Ole Sauerkraut." I knew they were trying to shark me in their own way so I played way below my speed and it was no trouble for the old man to win the first few games. But then he cracked smart and said, "Fat Boy, if you're a aiming to catch up, you better double the stakes." That's when I knew Ole Sauerkraut belonged to me.

I tapped out Ole Sauerkraut clean down to his overalls and then I played him for the watch and won that, too. He kept saying, "I know I can beat this Fat Boy, I know it, I know it." I've heard that lament many, many a time in my life because being fat seems to be an added attraction for most people. They all figure because you're fat, you must be something real special so everybody wants a piece of the Fat Man in the worst kind of way.

I stood around waiting to see what the old farmer was going to do next but he was dead silent. So I took out the watch, the same way he did, and I said, "Mr. Sauerkraut, I have time to play you one more game. What do you want to play for?"

He thought awhile and then he said, "Sonny, all I got left to wager is Heckle and Jekyll." He said Heckle and Jekyll were his team of plow mules and he said if I was willing to play for $100 against the mules, he was ready. I told him even though I loved animals of every kind, there was no way I could see my way clear to play for a team of mules, especially when they were named Heckle and Jekyll. So that was the end of that but I asked him how come he gave his mules names like Heckle and Jekyll.

"Sonny," he said, "it's like this. That Heckle is the happiest mule I ever knew. He never gives me nary a problem and always seems to enjoy his work, but the other one, the one I call Jekyll, is the hardest-headed son-of-a-bitch in the whole goll-dern state of Iowa."

That started the eyeballers on the feed sacks to hee-hawing again and Ole Sauerkraut got red-necked. So I took Ole Sauerkraut out and bought him an enormous ice cream soda, and just before he left I gave him back his watch because if there is one thing I never had a bit of use for it was a watch. That's most of the suckers' problem, the watches and clocks. They become slaves to the time tables and they get a little behind in their schedule and they start running and running to try to catch up and they never do. It's a lifetime grief. I wouldn't give a quarter for the finest timepiece in the history of the world.

I hustled all over Iowa that way. I made every town in the state—Cedar Rapids, Marengo, Des Moines, Waterloo, Iowa City, Guthrie Center and Council Bluffs and a hundred other stops. I remember Council Bluffs real well on account of it was right across the river from Omaha, Nebraska, and I went to Omaha one day and got tapped out real good playing poker. I got busted down to my last dime.

I walked out of the joint and was standing in front of a poolroom when a Salvation Army outfit came up and started playing music and talking about saving sinners. So this doll in the Salvation Army bonnet came up to me and said, "You look mighty low, friend." I told her that was exactly right, I was really low, about as low as anybody could ever get. So she told me if I joined in the singing she would help save me and then some mooch said that after the community sing they always put on a beef stew at the headquarters around the corner. So I sang like a canary and then I belted out two plates of beef stew. But the doll started smiling at me and when I smiled back she started putting on a pose and looking starry-eyed and twisting her toes, which is a very dangerous sign because it means the tomato likes you real good. That wouldn't have been so bad except this doll was the most forlorn creature you ever laid eyes on. She would have made Sophie Tucker look like Zsa Zsa Gabor. So I faded out of there real quick. That's on the square.

I headed back to my uncle's farm but over in Council Bluffs I noticed a picnic in progress and everybody was belting out the chicken and the potato salad. So I moved in and found out it was a church outing and after a little conversation, they all started shooting me the chicken and the potato salad. I told them I was a tourist from New York and somebody had picked my pocket in Omaha and they all said they were very sorry to hear that. But when I told them I was Emil Schaub's nephew, they all got excited because a few of them knew Uncle Emil. So one gentleman said he could let me have a fin to get back to Blairstown and I screwed out again, only I headed back to Omaha and got that mooch who cleaned me in the poker action and won some of my money back playing Rotation. By the time I left Omaha I really had a bankroll, so I headed down to Kansas City.

The high rollers in Kansas City were talking about a new game they had seen down in Tulsa and Oklahoma City. They called it One Pocket but nobody was playing it in Kansas City at the time, even though they said it was a tremendous gambling game. So now I'm bound for Oklahoma City looking for the fellow who invented One Pocket, a fellow by the name of Jack Hill.

Babe Emmett had a fantastic room on Main Street in Oklahoma City and I went there looking for Jack Hill but they told me I would find him in the billiard parlor at the Huckin's Hotel down the street. I must have stayed at the Huckin's Hotel for six months watching old man Hill playing One Pocket. He told me if I could play Three Cushions and Banks and straight pool, I would have a tremendous advantage in One Pocket so we played some Banks and Three Cushions and once he saw the way I could bank a shot he said I wouldn't have any trouble at all.

One Pocket is exactly what it says—one pocket. Each player gets one pocket. Nowadays in New York they call it A Pocket Apiece. The player has to pocket all his balls in one pocket, which means it takes a tremendous player to really master the game. I'll tell you what it's like. Say somebody's going to rob an apartment house, only there's just one door, so you have to walk all around the joint looking for that one door. Now it stands to reason the job will be easier if the house has six ways of entry. You can take your pick of how you want to get in. Another thing, in straight pool, you just shoot to pocket balls, but in One Pocket sometimes it's not smart to pocket a ball because it may be even smarter to roll the cue ball into a position where your opponent won't have a shot at all. It's a lot like chess, although I've never played chess. There's a lot of defensive moves in One Pocket.

When I left Oklahoma City, Jack Hill told me I played One Pocket better than anybody alive except him and his protege, a fellow by the name of Hubert Cokes who I met later on in New York. So I started back East, stopping off in every poolroom to improve my One Pocket game. I figured this was the proposition to crack out Smart Henny.

So now I'm back in New York, only I find out Hubert Cokes has already been there and has introduced One Pocket to everybody on Broadway, although none of the top players took it seriously at first. Then one day who walks in Kreuter's but a pool hustler called Jalopy who was from Brooklyn and he said he had played a little One Pocket himself and was taking on all comers. Jalopy and I played even at first but I hashed him real good so he wouldn't play me any more unless I spotted him a ball, then a ball and the break and then two balls. I kept stepping up the odds until I whacked out Jalopy so clean that he said there was no way on earth he would ever go to the table with me again. He was very sincere about his intentions because he did a fadeout and nobody saw Jalopy around for like three months.

Then one day he comes walking in with a tremendous bankroll and I started giving him the conversation about propositions but he said he would rather go to the gas chamber than play me. So I kept giving him the this-and-that and finally Jalopy said, "Look, Fatty, I wouldn't play you even if you said my scratches don't count." So I said, "What do you mean by that, Jalopy?" and Jalopy said, "I mean if I scratched I wouldn't have to pay a ball." So right there I invented a brand new proposition.

By scratches don't count, Jalopy not only meant he didn't have to pay a ball but he could roll the cue ball to any part of the table without hitting another ball or a rail. It was tremendous odds to give a man but I knew a player Jalopy's speed didn't belong on the same table with me. So I went to a room in Washington Heights and played myself scratches don't count for like six hours. I could see it was such a tremendous proposition that Jalopy couldn't turn it down but the way I banked I knew I had a mortal lock. So the next day I conversed with Jalopy again and this time I got him on the table. Now this is on the square. I beat Jalopy worse than when I was spotting him like a ball, or two or three balls. I mean I really cracked him out. After that he wouldn't even give me the time of day much less engage me in a cash proposition.

Word about the scratches-no-count proposition traveled all over Broadway and somebody put a tongue in Smart Henny's ear and Smart Henny said it was the biggest sucker offer he ever heard. So Smart Henny shows up around Kreuter's and wants to know if I'm on the level. Then he says will I give those kind of odds to Coney Island Al and I said that would be just fine.

Coney Island Al was an old-timer who was hard of hearing in one ear, although if he really wanted to hear what was being said, Coney Island Al wouldn't be hard of hearing at all. Like one day a mooch who was busted out comes up to Coney Island Al and screams in his bad ear, "Al, can you lend me $2?" Coney Island Al made out like he couldn't understand what the mooch was saying, so one of the eyeballers walks over and says to the mooch, "Use the good ear." So the mooch walks around to Coney Island's other ear and as he does, he sees Coney Island Al counting some cash he just won so the mooch screams in the good ear, "Al, can you lend me $5?" And Coney Island Al says, "Go back to the other ear."

So now Smart Henny comes around Kreuter's with Coney Island Al, who was the funniest looking little fellow you ever saw. He looked exactly like a little chimpanzee but he was a pretty fair shot. Everybody got down on Coney Island Al real good because it looked like the odds I was giving were so fantastic that Coney Island Al couldn't lose. Nobody dreamed I was going to bank those balls from every angle known to man.

I'll tell you what it was like. It was like the day the banks tapped out. You never saw so many sad-faced creatures in a hundred years. I ruined Coney Island Al and real quick everybody got off Coney Island, everybody except Smart Henny. Smart Henny kept betting higher and higher because he figured with the scratches don't count proposition there was no way I could win it. He just couldn't quit. He thought that sooner or later I would make a slip and then Coney Island Al would whack me out and Smart Henny would end up with all the cash. But I kept winning and winning until I thought I would have to call an armored car to get out of the joint. It was unbelievable.

Finally, Smart Henny said he had enough. "Fat Boy," he said, "I've been betting propositions around pool halls all my life but you cured me." Smart Henny never came around much after that.

All the eyeballers were real impressed and they started saying that if Smart Henny was the smartest fellow on Broadway, where did that leave the Fat Boy. "I'll tell you where it leaves him," one of the eyeballers said, "it means that Fatty is twice as smart as Smart Henny."

"That's exactly right," Titanic Thompson said, "he's twice as smart— why Fatty is double smart."

So from then on everywhere I went on Broadway the guys and dolls would say, "Here comes Double Smart Fats." And that was my first nom-de-plummer.

I won so much gelt off Smart Henny it looked like I was smuggling coconuts in my pockets, only every mooch on Broadway knew what a lovely bunch of coconuts it really was. I got bit more than a welfare worker.

So what I did a couple of days later was buy my first car—a Stutz Bearcat that was fabulous beyond compare. Then I really started moving among the Broadway Sociables.

CHAPTER 7

I Could Spot Einstein the Ten Ball

It was a real genuine pleasure to drive a car in New York City in those days because you never had any of this bumper-to-bumper grief you got today and you could even pull up to a curb and park without a hundred gendarmes swooping down writing out tickets. So I drove that Stutz Bearcat up and down Broadway like a big maharajah just off the boat from Bombay and the suckers would see me and say, "There goes Double Smart Fats in the car Smart Henny bought him."

After I ruined Smart Henny the way I did, I had to come out with a new motto: "I'll Give You An Out And Take Out After You," which meant I was giving the suckers such a cinch that they wouldn't quit and then I'd shoot their eyes out. And every proposition was for cash, not trophies. I never played for fun in my life. If I wanted to have fun, I would play with girls and when I was running around Broadway I played with a zillion fabulous tomatoes that were gorgeous beyond compare.

I was romping around with this fantastic redhead who was a musical comedy chorine and one night we're out driving. We stop at a restaurant for something to eat and the doll gets out one door and I jump out the other. So who is standing on the corner with a hurt look on his face but a pool player named Joe Toomey who was the most elegant gentleman on Broadway. He was a very proper man in the real sense of the word and he calls me over and says, real low, "Double Smart, you just committed a very grave error in social etiquette." So I said I didn't know what I did so wrong and Joe Toomey said, "You must always open the door for a lady," so after that I always did.

Joe Toomey was real particular about manners. He said he could see I was very young and unaccustomed to some of the high class company I was keeping, so he took me under his wing and said he would make a first class squire out of me, although I wasn't what you would call socially undesirable at the time. He took me to all the finest restaurants and showed me the proper way to use the silverware and how to act when I met elegant people, but most of all Joe Toomey impressed me with the importance of treating a doll like she was a real lady. He thought every doll should be handled like a piece of Bavarian china.

Now one night Joe Toomey and I are standing on the corner of 49th and Broadway and about six mooches all full of the juice are also hanging there and giving the dolls a hard time. Pretty soon one of the mooches said a very improper phrase to one of the tomatoes and Joe Toomey wanted to belt the mooch real good. He got so upset he said he needed a drink so we headed for one of those bistros where the Whoopee Set gathered every night. I told Joe I didn't smoke or drink but he said that was all right because I could have something to eat.

They gave us this tremendous table at the speakeasy and Joe said, "Double Smart, what will you have?" I asked Joe what he was having and he said he was having a drink so I said I would have a turkey. Joe wanted to know if I wanted a turkey dinner or a turkey sandwich and I said, "Joe, are you having a whole drink?" and he said he was so I said, "Well, I'll have a whole turkey."

The tomato who was the waitress brought out this fabulous bird and set it in front of me and I demolished that old gobbler the way Charles Laughton handled the breasts and drumsticks in those old Henry VIII movies. Joe Toomey said it was a pleasure to watch me eat because he could tell from the way I went straight down to the bone that I really enjoyed it. When I got through with that turkey, those bones weren't fit to give a dog.

The floor show was going full blast and I had finished the turkey so Joe Toomey says, "Double Smart, would you like something else?" So I asked Joe if he was having something and he said he was having another drink, so I said, "Well, in that case, I'll have another turkey." And I belted out that second bird like it was sardines. That's on the square.

Every now and then a newspaper reporter interviewing me will say, "Fat Man, what was the toughest match you ever had?" I always say, "My toughest match was the time I ate two turkeys in one night."

The propositions and the smarts were always my strong suit on the pool table but I won a lot of eating propositions in my time, too. There was this friend of mine named Onofrio Lauri who was a tremendous straight pool player. I figure he was one of the best there was because he's 70 years old this year and when he plays in those fun tournaments in New York, he always whacks out the top players. It never fails. The newspapers always write what a tremendous upset it is, but the way I see it, it's no upset at all because if Lauri can whip those bums now when he's 70, you can imagine how he would have stuck them up 35 years ago.

Old man Lauri was also a tremendous eater, in fact, one time in the 20s he was challenged to an eating contest by Enrico Caruso, the great opera singer. Lauri was a violin player who was nutty about opera and Caruso was an opera singer who was crazy about pool and when they got together they found out they both liked to eat so they had this big eat-out at an Italian restaurant. Lauri won everything from the salad to the grand finale, but when it was all over, Lauri was weeping like a jilted doll because Caruso had started singing and when Caruso hit those high Cs, Lauri had crying hysterics. It was unbelievable.

Lauri knew what a fantastic eater I was and he always had a deadly fear of taking me on at the banquet boards. But he had an Italian friend by the name of Tony Nicoli and Lauri said Nicoli could out-eat any man alive. So one day Lauri brought Nicoli around and we started discussing the eating proposition from every side. Nicoli said he would out-eat me for like a C note and I said you must be kidding, so he said make it two C notes and I said how about a grand. And it went like that, back and forth, back and forth, until finally Nicoli said he was so sure he could whack me out with the knife and fork that he was willing to bet his house on the proposition. So it was all set but what happened was Nicoli's wife wasn't so sure about betting the house so she set a trap for me.

Lauri invited me to an Italian club where they were having this big supper and he said we could have something to eat and then shoot a little pool. So I went to the club with Lauri and I met Nicoli's wife and we all sat at the same table, although we weren't eating for cash that night. They were serving chicken and spaghetti and seeing how Nicoli and Lauri and I were all tremendous eaters, they served us whole chickens. I belted out one chicken after another but I could see that Nicoli was keeping up with me pretty good so I started giving him the con. "Tony," I said, "I'm warning you, there's no way on earth you could ever out-eat me." But he had tremendous confidence in himself because he said, "Listen, Double Smart, if I didn't know for sure that I could out-eat you, do you think I would bet my house on the proposition?"

Now that was all Mrs. Nicoli wanted to hear because she had been watching me demolish those chickens for like two hours and she could see that no matter how much Tony might eat, there was no chance of his out-eating me. So she said, "Tony, the bet is off—do you hear me, Tony, the bet is off."

Tony went into a real tantrum and jumped up and started puffing like one of those marathon runners and he told his wife, "Madam Nicoli, you underestimate your husband. Anthony Nicoli is the greatest eater there is in all New York and Anthony Nicoli will out-eat Double Smart Fats just like Onofrio Lauri out-ate the great Caruso. It will be no contest, Madam, no contest."

So that made Mrs. Nicoli real mad and now she jumped up and started puffing, too, and she told her husband, "Why, you goddamned fool, Double Smart Fats will not only out-eat you and win our house, but he might really get hungry and eat you, too." So that was the end of that.

Once I had that Double Smart Fats handle, I was the King of the Hill on the propositions and every smart on Broadway was shooting for me. What they didn't know was they had to get up early in the morning to out-smart me, but something else they didn't know was I never went to bed. There was so much action on Broadway back then that I was afraid if I went to sleep I might miss out on something real good. I used to romp all over Broadway for like a week straight without a wink of sleep and some-times I would get so tired I was like the walking dead. Finally, I had to look for a gimmick to replace the sleep and that's how I discovered the Turkish baths.

The Turkish bath is one of the most tremendous inventions of man because it not only relaxes you and makes you feel real good, but it makes a human being out of you as well. I'll tell you what, if they really want to end all those war jolts, all they have to do is get all the big generals together in a first class Turkish bath and when everybody's real relaxed and feeling good, they'll crank out a peace treaty like it was a Christmas card. I always felt tremendous after a Turkish bath. No matter how tired I got, I could always run for the baths and get all steamed up and in a couple of hours I was as good as new. And that's the way it had to be because I never knew what Broadway Sociable I might meet or what kind of proposition some-body might stick in my ear.

The poolrooms in Times Square in those days were retreats for actors and authors and song writers and the doctors and lawyers and the manu-facturing tycoons. Every living human stopped in those rooms. You could look around and see maybe Eddie Lang or Bing Crosby and his brother, Bob, and sometimes Joe Venuti, who was Crosby's violin player. All the Yankee baseball stars hung in those joints and Damon Runyon, the writer, was always around picking up the poolroom conversation for his books and articles. You were liable to see a hundred celebrities there almost any time but the one I remember most was Milton Berle.

He was real young then and he was an out-and-out fanatic about pool. Every year Greenleaf would win the world tournament again and the photographers would be snapping a zillion pictures and Berle would get right behind Greenleaf so he could get his picture in the New York papers on account of he was hoping to be discovered and made into a star. Then Berle would ask the photographers what papers would the pictures be in and the next day he would buy a dozen copies, only they always whacked out his picture with the paint brush. Berle was nutty about Greenleaf and he followed him around like he was the Pied Piper.

One night on Broadway I met John Barrymore, the actor, but it wasn't in a poolroom. I met The Great Profile at Madison Square Garden where they were staging the six-day bicycle races. My uncle, Gottlieb Wanderone, was one of the racers in the six-day jolt, which is why I went in the first place.

So this night I'm in the Garden and rooting for Uncle Gottlieb and somebody says, "Double Smart, meet John Barrymore." Barrymore looks me over and says, "Sir, I am intrigued by your name, Double Smart. It implies singular distinction. I pray, sir, what circumstance or act of Fate might have prompted such an illustrious sobriquet?" Barrymore talked like a Senator or an Ambassador and he was the most handsome man I ever saw, even better looking than Greenleaf. So I told him about the pool proposition with Smart Henny, and Barrymore said his Uncle Googan was a pool player. I told him that was nothing, my Uncle Gottlieb was one of the bicycle riders down on the floor. So Barrymore said, "Double Smart, it is obvious that you come from a very talented family."

A lot of those show people were real pool nuts and they would bet good on their game, even though they knew they never had a prayer of winning the stakes. There was this accordian player named Jerry Coe who made fabulous money but he dropped like a hundred or two a week just shooting pool. Sometimes an eyeballer would ask him how he could afford to blow that kind of cash and Coe would say, "Pally, it's my pleasure."

Later on up in Harlem I played a lot of friendly money games with old Stepin Fetchit and Bojangles, the old dancer who made all those motion pictures with Shirley Temple in the 30s. They were both pool nuts of the worst kind and they spent a fortune on the table because they just loved to play. When I would whack out old Stepin Fetchit he would take out the cash and say, "Step and fetch it, Fat Boy." We were tremendous friends. Now Bojangles was the easiest going fellow you ever met but if he got an idea some mooch was giving him the filage, he would really blow high. Like one time he saw a mooch was trying to get position on him so Bojangles pulled out a knife and stuck it in the wood rail of the table and told the mooch, "Now shoot." But as long as you didn't try any skull-duggery with Bojangles, he was as harmless as a lamb.

Some of those show people were real wise to the propositions, too. There was this vaudeville performer named Walter Nelson who was one of the world's greatest unicyclists and I met him when he was playing The Palace. He was a big blond Swede about 6-4 and when he wasn't on the stage, you'd find him in "Scabuch's," a tremendous poolroom in the Palace building. He wasn't what you would call a top player but he knew how to handle himself on the table and he loved to roll real high, only he always demanded tremendous odds. One time I played him one ball in the side pocket for like three days and three nights and cracked him out cold. He got a little sleep and then he came back for more so we went at it for five days and five nights playing four fronts to a back.

Four fronts to a back were tremendous odds to give any living human because I had to sink all my balls in one back pocket. He had the four front pockets, and the other back pocket was dead. It was like playing Russian Roulette with four live rounds in a six-shooter but in those days I was such a devout money player, I could spot Einstein the ten ball. In short rack pool like four fronts to a back, a fellow like Nelson could win maybe 80 games but if the session was long enough, I would be ahead in the cash because I was like a half-dozen overcoats over somebody his speed. But he loved it and he couldn't wait to get off the stage and back on the table.

One day he brought Carl Dane and George K. Arthur, two headline performers of the day, to "Scabuch's" and they listened to my conversation and before they screwed out they offered me a spot in their vaudeville act. That's when I shut up, in fact, the only time I ever shut up was when somebody talked to me about work. I told Dane and Arthur there was no way I could go for the acting dodge but they said they wanted me to join their act in the worst kind of way.

They were a tremendous attraction back then and pulled down fabulous cash on the circuit. They had this army act about soldiers in basic training, a take-off on a movie called *The Rookie*. For a whole week they gave me the high-powered con about my taking the role of the sad sack private in the gimmick because they said I had the makings of a tremendous comedian. They moaned and groaned for days and nights—so to shut them up I joined up with the act.

First we played the Fabian Theater over in Jersey City and then another big house in Elizabeth, New Jersey, and then we went to Newark. Everybody in the act wore the old dogface get-up with the wrap legs and the Jack Pershing britches and the Boy Scout hat and I stood in the middle of the stage looking like the saddest soldier since Napoleon at Waterloo.

So Dane walks up to me and says:

"Private, how did somebody like you get in the Army?"

"I sure didn't volunteer," I said.

"Well, Private, you look very strong and healthy," Dane would say, "but why are you such a coward?"

"I'm a coward, sir," I would say, "because I have a very serious stomach condition—no guts."

There were a zillion corny gags like that and the suckers laughed themselves crazy but I never went for that kind of jolt because I never liked being hemmed up in any way. I would be playing pool between shows and just getting a sucker in the right mood for some serious action when it would be time to go on the stage again. So right there I realized that the acting dodge was a losing proposition.

I fought the footlights and grease paint and all the grief that went with it for exactly three weeks when one day I walk in my backstage dressing room in Newark, and who is there but a mooch from Broadway.

"Double Smart," he says in a real confidential tone, "guess who's back in town?—Daddy Warbucks."

So I went over the hill and headed back to Kreuter's on Broadway for some real shooting.

CHAPTER 8

The Night Rides to Harlem

Daddy Warbucks was what the smarts on Broadway called Hubert Cokes and, as the nom-de-plummers go, it was really descriptive because Cokes was big and bald and always smoking fat cigars and he looked exactly like Daddy Warbucks. Not only did he look like Daddy Warbucks, but he had so much cash that if Warbucks ever needed a co-signer, Cokes would have qualified hands down.

He was an enormous man, about 6-2 and 200 pounds and he had muscles like Dempsey. Charles Atlas wished he had muscles like Hubert Cokes. The real old-timers called Hubert The Giant because they said he was the captain of his own fate at all times. One time he was running a crap game out in the Southwest and one of those protective outfits tried to muscle in on the action but Cokes didn't like the proposition. So they sent a couple of real huskies around to make a believer out of Cokes and old Hubert whacked them out with his bare fists. But all the time I knew Hubert I never knew him to be a brawler because he disliked all forms of violence as much as I did.

The first time I met Cokes I was in Kreuter's playing a little nine ball and this fellow in a uniform who looked like he was a Bulgarian Scout-master walks up and says he had a message for me. "I am Mr. Hubert Cokes' chauffeur," he says, "and Mr. Cokes sent me up to see if any of you gentlemen would like a little friendly game of pool." So I told the chauffeur to go fetch Daddy Warbucks because our pool games were more friendly than a lonely hearts club.

So now Cokes walks in like a real gentleman and he don't say much more than hello but right away he sees me annihilating a mooch in Nine Ball so he starts betting on me. I'm talking about how I met Jack Hill in Oklahoma City and this and that and Cokes got real upset because he said it didn't look like I was paying attention to what I was doing on the table. Now I need that nine ball to win it all and I'm still talking so Cokes comes over and says, "Look here, Double Smart, kindly pay more attention to what you're doing because you're playing for my money." So I took Hubert over and sat him in a big easy chair and told him, "Hubert, old boy, don't you worry about a thing." Then I went back to the table still talking like I was before and I whacked that nine ball in the corner pocket on the most tremendous three-ball combination you ever saw. So after that Cokes said he realized that the conversation was as much a part of my game as the stroke, which is the way it was. Sometimes a little conversation, providing it's real good conversation, can win the proposition before you even roll a ball.

It didn't take too long before me and Daddy Warbucks got down to some serious action. He wanted to play One Pocket right from the start but I steered the conversation around to Three Cushions. Cokes said he was as good a Three-Cushion man as there was, so we got the show on the road. Cokes liked to bet real high and there was no chintz in him because if he happened to lose a proposition, he paid off quicker than Chase Manhattan. I'm telling you, Warbucks would bet with both hands and right away I saw he was the kind of man whose footsteps I could follow. We became tremendous friends and later on we even roomed together in Chicago. Hubert always reminded me of my old man because of the way he understood people and the propositions.

Even though Cokes was a tremendous player, I whacked him out real brutal-like because he grew up down in Arkansas and he never played on a big 5-by-10 (foot) table until he came to New York. Down South they were all weaned on little tables, like 4-by-8 and even smaller, so when those Southern gentlemen came to New York and tried to move around on those big tables they looked like they just got out of the blind men's home. We called the 5-by-10s Rebel Traps. Cokes moaned and groaned about the big tables, but there was nothing whatsoever he could do because 30 years ago you had a better chance of finding Paul Revere riding at Aqueduct than finding a 4-by-8 table in a top room in New York.

In the olden days all the world tournaments were played on 5-by-10s because that was the standard championship size. But later on in the 40s, the Billiard Congress of America, which conducts those fun tournaments, reduced the official championship size to 4½-by-9. And that's not all. Those big alphabet generals widened the pockets from 4⅞ inches to 5½ inches, which made soup satchels out of them. Every time I look at those fun tournament tables, the pockets look like they're getting wider and wider and pretty soon I guess they'll be big enough to handle cantaloupes. When they filaged around with the size of the tables and the pockets, those generals took a tremendous game that required fantastic scientific skill to play and reduced it to a farce. It was the biggest hornswoggle known to man. You've got out-and-out ham-and-eggers running around today claiming they're world champions, but on a 5-by-10 in the olden days, they wouldn't have beat Frank The Drunk, who cleaned toilets at Kreuter's. That's on the square.

Now to make my point about those big tables, I whacked out Cokes so bad in Three Cushions that he said he had enough unless I was willing to play him some One Pocket. So we played One Pocket from morning till night but poor old Hubert didn't fare much better. Finally, Hubert said he was packing it in so he and I jumped in his big limousine and he told the chauffeur to head for James Evans' place up in Harlem.

Evans was the best all-around Negro player in those days. In fact, Evans is the greatest Negro pool player who ever lived, and the only reason why he never won a lot of those world tournaments was because they wouldn't let him play on account of his color. He liked to roll real high himself, and back then he was running a little four-table room with the poker action on the side up at Lennox Avenue and 129th Street. His joint was open all night and if the action on Broadway happened to slow down, everybody would jump in cars and drive up to Evans' room. At daybreak you could always find the top stars of the game there.

Daddy Warbucks had a real glow in his eyes on the way up to Harlem because he had busted Evans like a year before when Evans went looking for him down in Hot Springs. They played One Pocket on a 4-by-8 table and Hubert won so big that he had to pay Evans' train fare back to New York. So now Hubert wanted another piece of Evans because he figured Evans was a real lamb.

We pulled up to Evans' joint and Cokes sent the chauffeur in and the chauffeur comes right back and says, "Mr. Cokes, Mr. Evans says since you and he are both Southern boys (Evans was born in Hopkinsville, Kentucky) to tell you that Southern hospitality is the order of the day." So Cokes and I walk in like a couple of generals and in no time at all he and Evans are rolling real high on One Pocket. Only this time they're playing on a big 5-by-10 and now Hubert couldn't win a game. I mean Evans really thumped him out, so it looked like it was time for me to get into the action.

Me and Evans got the One Pocket action going and every time I beat him, old James would say, "Double it, Fat Man." He said "Double it, Fat Man" so much that he sounded like a phonograph record that was stuck. I beat him like 30 or 40 in a row because I had added a new dimension to One Pocket. Those straight pool players were always looking for the safety play in One Pocket but I put the runout in the game. If two straight pool players tried to shoot One Pocket, one game might last for three days because all they did was balk and safe, balk and safe, and nobody was pocketing any balls. But I banked them off two and three cushions and I got so I could run out the first time I got to the table, which was what I did that night in Harlem.

"Fat Man," Evans said, "there sure must be some way to beat you in this game. Double it again." But there was no way Evans could handle me in One Pocket. We played for years and years but I always came out ahead in the cash.

The last time I saw Evans he was retired and living on Social Security and a World War I pension. He was staying in a hotel in Times Square and playing the horses when they were in town, but he never plays pool anymore. He's 72 and he's got cataracts on both eyes and he needs an operation. He said he never goes near a poolroom because he can't see the balls like he should. But he said the big reason he never sets a foot in a room is because his eyes are still good enough to see the pockets and those big pockets make him feel like crying. "They're sloppy pockets," he said, "and they've made the game sloppy."

The day I got together with James Evans, a magazine writer who was doing an article on me dropped in and he heard me and Evans cutting up the jackpots. So this writer says, "Mr. Evans, was the Fat Man really as good as he says?" Evans laughed and told that young writer, "Listen, sonny boy, 30 years ago this fat boy sitting here was the greatest One Pocket player I ever saw—especially for the cash. There was no way you could whip him." And that's the way it was.

I hung around Broadway making a fabulous living on One Pocket wagers and the proposition pool. The way I put the high run and out to One Pocket was so brutal that after awhile I couldn't get an even proposition anywhere. I had to spot a ball and then two balls just to get the action but the odds didn't matter because I'd run ten and out, ten and out like forever. Talk about high runs, I must have run a thousand straight in One Pocket a hundred times. It got so that everybody on Broadway thought I invented the game but I always told them the way it was—Jack Hill invented it down in Oklahoma, only the Fat Man was the one who refined it.

I was still romping around Broadway when the Depression set in real hard and the brokes were starving to death in the streets. A lot of those captains of industry weren't showing up around Kreuter's or the other joints any more and somebody might say, what happened to that little fellow with the manufacturing gimmick and somebody else would say he took the easy way out, like from 32 stories. Those were brutal days, brutal beyond compare.

Hoppe's room at 51st and Broadway had changed hands and an old man named White ran it for a few years. But he catered to the suckers and when the hard times came, the suckers didn't even have as much cash as the mooches. So one day I'm walking in the Roseland Building to have a few dances with the dolls downstairs and what do I hear but old man White has thrown in the sponge and Ralph Greenleaf is taking over the room. So that was a signal that all the top players would be making the move to Greenleaf's joint because Greenleaf was loved by every living human, the top stars and the mooches and even the multis. Like overnight the action shifted to 51st and Broadway, although Greenleaf didn't exactly encourage the gambling because if you were a legitimate champion in those days you had to push the choir boy image at all times.

On the opening day at Greenleaf's room it looked like the President was coming to give an award to the Ladies' Garden Society because all the big generals sent floral wreaths with best wishes for success and that kind of thing. The newspaper people started dropping in and one day I see this fellow taking notes on a pad of paper and I find out he's Robert Ripley, who happened to be a pool nut of the worst kind. One time Ripley gave James Evans a tremendous ovation after Evans ran a rack of 15 balls without the cue ball touching a cushion. Something like that was 100-to-1 proposition but Evans was a tremendous player back then.

I was involved in all kinds of propositions at Greenleaf's that might not have made Ripley's "Believe It Or Not" but they were very believable for the cash. Like one time I was sitting around and the conversation is about who has the greatest stroke. Now the greatest players in the world were in that room but the contest boiled down to me and Andrew St. Jean and Joe Chamaco, the Mexican Three-Cushion champion. Everybody got down and we shot a cue-ball nine cushion to see who could back the ball nearest the center of the table after it came off the last cushion. I won the proposition time and time again and I also won a lot of cash in shoot-out, which was a tremendous gambling game. Say you're playing and you don't have a shot on the table, well, you roll the cue ball into a position where you figure your opponent won't have a shot but at the same time you figure you can shoot out from that same position. He plays it safe, just like you figure him to do, and then you shoot out. I won a zillion of those propositions.

But the big attraction the first month Greenleaf opened was the All-Star Tournament he staged as a gimmick to bring customers into the room. Greenleaf was head and shoulders over anybody in straight pool in those days and nobody figured on beating Greenleaf. So the gimmick was a $100 cash prize for the player who ran the most balls against Greenleaf. He selected 14 outstanding stars, including me, and he played them exhibition matches afternoon and night. The suckers turned out like it was Dollar Day and Greenleaf whacked out one star after the other. After almost a week, the most balls run against Greenleaf was 87 and now it was my turn to get on the table. I not only ran more than 87 balls, but I beat Greenleaf at 125 points to win the match and the C note. The gimmick tournament ended up with Greenleaf winning 13 matches and losing one and that one loss was to Double Smart Fats. It was a tremendous honor to beat Greenleaf in an exhibition because he lost so seldom that when somebody did beat him it was the talk of Broadway for weeks.

Greenleaf asked me to play in a couple exhibition matches after that and I remember one in particular because he really whacked me out. He had this exhibition date at a fabulous Polish club down on St. Mark's Place right near The Bowery so that night he and The Princess and I hop a cab and on the ride down he tells me that my name is supposed to be Smigelski because I'm billed as the champion of Poland. So when we got there the big sign read: "Ralph Greenleaf, The World Champion, vs. Stanislaus Smigelski, The Champion of Poland," and when I was introduced, those Polacks really gave me an ovation. What happened was Greenleaf broke and left me with no shot at all but I studied the situation from all sides and saw I had a chance on a combination off the rail. So I gave the ball a zillion dollars' worth of Follow English and came off the rail like Man O' War and I made that combination like it had eyes, only I scratched in the corner pocket. It was the most fantastic scratch you ever saw. Then Greenleaf got up and ran 125 straight. And that was the end of Stanislaus Smigelski and Warsaw Fats because I was deader than General Pulaski. I think those Polacks knew I was an imposter because they didn't invite me to the big feast after the match.

Princess Nai Tai Tai was out of show business by then and she was in the room day and night and we would stand over by the counter and chew-chew for hours. I was crazy about her and sometimes she would ask me to go out to have dinner with her and sometimes I would go. One night she asked me about a quick dinner at a nearby Chinese restaurant but I was playing Erwin Rudolph Three Cushions for like a C note a game so I had to beg off and The Princess started out by herself.

Now just as she's leaving the room, this fellow walks in and says, "Good evening, Mrs. Greenleaf, and where are you going in such a rush?" So she tells him she's going to dinner and the guy says she can't go alone, which didn't exactly upset the Princess because she was real good at handling customers in the room. She talks with the guy awhile and first thing you know this fellow grabs her hat right off her head and runs out the room with The Princess running after him like they were playing cops and robbers.

The guy with The Princess' hat jumps in a cab and The Princess jumps in after him and nobody in the room knew what the angle was until like three hours later The Princess comes back all out of breath with her hair looking like she got nipped in a hurricane. I mean she really looked disheveled but at the same time she was smiling like somebody who had enjoyed herself.

So one of the fellows asked The Princess about the egg who snatched her hat and how she managed to get it back.

"Oh, dahlings, it was really nothing," The Princess said, "he was one of Ralph's admirers who insisted on taking me to dinner. It was a delightful dinner, once I talked him into returning my hat. He really is a mischievous little man but he wouldn't tell me his name."

Everybody in the room was relieved to see that The Princess wasn't harmed because one player happened to know who the hat snatcher was. He was Willie "The Actor" Sutton, the king of the bank robbers and he happened to be on the lam from Sing Sing at the time. Sutton loved the dancing dolls downstairs in the Roseland Ballroom and he even used his theatrical makeup kit to disguise himself like a tourist so he could waltz around with the tomatoes. Even though they called me Double Smart, I didn't know Willie Sutton was around the joint. I must have danced past that hat snatcher a zillion times, only he always looked like a salesman or something to me.

You never knew what might come off around Greenleaf's room in those days because nobody had any serious money. Even the generals were in hock, except the generals always managed to eat and a lot of the suckers and mooches didn't. I was always picking up old brokes and taking them to Washington Heights for a good meal. Sometimes I would take an old woman, or even a young girl, who might be down, and my sisters would feed them and give them a couple dresses. I brought a zillion brokes home in my day. My folks always liked to help people because the Swiss people really helped my mother and father when they first came to this country. So I was taught from the day I was born that you must always help other people.

Like one day in Greenleaf's room this old pool hustler comes in from Kansas City, only nobody knew he was a hustler because he sneaked in hoping he could win some money playing pool. So he just gets a game and before he even runs a ball he keels over and hits the floor like he's deader than Abraham Lincoln. The room was real crowded with like 300 people and 200 of them coming running over looking at this poor sucker stretched out on the floor. "He's dead," some mooch says and the other mooch chimes in "Yeah, he's already turning purple," and this and that, only nobody is doing anything to help the poor broke.

So I moved in to see what all the commotion was about. In those days I had the eyes of an eagle so I told everybody to move back and let the poor man have a little oxygen because there was no way that man could be dead on account of I saw his eyes flickering. So I took a good look at him and right away I knew what his trouble was. The poor mooch was starving to death and malnutrition had already started to set in.

I told the guy at the lunch counter to heat up a can of beans so in a minute one mooch runs over with the beans and another sucker digs a spoon into the can like he's handling a steam shovel. So I said, "Wait a minute, you can't feed a starving man like he's eating at the Waldorf Astoria or you're liable to kill him off from shock." So I took that spoon and threw it away and then I borrowed a match from somebody and I stuck the match in the can and speared one bean at a time, only one bean at a time, and I stuck it on the poor hungry mooch's tongue. "Now," I said, "wait and see what happens." So after the second bean the mooch's eyebrows started going up and down like a whorehouse shutter and after five beans he was able to get up.

"Now," I said, "I never saw this man in my life but I know he's a tremendous pool player, only he's been starving for like three days. Let him walk around for a little exercise and then let him whack a few balls and after that I'm betting anybody in the house this hungry man can run 50 balls."

Everybody got down and that bum went to the table and ran exactly 59 balls. He was a real old-time player named Willie Schmay and he hung around Broadway a long time after that.

When the suckers paid off on the bet, one of them said, "Gee, Double Smart, I never knew you were a doctor," and I said, "I'm no doctor, I just happen to know something about human nature. When a man is hungry he does things a man with a full stomach never would dream he could do. Understand?"

So now one of the eyeballers in the crowd speaks up, "No wonder they call you Double Smart," he says, "only I think you're smarter than that." So another mooch says, "Well, if he's smarter than Double Smart, then he must be Triple Smart." So right there I stepped up a notch in the nom-de-plummers and everywhere I went on Broadway after that I was called Triple Smart Fats.

I had been hearing that there was more action at some stops on the road than there was in New York, so I figured if I was really Triple Smart, I should build up a real big bankroll and take out on the road myself.

Then one day this big fruit and produce man came in Greenleaf's with a bankroll bigger than an eggplant. I gave him a little conversation about this and that and pretty soon I got him to the table with the four fronts to a back proposition. He said there was no way he could lose that kind of proposition so I told him he was right, only I was going to take out after him.

I whacked that vegetable tycoon like he was a punching bag and every time I won a game, he would take out the roll, pull off a big rubber band he had around it and peel off the notes. I kept winning and he kept pulling off that rubber band and shooting me the cash. And that's how it went, off with the rubber band again and again until now the bankroll was no bigger than a grape.

Now I whack him out cold for the absolute final time, because now when he took off the rubber band and hit me with the cash, he stood there with just the rubber band in his hand.

So I said, "Let's play one more game for the rubber band because you won't be needing it any longer."

With that bankroll I really put the show on the road because after that I was what you call a rolling stone—I mean a high rolling stone.

MINNESOTA FATS

Everybody says they can't figure out how a beautiful doll like Eva-line fell for me. I always tell 'em I was a pretty good-looking doll myself when I was young. This is what I looked like in 1935.

That's the old man, Rudolf Walter Wander-one, Sr., and me in 1919. I was six years old at the time and on vacation in St. Louis. The old man was a tremendous physical specimen and won jillions on strong-man propositions.

Hubert Cokes and Emmet Blankenship look like a couple of gay blades in this 1920 picture taken in Roanoke, Virginia. They just happened to be two of the world's top pool players at the time. Blank was the 1916 world champion.

James Evans

James Evans today. James was the greatest Negro pool player the game has ever known. He liked to roll pretty high for his own money.

Marcel Camp

Marcel Camp was another great player, but he was at his best playing for cash. I once turned Marcel into a pedestrian by winning his car in a proposition on the table.

Philadelphia Inquirer

Willie Mosconi

This is what Willie Mosconi looked like in 1937, before he became prematurely grey. Willie is one of the greatest tournament players that ever lived. I rank him second only to Greenleaf.

Andrew Ponzi

Andrew Ponzi ranks with the all-time greats of tournament play and money pool. He won the world title five times and he won and lost a lot of serious cash on money games, too.

Princess Nai Tai Tai

Princess Nai Tai Tai (Mrs. Ralph Greenleaf) was beautiful beyond compare. When she walked, she walked like a peacock. This is a 1932 picture.

Philadelphia Inquirer

Ralph Greenleaf

Ralph Greenleaf was not only the greatest tournament player in the history of pool, but also one of the handsomest men I've ever known. This is how he looked in 1925.

Philadelphia Inquirer

Mort Luby, Jr.

And that's Eva-line surrounded by some of my poolroom pals at Johnston City. Paulie Jansco and Luther "Wimpy" Lassiter are in the foreground and that's Tuscaloosa Squirrelly (Marshall Carpenter of Tuscaloosa, Alabama) and Cornbread Red (Billy Birge of Detroit) in the background.

That's me taking up the proposition in the back room at Johnston City, Illinois, a couple of years ago. Sometimes it takes hours and hours to discuss the proposition from every angle. I was always the past master in the elocution department.

Mort Luby, Jr.

Mort Luby, Jr.

The Jansco brothers, Georgie, left, and Paulie, are the fellows who brought competitive pool back in the early 60s with their All-Around Masters Tournament in Johnston City. I call 'em Heckle and Jeckyll. They're two of my dearest friends.

Daddy Warbucks was what pool hustlers call Hubert Cokes today. Cokes not only looks like Daddy Warbucks, but if Warbucks needed a co-signer, he has enough money to qualify for the job.

J. Bruce Baumann

That's Johnny Carson after I hustled him out of a dollar on the "Tonight Show." Johnny bet me I couldn't make the railroad shot after I missed it on the first try and I shot him down in cold blood.

"You must be Minnesota Fats," said Ann Sidlauskas of Indiana University when we met at the 1962 National College Tournament in Bloomington, Indiana. "That's right," I said, "and you must be Indiana Fats." Ann loved the repartee. She was the 1961 co-ed champion. This is Eva-line's favorite picture of me.

J. Bruce Baumann

Harrisburg Whitey is what they called Delmar Stanton on account of he was blond and from Harrisburg, Pennsylvania. Whitey and I traveled together on the road for years. He's an expert mixologist in Philadelphia today.

I was "The Greatest" at the end of a television debate in Chicago with Mr. Cassius Muhammed Ali Clay, the heavyweight champion. I told Cassius I had been whacking 'em out for 40 years and hadn't been on the floor yet. He said he couldn't make that kind of statement.

Ward Silver

Elwood Smith

J. Bruce Baumann

Detroit Free Press

I've played exhibitions in 48 states in the past two years and the eyeballers ogled from every angle. This is how I looked to a Detroit photographer from this particular angle.

My greatest relaxation is with my pets. I've got 27 dogs and 14 cats at my home in Dowell, Illinois. I also feed a groundhog and that's on the square. I love all animals. I wouldn't kill a mosquito — not even if it bit me.

This is your vice president in his working clothes. That's no trick photography; it's the Masse shot, one of the toughest on the table. The Masse is sure to impress the eyeballers because only the top players can pull it off.

CHAPTER 9

I Was the Daddy of Them All

When I quit Broadway for the road in the 30s, I left town like the biggest general you ever saw. I was driving a brand new Cadillac and wearing the most fabulous tailored clothes money could buy and I had enough cash to be a real genuine bon vivant. Everywhere I went the dolls were eyeballing me almost as much as I was eyeballing them because back in those days I was a pretty good looking doll myself.

The extra-curricular action I got with the tomatoes was fantastic beyond belief. It all went back to the conversation, which all dolls are automatically dying to hear, providing it's the right conversation. A tomato is a lot like a pool player. You have to know the right speed to use on each one. If a doll has been subjected to all sorts of brutality and skullduggery, you give her the honeysuckle and she'll fall for you like she's losing her equilibrium. But if a tomato has been cuddled and pampered too much, say by her grandmother or some sucker who don't wear the pants, then you can be disagreeable or even speak harshly to her and she'll love you just the same. The gimmick is knowing the proper conversation for the right doll, which is exactly the same as knowing the right speed to use on the different pool players.

All pool players play below their speed. That's the way it is. If I'm playing Detroit Whitey, who I can rob at will, I give him the conversation, but if I'm on the table with Mosconi, I go with the speed. I never use a hacksaw on mashed potatoes, which is why I never play my best if there's no cash up for grabs. If I'm playing for fun, I wouldn't care if Little Red

Riding Hood beat me, but if it's a cash proposition, I'm like Genghis Khan going through the Great Wall of China.

Now back then the greatest tournament players were Greenleaf, the all-time top banana, Willie Mosconi, Jimmy Caras, Irving Crane, Erwin Rudolph and Andrew Ponzi, but you take out Rudolph and Ponzi and none of them could do it for the cash. The one thing that separates the men from the boys on the pool table is when the proposition is for cash. You always hear those fun players cutting up jackpots about running 378 balls here, and 437 there, but if some eyeballer happens to ask how much they won on the proposition, the fun players say, "Oh, it was just an exhibition." That's the silliest thing I've ever heard because if it's not for cash, what's it worth? Listen, that's like swimming from here to Zanzibar and when they fish you out of the water, you tell the reporters, "Oh, it was really nothing." Nothing is exactly right if there's no cash involved. I never was an AAU player. I was always very devout about the money.

Those fun players are always looking for a crutch when they can't run more than two racks. That's when they tell the suckers they had an off day which is ridiculous beyond compare. If you're playing for cash, you can't ever have an off day or you'll end up singing "I Surrender Dear" at the War on Poverty headquarters. When you're playing for the gelt, you're like the knife thrower in the circus. If he ever had an off day, the tomato he throws those daggers at would look like she was massacred by a tribe of Comanche Indians.

The top pool players for the cash were myself, James Evans and Marcel Camp. We never needed any backers because we always played for our own gold. Andrew St. Jean and Rudolph and Ponzi and Chick Seaback and Arthur Woods and a few other old-timers would roll high, but they always needed financial assistance. They were all tremendous players who excelled at every game on the table, but when it came to doing it for the cash, I was the daddy of them all.

Marcel Camp was, and still is, a tremendous money player. The first time I met Camp was in Detroit in the 30s and we played One Pocket, Banks, Three Cushions, Rotation and straight pool for days and nights without stopping. Sometimes Marcel wouldn't miss a ball, but he always went home broke. Gambling is funny that way. You can win like a hundred times and still wind up sleeping in the park. If Camp played in those fun tournaments in New York and he could bet like a grand on every match, he would make those fun players break down and cry right on television. It would look like Peyton Place in the poolroom.

Camp made a trip down South in the 30s and got real adjusted to those 4-by-8 tables down there and then he sent the word around so I would know where he was playing. So I got in my Cadillac and headed for Edenton, North Carolina, where he was giving exhibitions and when I hit town all I saw were posters and pictures of Marcel advertising his appearance.

So I walked in the room and said, "Why, Marcel, isn't this nice running into you down here?" Then I told him he was very considerate putting his pictures all over the place to make it real easy for me to locate him. "Marcel," I said, "when the FBI is looking for a wanted man, they put his picture in the Post Office and offer a reward for his capture, but you even top that—you put your picture all over the country side so people won't have the slightest difficulty finding you." Marcel, who is kind of heavy like me, shilled in perfect and the suckers loved the dialogue so much they stayed around for days and nights watching the One Pocket action. It was nip and tuck but in the end Marcel won all the cash because what happened was the small table killed me dead. But I never counted Edenton a total loss because Marcel said he would see me in Philadelphia in a few weeks and we would get the show on the road again.

Now Marcel took all that cash he won in Edenton and bought himself the most tremendous Buick automobile you ever laid eyes on and when he drove to Philadelphia about a month later he really came to town like a multi. So now we're on a Big Bertha, which is what I call those 5-by-10s, and Marcel is having trouble adjusting back to the big table and I belted him out so brutal I felt like a sadist. Finally, I busted him smack down to his last quarter and then I said, "Marcel, I'll play you for the car." He said that would be just fine so then I won the Buick, too. Marcel handed over the keys and the title to the car and he walked out of the room the way Jimmy Durante used to exit on those TV jolts but just as he got to the door, I yelled:

"Marcel," I said, "you came to Philadelphia a motorist, but I made a pedestrian out of you."

I hung around Philadelphia off and on for years because most of the top players in the game were there and you could get as much action as you wanted. You never got any of that Who Shot John nonsense in Philadelphia because there were always enough well-heeled gentlemen from South Philly hanging on Market Street to keep the backroom economy moving real good. I always took a suite at the Bellevue Stratford Hotel and played all the big joints down around City Hall, but I never sneaked in and gave anybody the double-double. I always walked right in and let everybody know I was in town.

The Hudson Bowling and Billiards Room on North Broad Street was an elegant place and Harry Robbins ran a high class room at 15th and

● 73

Market. But the most fabulous spot of all was Allinger's on Market Street around 13th. The joint took in three whole floors and no matter what time of the day or night you dropped in there were so many tables going it looked like New Year's Eve on Times Square. Allinger's is still operating in the same block, only the whole room is on one floor now and compared to what it was 30 years ago, it looks like one of those Depressed Areas.

In the olden days, Allinger's was a real showcase, in fact, a section of the second floor was partitioned off in glass just like a showcase and only the elite players were allowed to perform there. I played in that glass house many and many a time. Phil Longo and his wife, Mamie, ran a beautiful old-style room upstairs at 5th and South. It was always as immaculate as a church and it still is. You could take your 12-year-old daughter there, that's how nice it is.

Later on Jimmy Caras, who was the World Champion off and on, ran a room at 11th and Chestnut and Mosconi had one in his old neighborhood at 7th and Morris in South Philly. I would walk in their joints and say, "Hello, boys, what's new?" and they would say, "Why, hello, Fatty, how are you?" But they never got off the chair. Some other sucker would drift in and they would snatch him like a butterfly, but all they ever gave me was that "Hello, Fatty" con. That's the way it was.

The room where you could always find the action was a walk-down joint at 16th and Market called Fox Billiards. It was a real trap. Before you walked in you needed a tetanus shot, a gas mask and a Flit gun. All the top players hung at The Fox and it was down in that decrepit hole that I played many a cash proposition with the king of the fun players, Willie Mosconi.

Mosconi grew up on the big 5-by-10s in his old man's room and he was already a top professional player in the 30s, which was years before he got a strangle hold on the world championship. His old man, Joe Mosconi, wanted Willie to be a dancer, only Willie fell in love with pool the way I did when Gans, the goose, ran into the amusement park pavilion.

Willie had a lot of real affluent friends in South Philly and they thought he was the greatest thing to ever crouch over a table and they liked to bet on him real heavy. I thought it was a splendid arrangement, only old Joe Mosconi had a different view.

Me and Willie are about the same age and back in our younger days we played every game on the table together, only every match was for the cash which meant I was the automatic winner. Willie Mosconi is a tremendous pool player; in fact, I rate him second only to Greenleaf among the all-time tournament stars. But when it came to playing for the cash I was in a class by myself. So everytime I played Willie for the gold in Philadelphia, I whacked him out clean. In fact, I beat Willie so much that his old man figured losing like that might not be good for Willie's ego. So he told Willie not to play me anymore. The old man even had a little talk with me and asked me not to play Willie for cash.

Now it wasn't that Willie was pampered or spoiled or coddled by his old man or anything like that. Willie Mosconi was always his own man. That's on the square. It's just that Willie really respected his old man the way kids respected their parents in the olden days so he didn't want to do anything to hurt old Joe. Now the thing with the old man was that he knew Willie was a tremendous straight pool player and he wanted Willie to win the world title the way some fathers want their sons to be President. So he figured Willie sure didn't need the experience he was getting losing the cash matches to me and he told Willie he should let me alone. But Willie didn't see it that way because he wanted to play me so bad that we had to sneak around to different rooms so we could play without his old man knowing it.

The reason Willie Mosconi was such a super star was because he was an incurable perfectionist and if he found something that he couldn't do real well, Willie would kill himself until he mastered it. Now back then he couldn't come close to whipping me in One Pocket, only Willie wouldn't quit. I would whack him out again and again and he would always say, "I know I can beat you at this game, I know it." But Willie never did.

I whacked out all the fun players in One Pocket, I mean every last one of them. I played Andrew Ponzi, who really liked to wager on his ability, two days and two nights in Vineland, New Jersey, and I busted him flatter than a praline. I had heard Ponzi won a zillion on the horses so I went to Vineland and I found him in a room over a gymnasium and an Italian restaurant. I walked up and said, "Why, hello, Andrew, what's new?" and Andrew said, "Why hello, Fatty, how are you?" Only after that Andrew and I put the show on the road. When Ponzi had the cash, he was exactly like Barkis—always willing.

We played One Pocket even for 48 straight hours in Vineland. Ponzi would run eight and out and I would run eight and out but in the end I stuck him up like he was a two-year-old baby, even though he was a tremendous player and World Champion like three times. I've got a friend in New York by the name of Nat Klein and he was in Vineland and saw it and every time I see Klein he says, "Fatty, I'll never forget the day you stuck up Andrew Ponzi in Vineland."

I was playing Ponzi in Philadelphia one time and Andrew had been sick with flu or something and he looked sort of pale and washed out. I kept winning and winning and Andrew kept paying off and first thing you know a friend of his walks in the room and says, "Why, Andrew, you look sort of sick—what's wrong?"

"I'll tell you what's wrong," I said, "Andrew is suffering from economic anemia." And he was.

Andrew's real name wasn't Ponzi. It was Andrew D'Alessandro only when Andrew was like 16 and already a tremendous pool player, the notorious Boston swindler, Charles Ponzi, was in the headlines and everyday you would read about Charles Ponzi swindling somebody out of zillions. So when Andrew started winning proposition after proposition on the pool table, his friends began calling him "Ponzi." Later on when he became a super star and played in the tournaments, the reporters would always misspell D'Alessandro so Andrew started using Ponzi as his professional name. That's all anybody called him anyway. If you walked in a poolroom back then and asked for Andrew D'Alessandro, those bums would think you were talking about some Italian painter from the Renaissance era.

Names around poolrooms are funny things. When I was on Broadway they called me Double Smart Fats and later on Triple Smart Fats but when I hit the road in the 30s, everybody called me New York Fats on account of I was fat and I was from New York. Then if I happened to pay a prolonged visit to a town, the local suckers would sort of adopt me and call me like Chicago Fats or New Orleans Fats or even French Lick Fats because I played around French Lick, Indiana, a lot of times. I played all over the country for 30 years.

I might be in Cleveland one day belting out Oklahoma Whitey, who hung at a room called The Bucket of Blood, and I'll hear about the action in Toledo or Detroit or Chicago or Pittsburgh. I played a fellow by the name of Harry Oswald in Pittsburgh but I never stayed around too long because Pittsburgh was the worst pool town in the country. The way I lived it cost me like $200 a week to break even, and I'm talking about the 30s, but if you spent a week in Pittsburgh you would be lucky to get $100 worth of action. So that's why I never was called Pittsburgh Fats.

In the beginning I looked for the action, but after awhile, the action was always where I happened to be. I would go to a town that was deader than a DAR tea but in two days I'd have the poolroom so crowded that the gendarmes would have to come around to find out why all those people were standing in line outside waiting to get in. Then when I left with everybody's cash, the room would be like the morgue on Sunday. That's how it was in every town I played from coast to coast. That's on the square.

I was in so many different parts of the country in those days that my mother and father were singing "Where Is My Wandering Boy Tonight" in duets. I went to Boston looking for Jimmy Mills, who was the top player in all New England, and I whacked him out like 30 in a row. Then I would drive to Newark and play Danny Gartner, who was the best player in the whole state of New Jersey. He was so tremendous they called him Young Greenleaf. Me and Danny Boy played for days and nights on end at a fabulous joint called Steele's but I annihilated Danny so many times that I forced him to make the most drastic decision of his life—I made him go to work. He became an insurance salesman and used a lot of the conversation he heard me belt around the poolrooms on his clients and Danny ended up a real shark with the double-indemnity dodge.

I never neglected any section of the country as long as the backroom economy was in a fluid state. I went all the way to California once to play Ray Kilgore, who was the Three-Cushion champion at one time, because I heard Ray was getting a little lonesome out there among all those movie stars. I played Kilgore in his own joint on Wilshire Boulevard in Hollywood and I pushed him around like he was one of the extras in a mob scene.

That was always my strong suit—beating the other guy in his own joint and on his own table. Playing a man for cash on his own table is always risky because the table is usually a trap of some kind. Maybe the rubber is real fast, or real slow, and maybe the cloth is brand new. There's a zillion different factors to consider, like playing the guy at his best game on his own table. That's where I always used the conversation to steer the action away from his best game to maybe my best game. If you're on his table and you play him his best stick right away, you're never going to leave with the cash, never in a hundred years. We would discuss the proposition for hours on end. I would moan and groan about what a patsy I would be on a strange table and this and that and when I finally convinced them I was willing to be a sacrificial lamb, the One Pocket action would get under way. It was all a matter of salesmanship, which is what the conversation is all about in the first place. Then once I had a real good feel of the table, I would take 'em at their best game and scramble 'em like souffle.

I played the best there was, the best anywhere, and it was never any of this stop and go, up and down, nip and tuck action. When I got the show on the road, I'd belt 'em out like 30 and 40 in a row and nobody ever got back any cash.

A couple of years ago my wife, Eva-line, and I were driving to St. Louis and a crooner on the radio was singing "The Days of Wine and Roses." Eva-line said, "Rudolf, you must have had your days of wine and roses when you were a bachelor on the road." But I told Eva-line it wasn't all wine and roses. And it wasn't. Sometimes you ran into a lot of heart-aches.

I saw a lot of grief in poolrooms. Sometimes when I was riding high without a worry in the world, I would run into one of the real old-time stars who would be on his last legs. Some of them were in such pitiful shape that a $1,000 handout wouldn't come near solving their problems.

The saddest spectacle I ever saw was down in New Orleans about 15, 20 years ago. I was playing Sammy Bales and a fellow called Baton Rouge Frenchy in a dive called Sal's Pool Room and who do I bump into but old Emmet Blankenship. Blankenship, who was originally from Oklahoma, was the world pocket billiards champion in 1916 and one of the most fantastic all-around players to ever pick up a cue. But after he won the title he started frequenting what James Evans used to call "them sportin' houses" and Emmet really went to pot.

Right after he won the title he got all juiced up and had a serious beef jolt in a poolroom somewhere. He hit a guy on the head with a cue stick and it killed the man. So they barred Emmet from all tournament competition and he went down and down until he was nothing but a help-less drunk living like an ordinary hobo. I hadn't seen him in years until that day we met in New Orleans, only now Emmet had just one arm.

Emmet lost the arm in another beef jolt down in New Orleans. He had an out-and-out brawl with some longshoreman and Emmet hit the fellow a shot in the teeth, only the fellow's teeth were so hard they cut Emmet's hand real bad. Instead of going to a doctor, Emmet went out and got drunk and the upshot was an infection set in and they amputated Emmet's right arm which happened to be his shooting arm.

But that didn't stop Emmet from playing pool. He learned to shoot with his left hand and won a zillion with the propositions. Those roaches in the poolrooms will snatch a one-armed man like he was a baby, only when they went to the table with Emmet Blankenship, they never dreamed they were up against a one-time World Champion. Emmet really stuck 'em up, except in the end, Emmet died broke.

Emmet was drinking so hard that somebody had one of those soul hustlers talk to him and he convinced Emmet that the juice was a losing proposition at best. So Emmet swore off all beverages but he got the shakes something awful and one night he went back to the $1-a-night scratch house where he was living and Emmet never woke up anymore. It was a real tragedy because Emmet Blankenship was a tremendous player and deep down he was a very fine person. When I told Eva-line the story, she cried like a child and said, "Rudolf, I know you would never end up like that." Now there's a doll for you.

I told Eva-line that Emmet Blankenship's trouble was he had been overcome by a tremendous fear and he hit the juice so he wouldn't have to confront reality. A lot of people are like that. I never went for that kind of action because I always had a real high regard for reality, only I never let it bother me. With me, it's always mind over matter, but I never made the mistake of losing touch with reality.

Most pool players have a deadly fear of busting out and ending up a dependent person. It's real odd because pool players are all rugged individuals who are smart enough to avoid the working dodge and call all their own shots in life. But sooner or later something happens and all sorts of neurotic fantasies start gnawing them inside. That's when the nerves go.

If a pool player has a $200 bankroll, it'll be buried so far down in the heel of his shoe that it might take four hours to dig it out. That's only a part of the neurosis.

I never was like that in all my life because I never let money worry me. I never romanced cash, I spent it. If I had money, I was happy, but when I got busted out, I never gave it a second thought.

The reason why I've always been able to live that way is because I've never known one of life's most terrifying passions—fear.

I'm the most fearless man who ever lived—and I'll tell you why.

CHAPTER **10**

Fear Strikes Out

When Franklin D. Roosevelt told all the citizens the only thing to fear is fear itself, he wasn't giving them any soft con. Fear is a hideous thing. It's a malignancy of the mind and the soul and if it really gets to you, it can turn your life into a deadly horror.

Fear can make a sucker do some of the most drastic things you ever imagined, things he really doesn't care to do at all—like taking a job, for example. But even after he's a working man, fear can prevent him from advancing up the ladder. He might run into an opportunity to make a real smart move, only he'll look at the proposition from all sides and then take the easy way out by not making the move at all. He'll pass up a golden opportunity to improve his lot on account of a deadly fear of falling on his face, which is what makes him a sucker in the first place. What happens then is he's not making enough scratch to stay alive so one week he stiffs the grocer and next week it's the landlord and then the milk man and the department store and after awhile the shylocks get into him real good and he's hemmed in the rest of his life. That's the way it is.

I never went the sucker route because suckers always end up getting seduced by what they think is security. Now everybody has a different idea about security, but the way I see it, the only real security is being free—mostly free of fear. I was always totally free of fear, which is why I was always untouchable when the cash was up for grabs. And I was just as devoid of fear if I happened to be busted myself.

I never knew fear from the beginning, not even when I was a baby, because I was never coddled or sheltered from the stark realities of life.

I remember when I was two years old my old man gave me this tremendous carpenter set for Christmas. It had a hammer and a saw and a pair of pliers and a screwdriver and one of those miter boxes and a zillion different nails. So one day I'm sitting on the floor in the living room whacking the nails in the miter box while my mother and sisters are busy changing the linens on the beds. Now my mother decides she's going to have a little fun with her little Roodle and what she does is put one of the sheets over her head and says, "I'm the Boogie Man and I've come to get Roodle because he's been a bad boy." Now, even though I'm only two years old at the time, already I was the most fearless son-of-a-bitch on the entire earth.

I had no idea who might be under the sheet but when this Boogie Man comes over and bends down to snatch me, I took that hammer and whacked him right on the head real good. And as the Boogie Man tippled over and fell smack flat on the floor, I jerked off the sheet and saw it was my mother. She was out cold. Listen, I put a knot on her head the size of a walnut.

I jumped up and ran to my old man yelling, "Mama's dead, Mama's dead." The old man came out and revived my mother and when she told him what happened, the old man said, "It serves you right, Rosa, you must not make our Roodle afraid of anything." And I never was. That Boogie Man con is one of the most vicious and grotesque propositions of all time. It's no wonder half of the kids grow up afraid of everything from butter-flies to the dentist's drill.

My old man set me straight on all those scare propositions when I was still learning to walk. I never heard any of that wicked witch or black Santa Claus or the goblins will get you if you don't watch out propaganda when I was a child because my old man always treated me like an adult. When I heard the proposition about George Washington and the cherry tree in school, I asked the old man if it was really true that George Washington never told a lie. The old man shook his head and said, "Roodle, it is impossible. If he never told a lie, how could he win an election?" The only politician my old man had any time for was Roosevelt. "The President is absolutely right about fear," the old man used to say, "always remember, Roodle, to fear is to die." That's what he said, even before Roosevelt put it out. What really was strange, though, was my old man and Roosevelt died on the same day—April 12, 1945. That's on the square.

My lack of fear was always a strong suit on the pool table on account of my attitude about money. At no time did I let money worry me in the least. That was the difference between me and the other players. Listen, I was wearing out $100-a-day hotel suites when those mooches were living in $5-a-week flop houses and eating at hamburger stands. They lived like animals because they were afraid to run up a bill living in a decent place. I always went first class. I took $100-a-day suites even when I was broke. I lived like a king at all times.

Once in the 30s I got into some high stakes poker action in Chicago and went busted so I borrowed like $50 from Daddy Warbucks and headed for Detroit where I heard the pool action was real hot at the moment. By the time I gassed up and stopped to eat at every roadside restaurant between Chicago and Detroit, I'm down to my last fin and the five went for tips checking into the Book Cadillac Hotel. So now I'm in this fabulous suite with only a quarter in my pocket and I'm so hungry I'm feeling faint. But since I felt no fear, I picked up the telephone and had room service bring up the best meal on the menu and after I belted out the calories I went to bed.

I slept for two days and two nights eating on the tab all the time, even though all I had to my name was a quarter. I had no qualms about not being able to pay the hotel bill, none whatsoever. Then after I was good and rested, I walked around to a room called Detroit Recreation, a fabulous joint with 144 tables, and got the show on the road.

All I had in my pocket was that quarter, understand? Just a quarter. By now the hotel bill is like $200 and I owe for parking the car too, but I walked in Detroit Recreation like a real general and started playing a fellow named Clarence Jackson, who was a very high roller. We played every game on the table and I took all the swelling out of Mr. Jackson's carbuncle; in fact, in the end I had a fair size carbuncle of my own. Then I went looking for another top player by the name of Paul Graham, who was called Detroit Slim, and I stuck him up, too, along with several others. When I got back to the Book Cadillac, which was like two days later, I not only squared the hotel bill, but I had enough cash left to make a down payment on an aircraft carrier. I told Zee the story and he said, "My God, Fatty, you really operated on margin."

The reason I could maneuver that way was because I never got emotionally involved over cash, or even the lack of cash. I was a ruthless, cold-hearted killer. I'd set 'em up and psyche 'em out and shoot 'em down in cold blood.

If I happened to be playing some mooch living in a scratch house and counting on a $5 Nine Ball game to get him through the day, it was like taking popcorn from a five-year-old child.

Since I never played my top speed against a mooch and since it always took me awhile to warm up to the table, the mooch would usually win the first few games. That not only got him all puffed up and feeling sure of himself, but also aroused the interest of whatever hairy legs might happen to be in the room at the time. The hairy legs would notice how well this mooch was shooting, and since they're always looking to get position on somebody anyway, the hairy legs would start backing the mooch, which meant there was serious money on the table. First thing you know the stakes were maybe two bills a game and commencing right then and there, that mooch belonged to me and so did the hairy legs.

Right away the mooch has to think about the two bills riding on every game because he realizes by his standard of living he can survive two whole months on that kind of money. He gets so carried away he starts thinking about the big steak he's going to put away that night and he even begins contemplating a move into a better class hotel. But then he considers the other side of the proposition—if he loses he ends up sleeping in the park. And right there the deadly fear takes him over. You can always tell fear in a man's face, first in his eyes then around his mouth when his lips start to tighten and get dry. A man with a deadly fear has a face like a cash register.

I always went along to the point where I figured the mooch was at the height of his dilemma. Then I stepped up the speed and sprung the trap. I did it a zillion times. I robbed 'em all.

Once in Norfolk I was playing a one pocket proposition with Andrew Ponzi, who certainly was no mooch in any sense of the word, and Andrew had me hemmed up in the worst kind of way, only I saw a chance to run out if I played a ball off three cushions. Now there was a zillion riding on the outcome and anybody with good sense would have played a safety in a spot like that. But I brought that ball off three cushions, rolled it between two other balls with maybe a cool quarter-inch to spare on each side and dropped it in a corner pocket like it was radar-controlled. Andrew almost fainted dead in his tracks he was so astonished.

"No wonder nobody can beat this son-of-a-bitch," Ponzi said, "why, he takes the most impossible shots on the table and he makes them every time."

I never knew any type of fear whatsoever in a tight situation and they all knew it, the high rollers and the fun players, too. That's why I couldn't get any serious action once I cracked 'em all out. They all knew I was absolutely fearless when the cash was on the line and after they all had a piece of me none of 'em would play me for a toothpick.

Now you might not find many of them who are willing to admit that they were whacked out by the Fat Man on account of pool players are a rare specimen. They all have very convenient memories when it comes to remembering the matches they lost. Some of them will look you straight in the eye and tell you they never lost a match in their life. It's unbelievable. The pity is there's no way on earth to find out who is telling the truth on account of nobody keeps official records of everyday matches, especially the money matches. Pool has never been run like say baseball or basketball. There's no box score in the morning newspaper reporting in black and white exactly who won and who lost the big match the night before. Everything about pool has been sort of run by ear and when some players get through romancing and improvising the outcome of their defeats, any similarity between the improvised version and the actual facts is an absolute impossibility.

In my particular case I'm all over the country year after year boasting that I never lost a cash match in my entire life. Now that just happens to be the brutal truth and if there are any Doubting Thomases who question my claim, I'll gladly prove it.

I say I've beaten every top player in the country, the fun players included, in the past 35 to 40 years. You name him and if he played me for the gold, I've whacked him out. Now if any of them claim otherwise, I'll tell you what I'm willing to do. I'll take a lie detector test.

Any living pool player, including those fun tournament champions and near champions, who says he beat me in a cash match can prove it by letting the gendarmes wire up both of us in one of those lie detector joints and if any one of those eggs says I never beat him for all the cash every single time, he'll electrocute himself. Listen, I'm so honest I could beat a monk in a lie detector test.

I beat 'em all for the gold. I'm the fearless, heartless Fat Man who turned Willie Mosconi snow white and made Mr. Luther "Wimpy" Lassiter, another member of the Tuxedo Set, prematurely grey.

I met Wimpy, which is how Luther Lassiter is known in the poolrooms, down around Washington, D. C. in the late 30s. He was real young then and he used to get into wrestling matches over who was going to carry my cue case. Wimpy idolized me. I took him under my wing as a protege, in fact, we traveled on the road together, and when I got through with Luther he was a tremendous cash player.

Wimpy would come up to Washington from his home in Elizabeth City, North Carolina, all the time and after a while he got so good with the cue he was breaking every living human in the District of Columbia, only when me and Luther got on the table the currency always changed hands. I sent him home penniless so many times that I almost needed a lobbyist to get him to play me.

Back then I had a friend named Jimmy Jones who owned a little room in Anacostia on the outskirts of Washington and Jimmy got real sick and had to go to a sanatorium so he asked me to run the place for him. I never like getting sewed up that way but Jimmy was real sick; in fact, he died, and in a situation like that I'm a regular social worker. I'm only cold-blooded for the cash. So I'm running the joint and Luther Lassiter is busting everybody because he's getting better and better all the time.

Now this one night Wimpy has cleaned everybody in the room and his backer says they should head back to North Carolina with the wad, only Wimpy keeps looking at me like he wants to try one more time. His backer got very upset and said, "Don't play him, Luther. He always busts us. Everytime we come to Washington we bust everybody and then Fatty busts us. Please don't play him, Luther." That's what the backer said, but Wimpy just had to have one more piece of the Fat Man.

So we played straight pool all through the night and Wimpy was shooting so good that at one point an old-time player named Johnny Irish says to me, "Fatty, there is no way you can beat the kid." Now it's like 9 o'clock the next morning and exactly all the cash is up for grabs when Wimpy plays a safe which happened to hem me in pretty good. I need the deuce in the corner pocket, only there's a zillion balls between the cue ball and the deuce so the only way out was for me to go to the masse, which is a very difficult shot to pull off. I put a jillion dollars worth of English on that ball and it hurdled right over the other balls like a rocket and whacked that deuce in the corner pocket for all the gelt. I had busted Mr. Lassiter again.

Now I turned to look at Wimpy and he's just standing there turning green and all of a sudden Mr. Luther Lassiter, a future World Champion, started yelling in that Southern drawl of his. "Oh, Lawdie," he said, "oh, Lawdie, the Fat Man has won all my cash again." Then he turned to his backer and said, "Oh, Lawdie, you told me not to fool around with the Fat Man. You told me. Oh, Lawdie, he has busted us again."

Wimpy is a real gracious boy and he tried to laugh it off, but all of a sudden he said, "Oh, Lawdie, I do believe I have to go to the bathroom." And he took off in a dead run for the john in the back of the joint and his backer took off after him.

"Luther, Luther, can I help you?" his backer yelled.

But Luther was already out of sight.

That was a long time ago but Wimpy remembers it real well. A couple years ago in Johnston City, Illinois, a mooch named Eddie Beauchene, who is called Detroit Whitey, was trying to heckle me and Wimpy was standing around listening. So Detroit Whitey says to a newspaper reporter, "Don't fall for Fatty's corny con."

Wimpy started laughing and he told Detroit Whitey, "Beware of the

Fat Man, Mr. Beauchene. If you play him for big money he makes you go to the bathroom." The newspaperman put it in the paper just the way Wimpy said it.

Mr. Luther Lassiter remembers all right, only sometimes he forgets, like in California last year when he was being interviewed by a reporter from the *Los Angeles Herald Examiner*. They were having a Tuxedo Set tournament in Burbank and this reporter is interviewing all the hot dog players, including Mr. Lassiter, the same Mr. Lassiter who I sent sprinting for the crapper.

Luther is telling the reporter there are maybe 100 players he can't beat unless he gets about two weeks of practice and the reporter asked Wimpy if that included Minnesota Fats. "Minnesota Fats?" Wimpy says, "why, I can lick him anytime, anywhere." Sometimes those fun players get so carried away with the double-double that they lose all contact with reality. If you catch them in the middle of their YMCA routine they're just liable to tell you their father was their mother.

Those hot dog players always had a deadly fear of me. I went to the World Tournament for years and just stood around hoping the top finishers would play me for a little cash but it was hopeless. They would be all dressed up in the tuxedos and when the subject of cash came up, they really gave me the old double-double. "Why, Fatty," they would say, "you know I never play for cash." The same mooches I had cracked out like eggs a couple of months before would look at me with a straight face and say, "Why, Fatty, you know I never play for cash." All of a sudden they were all patron saints.

In the olden days it was a different story. Arthur Woods and Chick Seaback and Andrew Ponzi and Erwin Rudolph and all the other stars would play in the tournaments all right, but when it was over they would give you all the action you desired at a C note or two a game. And they would play any and every game on the table. That's on the square. Today the tournaments are run like hospital wards, only today's fun players couldn't attract a crowd if they played in a telephone booth. Even the suckers are wise to the Lilliputian tables with the shopping basket pockets.

On the whole, the top pool players today are a lot like the suckers. They're scared to death to bet their own cash on their game. Oh, they'll tell you all about the tremendous pressure in those big tournaments but they create their own pressure. What pressure is there playing all week long for trophies? Now when you're playing for the cash to pay the hotel bill and the food tab at the best restaurant in town, then I'd say you're really under pressure.

One of those fun players told a magazine writer that when he plays in a big tournament match he bites his tongue and breaks out in a cold sweat and loses 10 to 12 pounds before it's all over. Well, when I play in a big cash match, I always gain 10 or 12 pounds and it's always in the carbuncle. If those hot dog players ever put their own wad on the line they would be so nervous and full of fear that they couldn't direct you to the subway if you offered them a $500 reward.

It's easy to be alert and gracious when everything is going good but it's a normal human instinct to run scared when things start sliding the other way. There was never a touch of human fear in my entire body when I played for cash, not even when I lost. That's why I could be so cold-blooded. It wasn't an act or a filage. That's the way I was and that's the way I am today.

The best way to tell if a person has a deadly fear is to watch them around animals. Animals are the most loveable and affectionate creatures on the face of the globe, even ferocious animals, providing they're not hungry. If a crocodile has just had lunch, he wouldn't bother a tourist in a hundred years, only most people are afraid of crocodiles, even well-fed crocodiles. I never fear any kind of animal, in fact, I'm crazy about them.

I remember one time in Detroit I won a zillion on an animal proposition. There was this fabulous looking tomato with a traveling circus and she had two lion cubs, the most beautiful baby lions you ever saw, and she carried them around in her arms on account of she was training them at the time. You see, she didn't want the lions to have a deadly fear of people and start snapping at the suckers so she was giving 'em all the love and affection she had.

The doll was stopping at the Book Cadillac and when the mooches saw her coming down the street with the baby lions they would all run for cover. I told them there was nothing to fear so one mooch cracks wise and says he will wager any amount I wouldn't walk up and pet the lions.

Now I not only went up and caressed those harmless little kittens and won all the cash, but I ended up with the doll as well. I went with her for months. Every day me and the gorgeous tomato would go walking the lions in Grand Circus Park right in downtown Detroit. We had 'em on leashes, just like they were poodles, and when the mooches saw me and the doll strolling with the kittens, they would start running and running and they wouldn't stop until they were clear across the border into Canada. The tomato kept the two cubs until they were too big to have around but by that time they were completely trained and as playful as canaries, so she took off. She went in one direction and I went the opposite.

I didn't know it at the time, but that was one of the last dolls I would be romping around with. I had been playing the pool and the propositions and the dollies all over the country from morning till night for almost 15 years. But my future travels were to take me to a little town down in Southern Illinois where I would meet the most fabulous looking tomato of all time.

Her name was Evelyn Inez, only I called her Eva-line.

CHAPTER 11

Love and Marriage and Fried Chicken

Chicago was really my kind of town back in the later 30s. I never was what you would call a permanent resident, but any time the action on the road slowed down, I headed back to the Sheraton Plaza where I usually shared a suite with Daddy Warbucks, only when I got back to Chicago in the early 40s, I discovered that Daddy Warbucks had pulled stakes and left town. He not only had left town, but he struck it rich in the oil fields down in Southern Illinois and Southern Indiana and now he was a real general. He even got married and was living like a Square John in Evansville, Indiana, where Titanic Thompson happened to be in residence at the same time. It was unbelievable about Hubert becoming domesticated because he always liked the dolls real good. In fact, one time back in New York he was the object of the affections of a doll by the name of Miss Texas Guinan. That's on the square. But now old Hubert was sold on the slippers and pipe proposition so I was on my own in Chicago.

The lakefront was like a big ocean resort inside a tremendous city and I spent a lot of time bicycle riding and swimming out there. I even joined a swim outfit called the Polar Bear Club which meant exactly what the name implied—we went swimming in Lake Michigan in the dead of winter. Of course, when it really got cold the Polar Bears would retire to the Turkish baths and hibernate in the stream boxes until the lakefront had that tra la, tra la look about it again. All the swimmers called me the Big Bear on account of I was the biggest Polar of them all and I had enough hair growing out my back and chest to be a gorilla. But in the poolrooms around the Loop I was known as Chicago Fats.

I hung out mostly in Bensinger's, which was palatial in those days, and Augie Kieckhefer's old room down around Randolph Street. Both were top action spots and every outstanding player who came to town could be found in one place or the other. Augie Kieckhefer was a top-notch player in his day, in fact a world champion, and he liked to shoot for the cash so I caught a lot of action with him and also with Rotation Slim and Rockford Lou and a tremendous old player named Johnny Saunders and a zillion others. Listen, I'd play for six months straight without losing a heat for the cash. I played every game on the table, sometimes even and sometimes giving outrageous odds, and I whacked 'em all out time and time again until they ran like deer when I walked in the front door. It got so that if I wanted a serious money match, I had to make a novena to the patron saint of impossible propositions. Sometimes I would back one mooch against the other and then take on the winner just to keep in stroke. I walked in Bensinger's 800 times in those days and not a one of those mooches ever made a move.

Finally for the want of something interesting to do around the poolrooms, I began making a study of the speeds of the individual players. I charted them like they were horses and after awhile I knew what each and every one could do under given conditions. It really wasn't such a difficult proposition at that, because back then all tables were a standard 5-by-10 so all things were equal at all times. You couldn't figure a proposition like that today because on those 4½-by-9 washtubs Lady Bird Johnson is apt to beat one of those fun players. After awhile my study was so thorough and complete that no one on earth knew as much about the players as I did. So I started making the odds for the World Tournaments, which happened to be played in Chicago in those days.

By the time the 1941 tournament rolled around, I had my system purring like a computer and when Andrew Ponzi defended his world title in Chicago, I booked bets on every match. I determined the odds and did business with anybody who had the scratch and when the 156-match tournament was over, I had won 154 of the bets. That's on the square. I lost only two bets the whole week. Willie Mosconi won the title, which was his first world championship, but I won all the cash.

I went out and bought the most fantastic looking LaSalle automobile you ever saw. It was a real deep, dark green, almost the same color as money. It was late February so I headed South for Hot Springs, Arkansas with Jimmy Castras, who was called Jimmy The Greek, along for the ride.

We cleared Decatur down in mid-state and as we're rolling into a little town called DuQuoin it starts sleeting and the roads turn to ice. Even that big LaSalle started slipping and sliding from one side of the highway to another and I ended up slamming into a couple of mail boxes which put a dent in one of my fenders. It wasn't a real bad dent but I didn't want to drive into Hot Springs anything but first class so we stopped in DuQuoin to have the fender repaired.

The fellow at the car garage said it would take a day or two to fix up the car so right away we ask about a poolroom and he told us there was one right behind a placed called The Beanery, which meant we could whack out two birds with the same shot. Now The Beanery not only served tremendous home-cooked food, but the room out back was a real action scene. You could get more action in that little four-table room right smack in the middle of nowhere than you could get on Broadway at times. It was unbelievable. In fact, it was so good that we never did get to Hot Springs.

DuQuoin was a coal mining community back then and pretty soon the word got around about this Fat Man from Chicago whacking out every living human behind The Beanery so every day there were more and more miners in the room. They were the funniest looking eyeballers I ever saw because I never had seen eyeballers with big lights on their caps before. They came in packs and they followed me around like I was John L. Lewis. Pretty soon they saw what tremendous odds I was giving my adversaries, so one of the miners wanted to play me, only I told him I never gambled with family men or working people. And I never did. I always stuck with the ones who were in my class and back then there were more top action players in DuQuoin than there were in Las Vegas.

Now one day who comes into The Beanery but a pair of high rollers named Frank Riggio, who was called Muzz, and Joe Scoffic, who everybody referred to as Scoffie. Muzz allowed that he was a fair pool player himself and said he was interested in taking some of the outrageous odds I was offering. The thing I remember most about Muzz was that he was a tremendous size, in fact, about a double for me in the waist, but he wanted a piece of me almost as bad as the rest of 'em. So I played Muzz a little One Pocket and after a few games, Muzz said, "Excuse me, sir, I have to run to the bank before it closes." He came back with a fresh bankroll and I took him for every last cent, so then he said we would have to postpone the competition until the next day right after the bank opened again.

I took a good look at Muzz and said, "Muzz, you look like a pretty healthy man and judging by your size, I imagine you can handle yourself pretty well with a knife and a fork. So if you'll recommend a good restaurant, I'll buy the steaks." So Muzz directed me to a joint on the outskirts of DuQuoin called The Evening Star and he said to "Tell Evelyn Inez that Muzz and Scoffie sent you." He also said that this Evelyn Inez was the best looker in the whole of Little Egypt, which was what they called Southern Illinois. So now I'm expecting this Evelyn Inez to be some kind of belly dancer.

Me and Jimmy The Greek got in the LaSalle and drove over to The Evening Star and just as we're walking in the front door, I pulled out a $100 bill and stuck it in my handkerchief pocket. Now who is standing just inside the front door but the tomato called Evelyn Inez, who happened to be the hostess and head waitress. She was beautiful beyond compare, a gorgeous doll without a flaw. She was a tall, dark-eyed brunette who went about 5-7 but she had just the right padding in all the right places. And legs? Listen, Betty Grable never had legs like Evelyn Inez.

"Why, you must be the high rollers down from Chicago," she said, and when she smiled she had teeth like a whole tray of pearls. So I said, "What makes you think we're high rollers?" and Evelyn Inez said, "Well, nobody in these parts carries pictures of Benjamin Franklin in their handkerchief pockets."

So she sashays across the floor of The Evening Star showing me and Jimmy The Greek to a table, and just watching that doll walk across the room was worth a couple of pictures of Benjamin Franklin in the pocket.

Evelyn Inez had all the waitresses jumping and they gave us fantastic service. Now Jimmy The Greek, who always had a much better approach than his follow-through, chimes and locks up Evelyn Inez for the next night, only she looks at me and says, "What's the matter, Mr. Franklin, aren't you interested in dating me?" I told her she was the most fantastic creature I had ever laid eyes on but I also told her there was no way I could date a doll, even a beautiful doll, with a name like Evelyn Inez. She got all red-faced and embarrassed and she said, "Well, then, what do you think my name should be?"

"Eva-line," I said, "your name should be Eva-line," and she seemed to like the idea.

Now it's the next night and Jimmy The Greek is engaged in a little pool action at The Beanery and when it comes time to pick up the doll named Evelyn Inez, Jimmy kept looking at his watch. He got so nervous that he started missing shots a child could pocket so I said, "Calm down, James, I'm volunteering to go fetch the doll for you."

Now I'm back in the LaSalle and headed for The Evening Star. I'm laughing like somebody who knows something real good because already I had decided on the conversation to use on Evelyn Inez and already Jimmy The Greek was out of contention. When I reach the joint, Evelyn Inez is all dressed up like she's going to model in a style show and she was very surprised to see me because she was expecting Jimmy The Greek. I told her that Mr. Castras had been detained by important business and that I would drive her around to look at the sights until James was finished with his undertaking.

Back then DuQuoin was just like any other little Midwest town, except it was a strip mining area and after all the coal was shoveled from the Earth, all that was left was a lot of little piles of dirt that looked exactly like the mole hills of Egypt. So Eva-line and I started talking about Egypt and Europe and world affairs in general because she said she was real worried about this Mr. Shicklgruber in Germany on account of she had a brother who was about to be drafted in the Army. We talked and talked and after we got tired of driving, I stopped in front of the movie house, the Grand Theater, on the main drag and we conversed for another hour or so.

By the time we got back to The Beanery, Jimmy The Greek was very perplexed, especially when Eva-line said it was too late to do any socializing on account of every joint in town was closed except The Beanery. So we ordered Eva-line a steak and I cut it up in little bite-size pieces and fed it to her like she was a Sultana. Jimmy The Greek kept trying to get a word in here and there but I shut him off like he was a Victrola so many times that he could not only see that I was hooked on Eva-line, but that the doll was overboard for me, too.

After that night, I never let Eva-line out of my sight. I hardly went around The Beanery anymore because I switched headquarters to The Evening Star, which happened to be a very high class restaurant and nitery and gambling rendezvous. It turned out that The Evening Star was owned by Muzz and Scoffie and it also turned out that Eva-line was keeping company with a bass player in the band at the joint. So right away I told Eva-line, "Listen, if you want to be my doll, you've got to give that fiddle thumper the double door," which she did.

The Evening Star offered all forms of recreation known to the gambling trade and I began making outrageous deposits at the crap tables and card games. In fact, the craps had the horns on me so bad that I was considering a return engagement at The Beanery when Muzz paid me a personal tribute by installing a pool table just to accommodate my business. So I would whack out everybody in the joint on the pool table and then lose my winnings back in craps and cards and then win it back in pool. It was a fantastic cycle that did much more for the economy of Little Egypt than it did for the individual entrepreneurs.

But the most fabulous attraction of all was the 30 gorgeous tomatoes who frequented The Evening Star for the dancing sessions after dark. Every night Muzz put on a dancing contest with the winners getting a bottle of champagne and steaks on the house and Eva-line and I won all the jolts hands down. Then we started something new with the marathon contests.

There was this dice dealer named Pop-Eye who loved to dance and he said he was willing to wager any amount that he could outlast me in the terpsichorean shufflings. So we got down real good and Pop-Eye and I danced and danced and danced all night until the sun came up. Sometimes Eva-line would get all tuckered out and I'd have to snatch another doll to keep going and Pop-Eye was doing the same thing. We wore out more dancing partners in one week than they did in a month at the Roseland. It was a nonstop marathon and me and Pop-Eye even had food served to us as we tripped about the floor. I would be two-stepping with a fabulous looking tomato in one arm and a drumstick or a breast of chicken in the other. It was fantastic beyond compare.

I was in the middle of a marathon proposition one night when who comes into The Evening Star but a coal miner I knew from The Beanery. He said he had bet a whole week's pay on me in an eating contest he had already arranged with a fellow named Little Tiny. Now this Little Tiny was real petite, like 6-5 and 440 pounds. I know he weighed 440 because later on me and Tiny got on the same scale down at the freight depot at the train station and we tipped an even 700. I weighed 260 at the time myself.

His name was Stripe Hampton and he came out of St. Louis where his parents had settled after coming from Syria. One of his ancestors had started a nonstop revolution over there that raged on and on for years and Little Tiny's people fled to America when things weren't going too good for their side. He was another real high roller himself and when he heard about all the action in DuQuoin, he quit St. Louis and opened a place in DuQuoin called The Plaza, which was a gambling paradise in every sense of the word.

Little Tiny had prided himself over the years at being able to out-eat any living human who ever came to DuQuoin and he made the gimmick stand up time and time again until this coal miner matched us up at The Evening Star. The miner had seen me demolish a whole pot of beef stew one night at The Beanery and although he knew Little Tiny had a tremendous consumption rate, he bet Muzz and Scoffie and another high roller named Louie Reed and Little Tiny himself that I could out-eat any man on earth.

It was a tremendous proposition, seeing how Little Tiny was such a tremendous physical specimen who might be capable of out-eating me at that. So I considered it from all sides because there was no way I could let the miner down and I decided the best means to winning the jolt was to psyche out Little Tiny right from the start. The proposition was to see who could eat the most of 30 tame rabbits Muzz had ordered special for the occasion so right before the bell rang, I decided to intimidate Little Tiny real good.

"Tiny," I said, "the rabbits are all here and ready for demolishing but I tell you what I'm going to do—I'm going to spot you a ham, a whole ham—and then eat more rabbits than you."

So Muzz brought over this tremendous 15-pound ham that was all cooked with the pineapples and cherries and I slapped it all over with butter and ate it like it was an appetizer.

"See, see," the little miner said, "I told you—why he ate that ham like it was an ear of corn."

Then we started on the rabbits, only Little Tiny surrendered after about six rounds because he said he kept thinking about how I ravaged that ham. So the little coal miner won the proposition and I finished off the rest of the rabbits. That's on the square.

I won many a proposition out-eating everybody in the fried chicken category, only even after I won all the cash I always ended up light as a cork anyway. Muzz's fried chicken was the most tremendous I ever tasted until I sampled the chicken cooked by Eva-line and her mother. I would walk into The Evening Star and put in my order and I would tell Muzz, "Now, don't rush—I'm in no hurry. Just take your time and cook it real good." Then I'd stroll over to a crap table or sit in the card game and I usually lost heavy. I always suspected that Muzz told the chef to really fry that chicken slow motion because most of the time that chicken really came high.

Later on during the war when there was a tremendous food shortage, Muzz had trouble getting chickens sometimes so I always bought up a couple of sacks of chicken for him when I was on the road. I would pull up in the car, drop the sacks of chicken in the door of the joint and then take off again. So this one day I come running up and dropped two sacks and yelled "Muzz, keep an eye on these sacks." Now about six hours later I come back and I ask Muzz about the sacks and he says, "Oh, you mean the chicken—they're right out in the kitchen."

"In the kitchen," I said, "why, my God, Muzz, that ain't chicken in those sacks—that's cash."

Those days in DuQuoin were the happiest of my life. I was so hooked on Eva-line that I wasn't giving any attention to my pool or the craps and cards. All I did was eat 24 hours a day and watch Eva-line prance about The Evening Star.

When it was time for the floor shows at The Evening Star, all the high rollers were featured in solo performances. Little Tiny always sang "Take Me Out to the Ball Game" and "Dry Bones," and Pop-Eye would do what he called an impromptu dance. When it was my turn I would belt out "Mexicale Rose" and "Poor Butterfly," only I always changed the lyrics to "Fat Butterfly," and the suckers would clamor for more.

That's how I was living 24 hours a day until one night I got a long distance call from New York. My sister, Rosie, had died. It was the first time in my life that I had ever known the sting of death and I came all apart. I broke down and wept right in The Evening Star and the only person I could turn to was Eva-line because she understood what I was going through. About five years before her father had been killed along with eight other miners in a tragic accident at the old Kathleen Mine in Dowell. We had talked about it a few times and she had told me that it was a feeling you just coudn't explain until you went through it yourself.

So Eva-line took me to her house and we got her mother, Orbie, out of bed. I was crying so hard I was unable to control myself and Orbie, who teaches Sunday School at the Methodist Church in Dowell, said, "Evelyn Inez, you'll have to accompany this poor boy to New York because if you don't, he'll never get there."

Eva-line said she couldn't go to New York because she was still paying on a new coat she had just bought so I told her if she would come with me I would pay out the balance on the coat. So she drove me all the way to Washington Heights and I told her I knew she really loved me.

When we got back in DuQuoin we never said anything about getting married, although something was always putting it in my mind. So one night I asked Eva-line if she would like to take a trip with me to Chicago and she got all excited and we went to her house to pack her clothes.

Now this time her mother, Orbie, comes into the living room in her nightgown and says, "Evelyn Inez, I don't want to tell you what to do, but when you went with Fatty to New York, you were performing a Christian charity. You have no reason to go to Chicago." That's all she said and she walked back into her bedroom.

So I said, "Eva-line, I think your mother wants me to marry you." But Eva-line said that was entirely up to me so right there in the kitchen of her house I proposed and she accepted. We decided to get married the next day, which was a Saturday, over in Cape Girardeau, Missouri.

The day was May 7, 1941, exactly two months to the day that I had met Eva-line at The Evening Star.

The next morning we got in the LaSalle and headed for Missouri, only I stopped in every gambling house on the road. Eva-line said it looked like they knew I was coming because everywhere I stopped they had a welcoming committee out to greet me. I dropped a real bundle at every place and by the time we got to Cape Girardeau it was late in the afternoon and there wasn't a Justice of the Peace to be found.

So I spot this poolroom right on the town square in Cape Girardeau and in I walk and I find a mooch who I had whacked out in Chicago and when I explained my predicament he said, "Hell, Fatty, there's a JP upstairs."

So I ran up three flights and found this JP and he said he would arrange everything within a matter of minutes. I went over to the window and yelled down to Eva-line who was double-parked.

"Eva-line," I said, "go park the car and come on up so we can get married."

The JP's name was Gus Schultz and he had us fill out a marriage license and then he told us to come back in 20 minutes and he would link us up. So Eva-line and I walked down to a drug store on the corner and had a dish of ice cream.

Gus Schultz told us when we got back that for an extra $5 he would give us a top-notch nuptial, including a prayer fitting the occasion so since Eva-line's mother was a very religious person, I accepted the prosposition. But as soon as it was over and he pronounced us man and wife, I bolted out of that place like it was on fire.

"Rudolf," Eva-line yelled as I ran down the stars, "you haven't paid Mr. Schultz."

"You pay him," I yelled back. "That was the most artificial prayer I have ever heard." And it was.

Then we drove back to Dowell and spent the first night at Eva-line's house and had the first problem of our married life.

It was my snoring.

Eva-line said she didn't mind and neither did Orbie because both of them said they were very sound sleepers. "Just give me a chance to get to sleep, Rudolf, that's all I ask," Orbie said. I snored so loud that night that I shook the chandeliers. I still snore a real shattering basso profundo.

It took Orbie awhile to get accustomed to my snoring but cooking for me was no problem at all because she cooked the lunches at the school in Dowell. "I cook for 70 children a day at school," she said, "so cooking at home for you will just about come out even."

Orbie and Eva-line were both fantastic cooks, only when they put on the fried chicken they were fabulous beyond compare. I mean nobody can hold a light to them. I even ate fried chicken for breakfast—fried chicken and about six bottles of Coca-Cola. I loved fried chicken since I was a boy but my mother never could cook it the way Orbie and Eva-line did. And when I ate fried chicken down on Broadway back in the 20s and 30s, which was before refrigeration is what it is today, the chicken always tasted half rotten. I always thought it had to taste that way until I started eating at Orbie's table.

The more food Orbie and Eva-line put on the table, the more I belted out and I kept getting heavier and heavier until like six months after the nuptials I had gained like 60 pounds. My neck size had puffed up to 19 and the waistline was 55 inches and when I hit the scales they read 283. It was the heaviest I ever weighed and that's when my neck just disappeared between my shoulders. With the neck gone my snoring became so hideous that it was waking up the neighbors. In fact, one night I slept at the St. Nicholas Hotel in DuQuoin during a long cash match and I woke up every guest in the joint. When I came down the next morning for breakfast there was a traveling salesman sitting in the lobby waiting to see if I was human.

"I just had to see for myself," he said, "I never thought a human being could snore that loud."

Right after the wedding the newspaper in DuQuoin ran a big article saying Mr. Wanderone and his new bride would honeymoon at Niagara Falls, only it was awhile before we got there. I kept getting involved in the serious money matches at The Evening Star and The Beanery and another poolroom named Curley's and we kept putting off the trip.

Every now and then I would make a short tour on the road and I always told Eva-line that each trip was an appetizer for the real honeymoon, only Eva-line didn't seem to care if we ever made it to The Falls.

We visited a zillion different towns all over the country in 1941 and 1942 and everywhere we stopped we heard tall stories about the tremendous action down in Norfolk, Virginia. So one night after we had been resting at Eva-line's house for about two weeks, I told her it was time to hit the road again.

"Any special place you want to go, Eva-line?" I said.

"Yes, Rudolf," she said, "this time let's see what's going on in Norfolk."

CHAPTER 12

Yes, Virginia, There Was a Norfolk

There wasn't anything extra special about Norfolk, Virginia, during the war years. It was like every other port city hit with an overnight boom and all the quick money that went with it, only Norfolk had a tremendous shipyard and Naval Base and when the shooting started in Europe and the Pacific, right away Norfolk was a 'round-the-clock proposition. The suckers came from all over to snatch the high-paying defense jobs and when it came time for recreation, they wanted to cut up worse than the Whoopee Set back in Prohibition. Norfolk back then was a lot like movies about wide-open towns during the Gold Rush and the Oil Boom days. It was exactly like that.

It wasn't the suckers that attracted me to Norfolk. It was the high rollers. Every big action man in the country had converged on Norfolk and wagering was nonstop, unlimited and gargantuan beyond compare.

I got real good pool action there and if I had just majored in the high runs and side pockets and let the other propositions alone, I might be totally rich today. But there were high stakes crap and card games all over town and what I didn't drop at the card tables I surrendered in the dice department.

It was the most fantastic exchange you every saw. The pool players would win a fortune with the cue and then lose it in cards and craps and the crap shooters and card sharks would win it back at their specialties and then lose it all over again on the pool table. There was so much cash changing hands that every day was like Gin Whistle Billing Day in Dixie.* It was fantastic beyond belief.

Titanic Thompson was one of the leading luminaries around Norfolk in the 40s. He had hit the gold roll in oil out around Southern Indiana and when he came to Norfolk he moved in like a real Sultan. He was on a brand new wife, a gorgeous doll named Maxine. But he also brought along Maxine's sisters, Betty and Bonnie, who were even more fabulous looking than Maxine.

Ty was always very particular about his wives. He insisted on being surrounded by raving young beauties at all times and when his wives got a little old, like maybe 26 or 28, he divorced 'em real quick. That's on the square. Ty's 77 this year and he's living down around Dallas and the last time I heard he had another new wife about 25 and a son about six.

When Ty first came to Norfolk he couldn't find suitable housing for his ladies so he moved out to Virginia Beach and took over one of those mansions the generals built right out on the ocean front. It was a fabulous joint and Ty entertained the way Perle Mesta wished she could. All the high rollers would call a recess on the weekends and drive to Virginia Beach just to be an hand for Ty's soirees. We would check into suites in the resort hotels and between Ty's social gatherings the dolls would take to the beach while the high rollers got the poker and clabbiash sessions going in the hotel.

Even though Ty was already in his late 50s, he never looked a day over 25 and when he entertained he loved to have young people around him, especially young tomatoes. He had a real tall, trim build and a full head of brown hair and dark, deep-set eyes that were always dancing. He would take all the dolls over in the corner and tell them how gorgeous they were and notice their clothes and make over them like they were Lana Turner. The tomatoes were crazy about him.

But the most fantastic thing about Titanic was his hands. He had the hands of an artist, which is as good a word to describe Ty as you can find. He could do almost anything with his hands, everything except play pool. One time I saw him bet a zillion that he could take a rock and hit a bird in flight. It sounded impossible, only Ty did it right before my eyes.

---

* According to Professor Minnesota Fats, "Gin Whistle Billing Day in Dixie is that mournful hour when the cotton gin whistle blows at harvest time and the sharecroppers have to come up for the seeds and supplies purchased on account at the general store—there's so much cash changing hands when the gin whistle blows that it's exactly like the currency exchange between the high rollers in the days of wine and roses in wartime Norfolk."

He could do all sorts of amazing card tricks and sleight-of-hand gimmicks on account of his fingers were long and agile. Just watching him perform was fascinating. The way he moved his eyes and his fingers at one and the same time was liable to hypnotize you on the spot. He was a regular Houdini.

Now when it came to propositions, Ty really dazzled his adversaries with the quick hands and the soft con. A lot of times the golfing greens were the scene of some of his greatest performances.

He would pick a mark and struggle through the first nine holes shooting right-handed and losing a sizeable bet in a real close finish. Then the con would start. Ty would moan and groan and berate the sucker's game in the worst possible way and at the height of the beef jolt he would go so far as to say he could do better playing left-handed.

Now the mark would figure Ty for the sucker so the bet would double and on the second nine, Titanic not only shoots left-handed but wins like Citation on account of he's a natural left-hander to begin with. Ty could have been another Ben Hogan on the pro tour.

Sometimes Titanic's artistic hands wouldn't figure in the proposition at all on account of sometimes Ty pulled it off with just a high voltage con job. One time in Evansville, Indiana, he made a fantastic killing on a watermelon proposition that on the surface looked impossible for him to win.

Ty was driving in from the oil fields outside of Evansville when he sees this farmer hauling a whole truckload of watermelons to market. So Ty stops the farmer and right away he buys the whole batch of watermelons for a very inflated sum. Then he pays the farmer to count each watermelon and pays him another tremendous price to drive the truck past the old McCurdy Hotel in downtown Evansville at an appointed hour.

Now Ty hustles to the McCurdy and all the high rollers are standing in the lobby and out on the sidewalk in front and after awhile here comes the farmer driving out First Street with the load of watermelons. So Ty gets the show on the road by allowing he will wager any amount that he can estimate exactly how many watermelons the farmer has on the truck. It looked like such a Hungarian lock that the high rollers all got down real heavy and when they stopped the farmer to inquire about his inventory, Titanic just happened to have hit the precise number. He won a fabulous bundle on the watermelon con but I obligingly relieved him of most of it on pool tables in Evansville and later on in Norfolk.

Ty had a natural weakness for pool on account of he got the name of

Titanic in a poolroom out in Joplin, Missouri, when he was real young and every time he saw a pool table he thought he was attending a college homecoming.

When he was 14 he ran away from the farm down in Arkansas to take up gambling and after he won a few dollars he bought a real flashy brown pin-striped suit and a brown derby and everybody called him The Derby Kid. Now one day in 1912, which was the year the Titanic went down, The Derby Kid walks into a poolroom in Joplin operated by a gambler named Hickory Jackson and sees Hickory is betting anybody $500 they couldn't jump over the pool table. It happened to be a big 5-by-10 and all the suckers were killing themselves trying to win the five hundred.

So Ty considers the proposition from all sides and says he can clear the table providing Hickory Jackson lets him take a running start. Hickory said that was all right with him. So The Derby Kid takes off and dives over the table head first with old Hickory rushing around to see how badly he is hurt, only The Derby Kid is kneeling on a mattress which he had put on the other side of the table.

Now The Derby Kid is flashing the five C notes and some old-timer asks Hickory who's the kid in the brown suit with all the cash and Hickory says, "I don't know the punk's name but it ought to be Titanic because every time we make a bet he sinks me." So after that he was known as Titanic and with the propositions he was absolutely unsinkable.

Ty, whose real name was Alvin Thomas, although he later changed it to Thompson, thought since pool was a game requiring good hands and a keen mind, he should be able to master it the way he mastered everything else. But Ty didn't realize that pool isn't just an ordinary proposition. A lot of people think pool is a joke, but it almost takes an Einstein to really play the game. It's actually a lifetime proposition. You never really learn it all, never in a hundred years, only Ty didn't see it that way.

He was always coming to the table with fantastic propositions and he would bet just as high as anyone cared to go. And when he saw some of the outrageous odds I offered, like four fronts to a back and scratches-no-count, old Titanic just couldn't see how he could lose. But when I got on the table Ty usually ended up with those fabulous hands digging into his pockets to come up with the cash. I made an extraordinary convert out of Ty in Norfolk and after awhile he quit the pool table and stuck to the cards and the propositions.

Most of the pool action in Norfolk was around a room called The Tuxedo which was right downtown. Any hour of the day you could find the top money players in the country there. The card games and crap tables were at a horse room operated by a fellow named Joe Olsen but the real action came after dark at a place called Whitey's, just plain Whitey's.

Back then there were about 300 high rollers all told around Norfolk and when the good times started in the early 40s, Whitey happened to be one of the high rollers himself. But Whitey hit a real hot streak and won enough cash to buy a piece of property about 14 miles out from downtown Norfolk and he built a fabulous joint to accommodate the 300 genuine high rollers and nobody else.

Whitey ran a very discriminating joint on account of he wouldn't allow a sucker near it. He always said suckers were good for one thing: trouble. So by word-of-mouth he let it be known that suckers were not welcome at his place, which was a tremendous arrangement because if you happened to break a guy down to his alligator-skin shoes you never had to worry that he needed the money to feed a wife and a half-dozen kids. Whitey only skinned his own kind.

His joint was run like a high class private club. Not only did he make the place off limits for suckers, he also frowned on the dolls, although I took Eva-line sometimes and Ty would occasionally bring Maxine and the two gorgeous sisters.

Whitey had every known gambling game at his joint and if you happened to be a pool player he even had a special billiard room where you could go broke in quiet and peace and with as little pain as possible. I never had a piece of Whitey's action, but I happened to be his number one executioner on the green cloth.

I stayed around Norfolk off and on for maybe six years. The first two years me and Eva-line lived at The Monticello, which was the only class hotel there at the time. But it was during the War and according to a wartime public accommodations law, every five days we had to move all our luggage out on the sidewalk and then check back in again. There weren't too many bellhops because of the War and I got so tired of dragging those suitcases in and out that one day I told Eva-line to go find an apartment.

So she leases this tremendous four-room place in the Calvert Park section and she furnished it in the most elegant and luxurious taste money could buy. I guess we must have been victims of Ty's social jolts because all of a sudden Eva-line was inviting all the high rollers in for dinner, in fact, one Thanksgiving Day we had 20 people assaulting the turkeys. It was the only time in all our marriage that Eva-line had the opportunity to come on as the hostess with the mostest because that was about the only time we were ever in one place long enough to establish what you would call a real home.

When the action would slow down in Norfolk, me and Eva-line would take a vacation to visit our folks or maybe take a quick trip to Washington or Philly or even New York to survey the wagering possibilities around the poolrooms. But we were always heading back to Norfolk where the serious money was.

Now one night after the big jolt with the Japs and the Shicklgruber Set is done, Eva-line and I are back in Norfolk and who is one of the fresh faces on the scene but my old protege, Mr. Luther Lassiter, who was just out of the Coast Guard. We had a joyous reunion and right away I put Wimpy through a strenuous rehabilitation program to make him a real stakes player, only right away Wimpy comes down with the most deadly malady known to man—the dolls.

Back then Wimpy was in his late 20s and as handsome a young fellow as you ever saw. He was just beginning to turn grey and he had a soft, Southern Gentleman manner about him. I always thought he looked like that movie actor Sonny Tufts but Eva-line said Wimpy was even better looking than Sonny Tufts. Wimpy also was a very religious boy because he could quote the Bible as well as some preachers and when he met up with a tomato he was always very polite and courtly. In fact, if a doll paid Wimpy the slightest compliment, his Bible training would come to the fore and he would say things like, "Bless you, ma'am," or "That's right Christian of you to say, ma'am." It always made a big hit with the dolls and Wimpy could have written his own ticket with any tomato in the whole state of Virginia, only he got hooked on the wrong one.

There was this doll from Norfolk, oh, she was a fantastic beauty, gorgeous beyond compare, and she gave Wimpy the idea that she had the sweets for him real bad. So naturally, Wimpy got the weak knees for this dolly, too. They would sit around in a corner for hours like a pair of lovebirds, holding hands and whispering sweet phrasings to each other, and then it would always happen.

Wimpy would come running over with his mouth covered up and say, "Fat Man, I got the swolls." I'd look at the kid and his lips would be all puffed out and at first I thought it was from wiping off the lip-stick, only back then Wimpy wasn't the kind of boy to smooch a tomato. Back then if he was to bump into Elizabeth Taylor in a bikini he would be more apt to recite the *Declaration of Independence* or "Invictus," or something like that. I would have to say that at that time Wimpy was more like Little Lord Fauntleroy than Errol Flynn.

The way this Norfolk doll affected Wimpy was brutal and first thing you know he was talking about getting married; in fact, he might have married her at that only he was what you call a late scratch. He was buying furniture and a refrigerator and a stove and even contemplating the purchase of a house, but the doll was giving him the double-double. She had Wimpy going home early to get his rest and then she was stepping out on her own, only Wimpy didn't know about it. Now when he discovered what was going on, the reaction was brutal. Poor Wimpy's lips got all puffed up and he really had the swolls for sure.

"Fat Man," he said, "I feel so bad I can't even go to a movie." Wimpy was exactly like the story going around at the time about Virginia's Senator Carter Glass—he was all broken up.

There was nothing he could do about it, so he finally gave up on tomatoes across-the-board by remaining a bachelor. Eva-line told Wimpy he should fall in love and get married but Wimpy would always say, "Bless you, Mrs. Wanderone, but I'm already in love—I'm in love with pool." And he really was.

Me and Wimpy had some tremendous sessions around Norfolk back then but as long as we were playing on the big 5-by-10 tables he was in trouble. I also engaged in some cold-blooded shoot-outs with Mr. Andrew Ponzi and Mr. Marcel Camp and a hundred others who happened to stroll onto the scene. I played 'em all and I robbed 'em all in Norfolk. I was really at the top of my game and shooting better than I ever have, before or since. And if things hit a lull in Norfolk, I hit the road for action elsewhere.

There was this tremendous One Pocket player in Baltimore named Wally Stodd, only everybody called him Baltimore Stoddey. He was a real big-time bookmaker and he had lots of confidence in his own game and he would go real good for the cash. So this one time when things were dragging around Norfolk I took a trip to Washington and me and Baltimore Stoddey had a real nonstop session only it was one of those in-and-out affairs that lacked what you would call a decisive conclusion. In other words me and Baltimore Stoddey split pretty even.

So what happened was there was a fellow in the room from New York by the name of Abraham Sunshine, which happened to be his real name even though it sounds like a nom-de-plummer, and this Sunshine was real sharp. Me and Sunshine palled around together back in the olden days when he was known all over New York as "The Kid in the NYU Sweater." Sunshine was a top baseball and basketball player, even good enough to play for a college, only he was crazy about pool and he fashioned his life around the game. But being a good athlete he was on an intimate acquaintance with the top basketball stars at NYU so he would borrow their violet-colored sweaters with the big white NYU letters on front and he'd make all the poolrooms around New York posing as an innocent college youth. The mooches in the rooms would see this kid in the sweater with all the cash and they would snatch him real quick, only when the money was exactly right Sunshine would run the table and take off with all the gelt. He hustled 'em so much with the Joe College image that after awhile the word went all over New York: "Hey, be careful of the kid in the NYU sweater."

Now Sunshine being real wise to the situation offered to act as a go-between to set up a showdown with Baltimore Stoddey but the best Abraham could manage was a return engagement on Stoddey's home table in Baltimore. He said it didn't look very good for me on the other guy's table but I told Sunshine I didn't care what table we played on. "Listen," I said, "you tell Baltimore Stoddey that if it'll make him feel any better, I'll bite the ends off a kitchen table and play him on that." So Sunshine delivered the message all right, only he failed to heed my words and bet on Baltimore Stoddey instead.

Well, I drove to Baltimore and scattered Mr. Baltimore Stoddey like he was confetti. I beat him 30 in a row until he finally coughed up all his cash. So here was poor Sunshine looking exactly like he had too much Moonshine. He was as pale as an albino but on account of I felt a little sorry for him, not to mention that he set up the action in the first place, I walked over and said, "Mr. Sunshine, here is the money you lost but never again make the mistake of betting against the Fat Man because that is like taking the pipe—it's automatic and total sorrow." So Sunshine bet on me at all times after that.

I won a zillion propositions like that in Norfolk and all over the East Coast in the 40s, only I had this terrible craving for craps and I ended up like most every other high roller in Norfolk—which was broke.

For some ridiculous reason I thought because you handled the dice with your hands you could automatically control 'em. Even Eva-line was smarter than that because she told me it wasn't the same thing, only I never paid her any mind because any time you let the doll call the shots you're an instant disaster case. So I kept the crap tables busy.

One time I figured I had the Hungarian lock-up going for me in Norfolk because I kept rolling hot for like eight straight hours this night at Whitey's and if I told you the wad I had built up, even a social worker wouldn't believe it. I could have been a five-star general.

So now I'm still rolling hot and it's almost daybreak and outside a snowstorm is howling like a Caribbean hurricane, which was enough to cool off the dice to start with. But I kept rolling real hot until finally I had this overpowering urge to get totally rich on one big roll. So I pushed every last cent out on the table and picked up the dice.

What came up was the most hideous and appalling pair of snake eyes of all time. It was unbelievable. That quick I was as busted as an ordinary sucker.

So now all the mooches start heckling and berating me as mooches always do when a high roller has the horns on him real bad and since I wasn't in the proper frame of mind to engage in a lot of verbal grief I walked out of Whitey's joint into the snowstorm. I didn't even take my coat.

It was really coming down and I didn't have the car on account of Eva-line had driven it back to town the night before. So I started walking to Norfolk—14 miles away—in my shirt sleeves. That's on the square. The mooches all got worried and jumped in their cars and came after me saying I should get in and they would ride me home. Luther Lassiter was one and Andrew Ponzi was another and even Whitey himself came up in his big bus, only I told them all to evaporate.

I walked those 14 miles back to Norfolk in that blizzard and before I went to bed Eva-line prepared the calories and I belted out a tremendous breakfast. I never allowed adversity to interfere with my eating and sleeping.

"Eva-line," I said, "you were exactly right about the dice. Craps is a losing proposition, only it cost me a fortune to realize it."

A couple years ago one of those fun players was being interviewed by a big magazine and the writer asked him what was the biggest pool bet he ever saw made. So he tells all about the day I walked 14 miles in the snow after losing an outrageous sum in a pool match in Norfolk. He came up with some ridiculous story about how I lost jillions over-cutting the nine ball, which was ridiculous beyond compare. He even inflated the amount of cash involved.

I lost jillions all right, and I mean jillions, and I did walk home in the snow, only I lost it shooting craps and not over-cutting any nine ball. Listen, I never lost a pool game for cash in all my life, not in Norfolk or Siberia or Zanzibar or anywhere else.

The show in Norfolk had a tremendous run, even longer than *Gone with the Wind* and *My Fair Lady* put together. But in the late 40s, a general by the name of Senator Estes Kefauver threw his coonskin cap in the presidential stakes and he started wolfing the gambling industry real steady. He kept pushing and pushing until it was the third act from *Camille* and before long the oldest established permanent crap and card and pool game Norfolk, Virginia, ever knew was shut down tighter than a drum.

The high rollers took off for Hot Springs and New Orleans and a few other action spots still operating. Some even went legit in Vegas which was about the last port before the storm because after Norfolk, wide-open gambling was a basket case. Even the suckers could see it.

Now about the same time the generals of the Billiard Congress of America fractured the last classical standards of pocket billiards by reducing the size of the tables to 4½-by-9 fun boxes with washtubs for pockets. It turned the game into a farce, exactly a farce. After that you couldn't get a real smart roller to bet on a pool game anymore than you could get the Daughters of the American Revolution to quit having tea parties.

So me and Eva-line headed back to Little Egypt and I went into semi-retirement, in fact, almost a total eclipse.

I got a little action around DuQuoin but it was peanuts compared to the olden days. Even Muzz and Scoffie had gone legit. The Evening Star had set and was now called the Perfection Club. Muzz and Scoffie had been reduced to pushing food. A whole era had vanished. Big-time gambling was out of this world—and it wouldn't ever be back.

So me and Eva-line settled down in Dowell with Orbie and the cats and dogs and every few days I would pick up another starving hound or kitten and bring it home. I kept picking up more and more brokes and strays until after awhile I had a regular kennel, and Eva-line said I should give every one a name, just like I did all the pool hustlers.

We named one mutt for Wimpy because it was always following Orbie to her Bible Reading Class at the Methodist Church on Sundays. And we called another one after Weenie Beanie, who is a young pool shark from Washington, on account of this little puppy ate leftover beans like he was a stockholder in Campbell Soup.

I found out that cats and dogs are the greatest creatures on earth to have around because they surpass humans on all counts. I went crazy over them and after awhile I had so many out in the back yard I forgot all about pool and was off on a real high run as a dog catcher.

CHAPTER **13**

Dogs and Cats Unlimited

I'm crazy about every living creature, it doesn't matter what it happens to be. I even love insects; in fact, I wouldn't swat a fly or a mosquito for a whole barrel of gold. One time I drove all the way from Mobile, Alabama, to Dowell and it was like in the summertime and my car was loaded with a zillion mosquitoes but they didn't even bite me. It was unbelievable because if you happened to drive from Mobile to Dowell with a carload of pool hustlers, you would get bit so hard and so often that you would need a malaria vaccine and a new bankroll as well.

Animals surpass humans on all counts. They not only never talk back, but animals appreciate kindness and affection in a way that most humans wouldn't understand to start with. If you can take an animal and tame it and make it next to human by showing it love and tenderness, like the doll with the lion cubs in Detroit, think what you ought to be able to accomplish with a human being who is supposed to have an intellect.

Why, a human being should be the most fabulous creature of all, which is the way The Man Upstairs intended when he put the show on the road in the first place. But what happens is one human gets to plotting with another human and maybe another and another and after awhile they all decide to be generals. So right away they form a combine in order to get the Hungarian lock on the mooches and the suckers and that kind of action touches off all the war jolts from here to Zanzibar. That's human endeavor for you.

The way I see it, human beings could learn an awful lot from lesser creatures like cats and dogs and even crocodiles. But instead they take these helpless animals and use them for experiments to hatch the most deadly and hideous problems the world has ever known. You take these advanced scientists and mathematicians. They're always putting poor help-less dogs on machines and torture racks in the interest of what they call progress, only sometimes it's the wrong kind of progress. It's this wrong kind of progress that I'm against because it has the entire earth in a state of permanent grief, exactly a state of permanent grief. Most of those scientists can't get out of their own way unless they're rattling test tubes. They not only wouldn't have enough common sense to come in out of the rain, they wouldn't even know how to open an ordinary umbrella.

Now I'm not against progress, unless it gets ridiculous. I'm not against politics, but when politics gets absurd beyond compare, then I'm really against it. What's been happening here lately is the scientists and politicians have been getting together more and more but instead of just rattling swords the way the old generals did, what they're rattling is test tubes. They keep testing and testing and screaming about all sorts of progress, only they never know when to stop. Those test tube generals have the world in such a frantic state with the atomic bombs and nuclear devices that all we need is another fiend like Mr. Shicklgruber to step forward and press the button. Then everybody ends up in the crapper.

Talk about social behavior, listen, those scientists and generals in Washington ought to take time out and just sit around and watch animals operate. When big-time gambling went to the laundry for good, I had a lot of time to think and observe things happening all around me, things I never had time to notice before. Most of my observing took place out in the back yard in Dowell just watching the cats and dogs. Now I know anybody in their right mind wouldn't believe that cats and dogs can live together without a lot of grief, but that's exactly the way it is in my animal kingdom in Dowell.

One time a guy gave me a chicken. I didn't even know the fellow, only he knew how crazy I am about animals of all kinds. So this night I was playing cards in DuQuoin and this guy comes up and throws this chicken in the middle of the card table. He says, "I brought the chicken for you, Fatty, I just found it out on the road and I don't know what to do with it." I took that chicken and locked it in the men's room so it couldn't fly away and when the card action was over, like around daybreak, I took the chicken home with me. It was real cold like in the wintertime and I didn't know what to do with the chicken so I went to this great big dog house in the back yard where there was 30 or 40 dogs and cats all sleeping together. So I threw the chicken in the dog house and went in and told Eva-line the story.

"Rudolf," Eva-line said, "you must be out of your tree. Just because the dogs and cats sleep together, you can't put a chicken in there, too." So I told Eva-line, "Is that so? Well, we'll see." So we tiptoed out there and peeked in and this chicken was sitting sound asleep on top of this big dog's head. That's on the square.

Now the reason the chicken was accorded immediate acceptance in the dog house was on account of my dogs and cats are accustomed to total kindness and affection and therefore aren't looking to touch off any beef jolts, not even at the drop of a live chicken. If you were to drop a Seminole Indian smack dab in the middle of Park Avenue or maybe snatch one of those society notables and deposit him in Big Chief Sock-In-The-Wash's tepee, you would touch off an automatic revolution. The generals say there will be no Seminole Indians in the Perfume Stockade and, likewise, no sociables are to be caught mingling around the wigwams. That's exactly what the Civil Rights revolution is all about when you get down to it. The real trouble is that people never take time to socialize and fraternize on levels other than their own.

Out in my back yard everybody is just one of God's little creatures. There's no discrimination of any type.

I'll tell you something else. You can talk about all your YMCAs and brotherhoods and fraternal orders, but if you really want to see something, just drop by my place in Dowell in the morning when the cats and dogs get up and you'll see the damnedest show you ever imagined. I've got this tremendous big old dog named Spotty and he watches over the rest of 'em like he was a shepherd. I don't even know what kind of dog he is. He's just short and stocky with a heavy fur and enormous weight, only he don't throw his muscle around out back. He just gets up every morning like he's the top general and the rest of the dogs and cats fall in line like they were privates in the Army and Spotty goes by each one and washes their faces by hitting them a lick with his tongue. It's amazing. The dogs and cats just stand there like a five-year-old waiting for the Mama to come scrub him clean and old Spotty licks every face until he thinks it's washed. Then he dismisses the whole outfit for breakfast. It's fantastic beyond compare.

Every one of my dogs and cats lives like the King and Queen of England. When I'm home every night I stop in at the Perfection Club and pick up maybe a 100 or 150 pounds of bones and leftover steaks. Sometimes a patron might leave a whole steak on the plate and Muzz drops it in the sack along with the bones. I'm always hustling like that. And when I happen to be on the road, Eva-line drops by to pick up the calories. One time Eva-line got carried away at a card party and forgot all about the cats and dogs and when I found out about it we had a beef jolt that ended up just short of the divorce court. That's on the square.

I feed 'em all on a pair of metal lids off a couple old septic tanks and when they start belting the food it looks like round tables at a high class feast. I walk around like the maitre d' seeing that the weaks and strays get the best of the grub and the big dogs get the heavy bones. Then for the second course I come out with the bone meal which looks exactly like ground hamburger. I buy it like 50 or 60 pounds at a time at Kroger's supermarket where they grind it from thousands and thousands of scraps and I dish it out in individual servings. In fact, each one of the guests knows his special place at the table because sometimes we feed 'em 30 or 40 at a time and they belt out the food without bumping into each other.

So now when all the regulars and the supernumerary strays from the neighbors' places are finished, there's always enough left for any new faces that might happen to be in the vicinity. I always put out like two or three times the normal consumption because you never know who might be coming. In fact, hundreds and hundreds of birds wing down to belt out the off-fallings. In a week there might be a million birds eating out there. They're crazy about meat and bone meal and when they get their fill they fly off chirping like a whole choir of sopranos.

Now to top that off, early in the morning, like around daybreak, the possums and the rabbits come in from their little bungalows out along the branch, which is a stream of water a hundred yards behind the house. They sneak around and whack out the bone meal and the beef like they were doing something wrong. Sometimes I see 'em when I get up to go to the bathroom and I'll wake up Eva-line and we'll stand at the window and just watch 'em like we're peeping through a keyhole. You couldn't give me a zillion dollars to miss it.

So one morning me and Eva-line are watching the show outside when here comes an animal that was so big I thought it was a police dog. Eva-line said she didn't know what it was but she thought it might be a ground hog. I didn't know on account of I never saw a ground hog before then in my life. Now every morning I'm getting up early and waiting for him and here he comes sneaking out of the shadows and looking around like he's a house burglar to see if the coast is clear. Each day he got bolder and bolder until finally he just walked up there like he was one of the regulars. He got more and more enormous cleaning off the banquet boards until he was the biggest rascal I ever laid eyes on.

Early one Sunday morning, my brother-in-law Junior Morgan, who happens to be a Baptist preacher and is known all over Little Egypt as the Reverend Mr. Silas Morgan, Junior, drops in on his way to the morning service at church. So I asked June to look at the animal and he said, "You're mighty right, Fatty, that is a ground hog, the biggest ground hog I ever saw in all my life." Then he said something like he wished he had a shotgun and I stopped him right there. I said, "Look, June, I like you real good, see, but don't you at no time shoot one of those animals. Some people think that might be legitimate, but I'm funny about that sort of thing. I don't want any animal shot on my property. I don't even want anybody stepping on a roach around here." So Junior said he was very sorry and he left and went on to church and about a month later, he told me he talked about the ground hog in one of his sermons.

A lot of people think it's real fun to kill and torture animals. Like one time in DuQuoin a fella pulls up to the poolroom and says, "Fatty, do you like turtle soup?" I told him I sure did. So he says, "Well, go out in the back of my truck and get yourself a turtle." Now I figure the turtle is dead, only when I get to the back of the truck the turtle is alive and kicking, I mean really kicking. The fellow had baling wire around the turtle's neck so he couldn't get his head through and he was tied around the feet and anchored between some barrels and cans in the back of the truck. It was brutal. I took that turtle down real quick and put him in a box and when I climbed down out of the truck with this enormous turtle this fella says, "Take him home and kill him, Fatty. He'll make tremendous turtle soup." I told him there was no chance of that turtle getting killed. "I could be starving and I wouldn't kill him," I said.

So I put the cardboard box on the front seat of the car and drove home, only on the way, the turtle climbed out of the box and I almost tipped the car over trying to get him back in. I put him back in and started driving again and now he climbs out again and slips down between the door and the seat but by this time I was home and I called Eva-line out to the car. Now she had a carpenter who was doing some work at the house and he looks at me petting the turtle and he says, "Be careful, Fatty, he'll bite your fingers off. Let me kill him for you." And I said, "You be careful or I'll have him bite your fingers off."

I told Eva-line I was going to take him over to Big Muddy, which runs into the Mississippi River around Murphysboro, but Eva-line said we should take him down to the branch because it had been raining a lot lately and the water was almost coming over the banks. The poor turtle looked dry and hungry so I put a little food in the box and me and Eva-line walked down to the branch with him. The water was all brown and muddy and swirling and when that turtle saw that swirling water he went down like a two-year-old. It was a picnic just to watch the way he took to that water. Nothing on earth would have satisfied me more, not a zillion dollars or even a date with Elizabeth Taylor. Eva-line got a big kick out of it, too.

"He'll likely be free forever now, Rudolf," Eva-line said. "He'll follow the branch all the way down and end up in Big Muddy."

I always loved animals, ever since the day my old man won Gans, the goose, at the Swiss Verein outing in New York. We always had a dog or a cat around the house, but keeping a pet caged up in New York is brutal beyond compare. Animals have to be free to roam about, just like humans. That's why you got so much trouble in those big cities. People are so cramped on top of one another it's like living in a telephone booth.

I remember in the summer my old man used to take the whole family to the Catskills for vacation and one time I saw this beautiful little calf and I really fell in love with it. The old man said I should give it a name so I called it Woodrow after President Woodrow Wilson who was in the White House at the time. I played with Woodrow from morning till night. When it came time to go back to Washington Heights I got a rope and put it around Woodrow's neck and was going to take him home, only my mother said it was out of the question. My old man said since we lived in a democracy we should put the proposition to the entire family for a vote. Everybody lined up against my mother and the tally was five to one in favor of making a New Yorker out of Woodrow but my mother vetoed the move. She said in a couple of months Woodrow's name would have to be changed to Bessie on account of he would be a milk cow and since she knew I wouldn't milk him she sure wasn't going to be the milkmaid. So I left the Catskills broken-hearted because I never saw Woodrow again. It was one of the greatest disappointments of my entire life.

I've always had special pets that travel with me, mostly dogs, because a dog can be a lot of fun on the road. One of the most tremendous dogs I ever had was a little mutt I called Pinky on account of she was the color of French ivory with pink spots all over her body. I picked her up in a rainstorm down in Biloxi, Mississippi. She was all cold and shivering and I put her in the car and she growled at me a couple of times but I gave her an affectionate pet and I told her, "You little thing, you'll never have another bad day as long as you live." She must have understood what I was saying because right away she started licking me like I was something special.

I took her back to the Broadwater Beach Hotel and put a fin on the maid to give her a real good bath and then I called room service and ordered two $5.50 steaks, one for me and one for Pinky, and that dog ate that steak like a human. I kept her for maybe a year and she turned out to be the smartest dog I ever had. Pinky was so smart she even answered the telephone.

I was stopping at the St. Francis Motor Inn in Mobile where I always occupy the Gene Autry Suite, which is right next to the swimming pool. Now I leave Pinky alone in the suite and just after I leave the phone happens to ring so Pinky knocks the phone off the hook and hollers smack in the receiver—"Waa . . . waa . . . waa . . . waa . . . ." The operator got all excited and told the bellhop there was a baby crying in the Gene Autry Suite. "There's no baby in the Gene Autry Suite," the bellhop said, "because the Fat Man is in there and he ain't got no baby." But the operator made him check anyway and he found out it was Pinky talking on the phone.

I finally had to get rid of Pinky on account of she was the most destructive dog I ever knew. She was tremendous as long as me or Eva-line was around, but if you happened to leave her alone, she went plumb berserk trying to break out. Pinky ripped out more mattresses and arm chairs and yanked off more Venetian blinds than you ever saw. I must have spent $5,000 paying for damages. So I had to give her up.

I found Pinky a tremendous home in Augusta, Georgia. I gave her to a couple who had a 14-year-old daughter and they treated Pinky like she was a queen. I missed Pinky so much at first that I called these folks in Augusta every day to see how Pinky was doing and she seemed to know it was me talking on the phone because one night the lady said, "Mr. Wanderone, I think Pinky wants to talk to you." So she put the phone down by Pinky and Pinky went, "Waa . . . waa . . . waa . . . waa . . . ." like she was talking to me. You see, that was because when me and Pinky were on the road I would call Eva-line and Eva-line would say put Pinky on the phone. So I trained her to talk into the receiver.

My Number One dog today is a tremendous little terrier I call Fuzzy. I picked her up around Dowell about a year ago because she reminded me a lot of Pinky, except her spots are black. Something else, Fuzzy don't answer the telephone, only she don't rip hotel rooms apart either. But she gave me a lot of grief last winter when she got in the family way. In fact, Fuzzy turned me into an instant midwife.

I had been out on the road for a spell and when I got to Dowell, Eva-line put on a real feast for me and Fuzzy, only Fuzzy kept sneaking out every time somebody opened the door. The reason Fuzzy was sneaking was because that old rascal Spotty was right outside the door and in the mood for some serious romancing. He knew what a tremendous female little Fuzzy was so he snatched her and really exposed her to the sweet mysteries of life.

Fuzzy got in brutal shape, only I wouldn't think of leaving her at home, so I ended up like the Dr. Kildare of an animal hospital. I had a vet look her over in every town I stopped, but when Fuzzy was ready to deliver there wasn't a vet for miles around. I was playing an exhibition in Buffalo, New York, and when I got back to the motel Fuzzy had delivered three gorgeous little puppies while I was out and later on the same night she had a fourth one. Then Fuzzy came down with a milk disease and she required a lot of loving care. I looked like a real scientist mixing up the egg yolks and the lemon water and Karo syrup and liquid vitamins but I shot it to the puppies twice a day and they came along real fine. I took 'em to Chicago and found tremendous homes for them but before I gave 'em away, I investigated each family like a social worker.

I had a zillion pets but the most fabulous one of all was a little squirrel I picked up down in Tuscaloosa, Alabama. In fact, this little squirrel led to my giving one of my proteges—Marshall Carpenter—the nickname of Tuscaloosa Squirrelly.

I was playing in a joint on the town square in Tuscaloosa and right outside there was this little boy about 12 or 13 who was selling watermelons, only every time you turned around this little fella had deserted the watermelon stand and was sneaking in the poolroom. But the owner, a Mr. McHenry, who happened to be an outstanding church member, kept throwing the kid out. I put in a few words in the kid's behalf by telling Mr. McHenry that no harm would come to the boy, only he wouldn't hear of it. Now two days later Mr. McHenry walks in carrying a little baby squirrel with a tail twice as long as its body and he says to me, "I don't allow kids in the room, Fatty, but squirrels are all right." He said the squirrel had just fallen out of a tree and seemed to be hurt so he brought it to me because he knew how I loved animals. So Eva-line took that squirrel back to the motel and I went over to a store and brought a little doll bottle with a little nipple and we fed that squirrel and raised it until it could do anything but talk.

The squirrel was crazy about Eva-line; in fact, he used to sleep around Eva-line's neck every night just like a necklace, exactly like a fur necklace. He was crazy about me, too, and every time I would let out a snore, the little squirrel would come running in and jump up on the bed and twick my nose like it was a hickory nut. That's on the square.

Everybody said the squirrel would get mean when it got older and it would bite me and Eva-line but that squirrel was just like a member of the family.

Me and Eva-line would call room service for breakfast every morning and we would belt out the ham and eggs with the coffee and toast and marmalade and the squirrel would eat right along with us. Eva-line would take the corners off the toast and slap butter on it just as thick as you could, like as thick as my finger, and then she would add the marmalade and shoot it to the squirrel along with a cup of coffee. That squirrel would whack out the coffee and buttered toast and marmalade like it was human. It was fantastic beyond belief.

We took that squirrel all over the country. I even took it in the pool-room in my pocket and that squirrel would run out of one pocket smack into the other. So one day a pool player by the name of Delmar Stanton, who was called Harrisburg Whitey, said, "Look, even Fatty's squirrel plays One Pocket." We had that squirrel for years and when it finally died, I couldn't sleep for seven days and seven nights on account of that little squirrel had the most unbelievable death you ever heard.

He fell off a bar. That's exactly right—he fell off a bar.

We took him to the Perfection Club in DuQuoin one night and he was romping around that bar like it was a tree and all the patrons were amazed. But this night the little squirrel scampered down to the end of the bar real fast, only its judgment must have been a little off because it tried to put on the brakes too late. It just sort of backed up and went right over the front of the bar.

He tried to dig his little claws into the bar, like if he was in a tree, only the bar was highly polished and real slick and the squirrel went all the way down to the concrete floor and landed on its back. It was in brutal shape after that, even though we did everything imaginable to cure it, and it went down and down until it finally died.

The funny part about the way it died was that it lasted for months and months until we happened to be in Tuscaloosa again. That's where the little squirrel died, right in the poolroom in Tuscaloosa, exactly the same place where we found him. That's a true story.

Now on that same trip to Tuscaloosa, the little boy who was hustling the watermelons had quit the selling dodge and was now a tremendous pool player for a kid 16 years old. His name was Marshall Carpenter and he was one of the regulars at Mr. McHenry's room and right away he went crazy over me. He begged me to make a top-drawer player out of him, so I worked on him for months and pretty soon he was better than anybody around McHenry's place.

So when I'm ready to hit the road again, the kid turns up at the poolrooms with his clothes all packed and he said he was coming on the road with me. He even brought his parents, who are in the plumbing business down there, to the room to tell me it was all right and Eva-line said we would take care of the boy like he was our own son.

He was the happiest kid you ever saw and just before he told his folks goodbye, he said, "Fat Man, if I'm going on the road, I'll need a nickname." So since I was still very upset about the squirrel and seeing how Marshall Carpenter was just about two sizes bigger than a squirrel to start with, I said, "All right, sonny boy, I'll call you Tuscaloosa Squirrelly." That's what he's called today all over the country. He's one of the best One Pocket players and top action men in the game.

Me and Squirrel spent a lot of time on the road together but the money wasn't in the rooms like in the olden days. So Squirrelly was always packing it in and heading back for Tuscaloosa and I was always going home to Dowell.

But Mr. Marshall Carpenter was exactly like that little squirrel from Tuscaloosa—he died hard. He was always out on the road looking for the action. If he happened to be in Hot Springs or Blytheville or Mobile or Macon or Fort Worth or New Orleans and the action possibilities looked promising he would grab a telephone and long distance me in Dowell.

"Fatty," he would say, "every high roller in the country is down here but nobody can get the action rolling. Come on down and start us a jamboree."

CHAPTER 14

The General of Little Egypt

A jamboree was what we called the high rolling sessions that are always sure to come off when a couple of pool hustlers and their backers are holding some serious cash. You're liable to hear about a jamboree almost anywhere, even in Zanzibar if there happened to be enough gold. Hot Springs, Arkansas, for example, was always a tremendous jamboree town, especially during the racing season when there was a lot of currency in circulation.

The reason Squirrel was always telephoning me to come down to get the show on the road was because he knew I was a past master at the art of conversation and a jamboree without the right kind of conversation is sadder than a graveyard. You could take all the pool hustlers put together, regardless of how much cash they might have on hand, and there's not a single one of them intelligent enough to convince a five-year-old child that the White House in Washington is painted white. That's why I was always the indispensable man at jamboree time.

Squirrel was real wise to the ways and means I used to talk up the propositions on account of he saw me perform a zillion times when we were on the road together and it wasn't always in a poolroom either. In fact, many times I used the conversation on the dolls with Mr. Tuscaloosa Squirrelly as the sole beneficiary of the continuity.

Squirrelly is a handsome fellow, even though he's no bigger than Mickey Rooney, and he always liked the dolls real good, except when he was real young he was almost as bashful around tomatoes as Wimpy—only Squirrelly never was bothered with the swolls or anything like that. He might see a tremendous little looker about his size and he would say, "Fat Man, I sure would like to know that doll there because she's a beautiful tomato." So I would tell Squirrel to give her the conversation, only every time he tried using words he would end up redder than those watermelons he used to peddle. Then he would say, "Fat Man, I can't do it—you show me how it's done."

So I would walk up to the little doll and tell her how I had been admiring her fantastic beauty for some time and maybe I would say she had the face of an angel and eyes like a lapis lazuli. Now the doll is all interested in the conversation so I whisper to her real low that I happen to be a married man but I'm speaking in behalf of Mr. Tuscaloosa Squirrelly who is carrying such a torch for her that he is beginning to feel like one of those Buddhist monks. So I call Squirrel and I say, "Squirrelly, is this the young lady you've been raving about?" and Squirrel would blush worse than the doll. But the ice would start to melt and after awhile Squirrelly was making out with one tomato after the other like that.

I was a regular John Alden for the Squirrel, only I always spoke for him and him alone on account of Eva-line never allowed any extracurricular romping once Gus Schultz prayed over us back in Cape Girardeau.

The conversation is just as important in the poolroom as it is with the dollies. It's a matter of salesmanship, only it all depends on which side of the proposition you want to take. Take automobiles, for example. I happen to drive a Lincoln Continental which I know surpasses any wheel on the road, but in a wagering proposition I might cite 40 reasons why a Honda is a superior wheel to a Lincoln. On the other hand, it would be real easy to prove that the Lincoln is like a zillion overcoats over the Honda. It all depends on which side you're taking.

I learned that years ago from Titanic Thompson. Say Ty was going to play a little coon can, which is a tremendous card game. He might take 11 red cards, some diamonds and some hearts, and lay you 20-to-5 that you couldn't win with the red. Then he would play the red hand and lay you like 40-to-5 that he could win with it. And he would. Now jamborees are exactly the same thing. You need the conversation to discuss every side of the proposition before going to the table. Sometimes you might have to convince a pool hustler that he not only couldn't lose, but that there was no way that you could win.

The jamborees might come off anywhere in the country, but most of the time it would be a Southern town like Hot Springs or Tampa or Mobile or Macon, Georgia, or even Blytheville, Arkansas.

Blytheville was a fantastic spot for jamborees. Cleo Vaughn, who liked to roll real high, had his own room there and if Cleo happened to build up a sizeable bankroll, every pool hustler in the country would hear about his good fortune and turn up in Cleo's joint like it was election day. But even after everybody had arrived, none of those mooches had the slightest idea of how to get the show on the road. Cleo could be sitting on one side of the room with a fabulous amount of gelt in his pockets and maybe Earl Schriver, a pool hustler from Washington, D. C., is over in a corner with some serious money himself, only nobody could arrange the summit meeting on account of none of those hustlers could sell a doughnut to a starving man. So after a week of sitting around 24 hours a day just eating themselves broke, Mr. Tuscaloosa Squirrelly steps up and says, "Let's not kid ourselves, there's only one thing to do—call The General in Little Egypt."

Squirrel would get a whole barrel full of quarters and dimes and call me on the phone, sometimes at three or four o'clock in the morning, and tell me about the tremendous gold deposits in those faraway little towns. He would put every mooch in the joint on the line and they would all tell me the action was so dreadful that nobody could win enough to buy peanut brittle. They would moan and groan for an hour until I told 'em I would start out first thing in the morning.

Pool players are the most amazing people in the history of civilization because even after they call me in the middle of the night and con me into driving like 800 or a thousand miles, when I arrive on the scene all I would hear is this Who Shot John nonsense. I would drive all the way to say Blytheville with a sizeable carbuncle of my own, only when I'd get there, Cleo or maybe Handsome Danny or the Knoxville Bear or even Squirrelly himself would say, "Who, me? What makes you think I want to play, Fatty?" It was unbelievable.

"Listen," I would tell 'em, "you must take me for Topsy. I sure didn't drive 600 miles for no beef stew."

Those pool hustlers are exactly like the sucker who goes to a hotel room with a top action tomato who might be on the lam or is maybe just a natural swinger, only when she gets to the room she says, "Look, I need a few drinks first." It happens all the time, only if I happen to be in a situation like that I would grab that top action doll and caress her and say, "Let me tell you something, girlie, I happen to be an expert at my work so there will be no dodging around with me, understand?" And then if she didn't get down to the overture, I would head for the door, which is exactly what I did a zillion times at those jamborees, only those hustlers would snatch me like I was the Hope Diamond and then the merry-go-round would really go round and round.

Sometimes I would play for like six days and six nights without a letup. I even ate my meals at pool side; in fact, whenever we had a jamboree in Hot Springs I had my calories brought to the table by a friend of mine named Beef Stew who happened to be a bouncer in a night club down there. But most of the time we would be playing in a small room with a little stove behind the lunch counter and I would double as the head chef and chief dietician.

I would send out for one of those old Tennessee iron pots and dispatch an eyeballer to the nearest grocery or poultry market for the supplies and then direct the cook in the proper preparation of my favorite recipes without even putting down my cue stick. My top dish was fried chicken cooked in the same pot with Louisiana yams. The chicken would come out tasting like the yams and the yams would taste like the chicken. It was a fantastic collation and you could smell it simmering for blocks because after awhile all the mooches would stumble in sniffing a free lunch on account of they knew the Fat Man was back in town. I fed a zillion hungry, scraggly mooches in poolrooms that way.

I always bankrupted every living human at those jamborees, especially as the cash pots grew bigger and bigger, only I had to be real, real careful to get out of town with the loot. I would be at the table for like five days and five nights without a stop and pretty soon my game would naturally start to drop off, which the mooches were quick to observe.

So what they would do then was elect one of the powerhouses of the industry and rest him real good to catch me when I really started to tire. They would take him to the hotel and see that he had a good shower and a tremendous meal and they would even tuck him in bed and pat him on the head and tell him to stay there and rest himself until the phone rang. Now they would double back to the joint and keep like a fatigue chart on me and the first time I so much as let out a yawn, they would send for this powerhouse back at the hotel.

Now one time the powerhouse is all rested and ready for the kill when this friend of mine comes over and says, "Fatty, I've been watching you; in fact, I've been betting on you, but you better take a rest. Your game is getting worse and worse and now they're bringing in this well rested player to take advantage of your weariness."

"Is that so?" I said, "well, you just go fetch me a few breasts and drumsticks and about six Coca-Colas and then you tell 'em to bring on the powerhouse."

So here comes this Hercules who is dead fresh and he looks at the poor old Fat Man across the table and already they're counting the cash they're figuring on winning, only I whacked that powerhouse so clean the first game that they all ran like antelopes. I'll tell you who the power-house was on this particular occasion: Mr. Tuscaloosa Squirrelly himself. But instead of being a powerhouse, Squirrelly was just another pigeon.

Sometimes the jamborees might be few and far between and when that happened I would drive over to Evansville, Indiana, which is like 100 miles east of Dowell, for some serious money games with Daddy Warbucks or Titanic Thompson when he was living there. A lot of times I played a wealthy oilman by the name of Ray Ryan, who just happens to be one of the richest men in the world today. That's on the square.

Ryan is what I really call a five-star general because he is the only millionaire I ever knew who lived like a millionaire. He never moaned and groaned like the rest of the multis on account of he knew the cash was just for spending and not for caressing. Listen, if you happen to go to the bathroom at his mansion in Evansville and you look real close you'll find out the throw mat on the floor and the cover on the john are pure mink. Raymond really knows how to live.

Ray Ryan loved to play pool, only he wasn't anything near a top player but he was as fearless as any man I ever knew. He would risk a zillion on one more roll and if he happened to bust out he would just laugh and start all over again. He did it many times.

Raymond came out of Watertown, Wisconsin, back in the 20s and got to be a real Sociable around the gaming rooms in Chicago. In fact, one time Raymond lost a real bundle, like maybe $19,000, to one of those Chicago gentlemen who wore the striped suits and Ray gave the gentle-man his marker. Now what happened was Ryan happened to have the shorts real bad when the Chicago gentleman sent word that the account was getting long overdue.

He happened to be in Centralia, Illinois, when he got the message. Ray had bought the leases on two 10,000-acre fields where the oil possi-bilities looked real good and he was raising capital to drill when the word came down from Chicago that he should make his marker good. So Ray walks in a big oil company office in Centralia and offers to sell one of the leases for $19,000 so he can pay off the marker, only this general at the oil company figures he has position on Ray so he says both leases for $38,000 or he'll do no business. The general had the Hungarians on Ryan so the only thing Ray could do was sell out. Now he paid off the Chicago account and then he blew the other $19,000 in a single afternoon of craps and romancing the roulette wheels so now he was really tapped clean.

Later on the two oil fields came in like gushers, I mean real gushers, like $15 million apiece. But that didn't discourage Ray Ryan because like six months later he hit it real big in oil himself and became a 100 per cent

Grade A tycoon. Raymond still calls Evansville home, but the last few years he was spending most of his time at the Mount Kenya Safari Club, a fabulous Jet Set hunting lodge in Nanyuki, Kenya in East Africa, which he owns along with William Holden, the cinema actor. Raymond loves the spot so much he says he wants to be buried there.

Raymond loved to shoot pool with me because he said I offered the most tremendous odds he ever heard of, even better than the oil fields, and even Daddy Warbucks said the same thing. Me and Daddy Warbucks played most games even but when me and Ray Ryan went to the table for a straight pool proposition I had one pocket, only one pocket, and Raymond had six. That's exactly right. I was actually playing One Pocket to his straight pool, only I always won the cash because I hardly let Ray get to the table.

Now the hustlers heard about the Evansville action and they would drop in every now and then, but they never had the kind of cash to get on the same table with Ryan. After awhile I was getting so much play around Evansville that when Mr. Tuscaloosa Squirrelly picked up his favorite night weapon—the dial—I would tell the mooches I was too busy to drive all the way to Mobile or Tampa so what they did was stage a pilgrimage to DuQuoin. They knew that wherever I happened to be the action was sure to follow, only sometimes they got a little action they weren't planning on.

Like the time in DuQuoin about 15 years ago when this band of deadly killers pulled off a heist that Mickey Spillane wished he had thought up first.

A couple dozen of the highest rollers in the whole country happened to be in DuQuoin at the time and the play was so fantastic that they dismantled the kitchen at the St. Nicholas Hotel and turned it into a private poolroom. The action went on and on right around the clock and for awhile it looked like a re-run of the Norfolk days, only these heisters set off a deadly recession in the kitchen economy.

It was about three o'clock in the morning and the kitchen was loaded with high rollers when all of a sudden the robbers swarmed in from all over. I happened to be out of action at the moment and was leaning against the wall right next to the swinging doors coming off the old dining room when suddenly I felt a real start. I turned around like I knew something was behind me and sure enough there was, on account of I was staring into the most brutal pair of Thompson submachine guns you ever saw.

The bandits walked in and sent everybody to the wall with instructions to put their hands up as high as they could and keep 'em pinned flat against the wall. The ceiling in the joint happened to be like 20 feet, only

Tuscaloosa Squirrelly, who goes maybe five-feet-four, left a pair of palm prints that made it look like Jack In The Beanstalk was one of the victims.

I happened to be holding my hands as high as I could reach myself and with all my weight, it was killing me. So I went to the conversation. I told one of the intruders with the Thompson subs that there was no way I could hold my arms up anymore on account of it was putting a deadly strain on my pump. So what happens but one of the stick-up artists recognizes me.

"Well, well," he says, "if it isn't the old Fat Man."

I had no idea who the gunman might be because he was wearing a mask over his face but I told him the way it was. "You sound like a friend," I said, "but if you're a real friend, kindly let me lower my arms."

So he said I should drop my arms and grab on to the cue rack, which I did. Then he turned and yelled at everybody in the joint to get their hands up higher. I thought Mr. Tuscaloosa Squirrelly was going to crawl up the wall.

Now the holdup men whistled in a couple of helpers with a tremendous blanket and they spread it out like a fire net and went from one high roller to another relieving them of the cash exactly like they were passing a collection. By the time the collectors got to me that blanket had a sag in it like a sway-back mule. But now the fellow with the Thompson sub comes up to me and instead of snatching my cash, he starts laughing and laughing like he knew something real good.

"Fat Man," he said, "you've robbed a lot of people in your time, haven't you?"

"That's exactly right," I said, "I robbed 'em all."

"Well, in that case," he said, "we won't take any of your money. You are a brother." That's what the gunman said and nobody touched my carbuncle.

When the collection was completed the heist gang made every high roller strip all the way down to his skin. Then they tied everybody's wrists behind their backs with electrical wire and anchored the wiring to the ankles which they tied up, too. Then they ran off with all the gold.

So now I'm rolling around on the floor on my belly like one of those old roly-poly clowns, only when I look across the room Muzz, who is heavy as me, is in a similar predicament.

"Muzz," I said, "you look like a stuffed turkey."

"Oh, yeah," Muzz said, "well, you look like a big fat pig ready for roasting, Fatty. All you need is an apple in your mouth."

That started all the high rollers to giggling and we just rolled around the floor laughing and cracking smart for maybe ten minutes until Muzz happened to break loose. Then he untied everybody and the hotel owner called the fuzz.

The gendarmes came around and asked how much was heisted but one high roller after another said, "Oh, I just lost $10 or $15. I was sort of thin anyway." So now the gendarmes asked me how much I surrendered and I said, "I never lost a dime, but that mooch with the Thompson sub sure ripped hell out of my beautiful new imported pink wool shirt."

If the average sucker was subjected to a horrifying experience like that he might be in shock for days. But 20 minutes after the robbers bolted through the swinging doors, every high roller in the joint was betting on markers. But a couple of months later when they nabbed the heisters, everybody around DuQuoin had a marked expression of horror on their faces. The bandits were real killers; in fact, they murdered a policeman and another person in a robbery down around Cairo and they got a long stretch in the pokey. One of them happened to be a high school basketball coach and another one was a preacher. The plundering and the killing was just a moonlight kick with them. That's on the square.

The big stick-up at the St. Nicholas didn't dampen anybody's enthusiasm for the action. I hardly ever went South anymore because every time I turned around the hustlers were in my back yard.

Then about six years ago Squirrel and Earl Schriver decided to strike out on their own and stage a jamboree in Johnston City, Illinois, which is like 60 miles southeast of DuQuoin.

Squirrelly and Schriver were playing golf around Johnston City one day and who did they happen to bump into but an old friend and high roller by the name of Georgie Jansco. Jansco was a retired bookmaker and he was wise to the jamboree possibilities on account of he had taken in a few at DuQuoin. So Jansco, who happens to be full-blooded Hungarian, decided to apply his native lock on the jamborees by switching the operation to Johnston City, only his initial effort wasn't what you would call an auspicious occasion.

Georgie and his younger brother, Paulie, who is called Joey, too, are partners in several business enterprises in Johnston City. Paulie operates this real swanky nitery called The Show Bar and Georgie runs a little road-house on the other side of town which he calls the J & J Ranch. One time somebody asked Georgie what the J & J stood for and Georgie said, "Why, it stands for me and Paulie."

Now Georgie took Squirrel and Schriver on a tour of Johnston City to survey the jamboree facilities, but they discovered there was only one poolroom in town and it was such a trap it wasn't even good enough for a jamboree. They were about to forget the entire proposition when Georgie, who was never one to miss out on something real good, said they could hold the jamboree in the garage behind The Ranch, where all the beer was stored. So now Georgie hauled out all the refreshments, only he discovered the garage was so small that there was no way for it to accommodate a pool table. But Georgie don't quit easy.

He got ahold of a tremendous carpenter by the name of Moore who happened to be drinking beer on credit at The Ranch and Georgie told Moore he would call the bill square if Moore would enlarge the garage. So now Moore is ripping out the walls and Georgie is feeding him the juice, and the more juice Moore consumed the harder he worked. In a couple of days he had the place looking pretty good. Then Georgie gets ahold of a secondhand table somewhere and the jamboree was ready to be launched, except there was one more real serious problem. Everybody was busted.

Squirrel and Schriver and the rest of 'em were thinner than a dime because they had been out of action for quite awhile and without the cash they were in worse shape than they were before. So Mr. Tuscaloosa Squirrelly spoke up again.

"Listen, let's face it," he said, "we've got to call The General."

I drove over to evaluate the possibilities but with just a room full of brokes for bait, there was no way on earth to attract serious money men. The situation looked hopeless, but I went ahead and called Daddy Warbucks in Evansville and gave him a little conversation, only Daddy Warbucks seemed about as hard of hearing as old Coney Island Al back on Broadway.

"Why should I drive all the way to Johnston City to play a bunch of brokes?" he said.

Everybody in the joint figured the jamboree would be called on account of a lack of gold reserves, but a couple of top-action men in Knoxville, Tennessee, said they would be real interested in driving up if I could assure them Daddy Warbucks would be on hand. I called Hubert and he said that being the case he would jump in his big Cadillac and head for Johnston City at once. So the show was on the road at last.

The jamboree out in Georgie's beer shed six years ago was by no means a staggering success. As jamborees go, this one lacked the most essential asset—a flow of liquid cash. But it was the start of something real big because a year later every pool player in the country was talking about Johnston City, Illinois.

Back then at the start of the 60s, pool was stone cold dead, I mean dead enough to call in the embalmers. Even the fun tournaments were a thing of the past. The game might have perished for all time, only a fellow named Walter Tevis wrote a novel about pool called *The Hustler,* and one of the central characters, a high rolling pool shark named Minnesota Fats, was fashioned after me. It was a tremendous book but it was even more fantastic as a movie because it won all sorts of nominations for the Academy Awards.

The movie starred Jackie Gleason and Paul Newman and it had the suckers jumping up from their theater seats and rushing for the nearest poolroom. Overnight the demand for pool tables and cues was unbelievable beyond compare. Even Georgie Jansco got bit by the bug.

Georgie went to see the movie and right away he called me at home and said, "Fatty, let's stage a World Tournament right here in Johnston City."

"Listen, Georgie," I said, "you must be off your trolley—you can't hold a World Tournament in no beer shed."

But Georgie said he would take care of all that on account of he was starting construction immediately on a private joint called The Cue Club and he would stage the tournament there if I could get the players.

So the next day I drove over to Johnston City and Georgie and Paulie were in their working clothes and already staking out the foundation for a building behind Paulie's joint, The Show Bar. They had on old bib overalls and straw hats exactly like Old Sauerkraut, the farmer I hustled out in Iowa in the olden days.

"Well, well," I said, "if it isn't Heckle and Jekyll."

"Don't give us any of that Heckle and Jekyll stuff," Georgie said. "Get some overalls and help us with the work."

"Work?" I said, "Why, I'm no common laborer. I'm the General— The General who re-jived the entire pool industry."

CHAPTER **15**

Exposed by Hollywood

When the novel *The Hustler* was published in 1959, it never made the best-seller list but it sure started an earthquake in the poolrooms. Nobody had ever written a book about money pool until this fellow named Walter Tevis came along and exposed every pool player on the hustle from here to Hong Kong.

Tevis did a tremendous job on the book because he happened to know a whole lot about the big action games in the top rooms around New York and Chicago. I never knew Tevis but I figure he must have been one of the eyeballers in the crowds when I played for the big cash back in the olden days. Listen, when I read the book I found out this Tevis knew more about me than I knew about myself.

The hero of *The Hustler* was a young pool player called Fast Eddie and he just might have been fashioned after somebody like The Knoxville Bear or Tuscaloosa Squirrelly or maybe Handsome Danny Jones. You'll find the Fast Eddie type in almost every poolroom in the country. But there was no question that the character called Minnesota Fats was fashioned after the one and only New York Fats, who just happened to be me.

Now I know those novelists always insert a crutch in the front of the book claiming that any similarity between characters in the story and actual persons living or dead is purely coincidental. That's the usual dodge but the similarities between me and this Minnesota Fats were so glaring and obvious that even the dumbest mooches in the poolrooms knew who the real Minnesota Fats happened to be. Right off, Cornbread Red, who's no threat to Einstein, started calling me "Fat Minnie."

If you saw the movie you already know this Minnesota Fats was the best pool player in the whole country and also a fearless gambler who played serious money matches for days and nights without a letup. That sounds a little like me, I think. But that's not all. This Minnesota Fats was also a tremendous dresser who wore fabulous diamond rings, ate in the top restaurants and was always stopping the games to wash his hands and dust 'em real good with the talcum powder. Just a coincidence all right, only there was something else. This Minnesota Fats also happened to have a neck twitch exactly like me. Gleason didn't use the twitch in the movie but in the novel Minnesota Fats was described as having a "sudden, convulsive motion of his head, forcing his chins down toward his left collarbone" about every ten seconds. Now, I just happen to be guilty of that sort of twitch; in fact, I've been twitching like that ever since I was a child.

Now let's say all those characteristics that me and Mr. Minnesota Fats seemed to have in common just happen to be purely coincidental, exactly coincidental. Let's say that. But when they filmed the movie, the technical advisor admitted that the Minnesota Fats role was fashioned after me.

The technical advisor just happened to be my old pal Willie Mosconi and he just happened to state in print that "Gleason's character" was "patterned after a real-live pool hustler known as New York Fats."

Willie let the cat out the bag in an interview he gave Dave Lewis, the sports editor of the *Long Beach* (California) *Independent-Press-Telegram*, during the filming of the movie in 1961.

Dave Lewis asked Willie if he knew "the real New York Fats" and Willie said, "Know him? He hustled me once." Then Willie told the story and Dave Lewis printed it in his column:

> Willie recalled "I was managing a room in Philadelphia one time when New York Fats came to town and set up headquarters there. He was big and fat and with those diamond rings he always wore, he created a lot of business. Naturally, he began hustling everybody he could.
>
> "It was good for business but pretty soon he ran out of people. There was nobody left to play, so he decided to hustle me. I told him I didn't want to play him. This infuriated him and he accused me of being afraid."
>
> At this point, the story goes, the owner of the room asked Mosconi to play him. "Well, all right," he agreed, "but I don't want his money. Why don't I just lose a few games to him and keep him happy and around because he's good for business."
>
> "No," the owner said, "you play him and if you can beat him, do it. You're the champ and you're good for business, too."
>
> So the match was made and New York Fats named the game—One Pocket, his favorite.

I remember the day Willie was talking about and I remember the room where we played. It was a joint at Seventh and Morris Streets down in South Philadelphia and Willie was managing the place exactly like he said he was. This was all back around 1948.

I remember something else, too. I whacked Willie out again, exactly like I did in the olden days. That's on the square.

The movie was a tremendous flick, I mean real swell entertainment. Everything was exactly the way it was, all except the last scene where Paul Newman beat Gleason for all the cash. That was fiction, I mean the worst kind of fiction, on account of I never lost a cash match in my whole life. But the most brutal part of all was the way Hollywood made pool players look like a pack of bums.

I've seen one or two pool players treat their dolls like the scum of the earth but never in all my life did I ever see a pool player push a tomato around the way this Fast Eddie handled that little doll Piper Laurie. Let me tell you something about pool players. Deep down 99 out of every 100 pool players are A Number One gentlemen. I've taken Eva-line into some of the most hideous poolrooms in the country, I mean real flea traps, and she was never treated like anything except a lady. That's on the square.

Now right after the movie hit the theaters all over the country, every living human started calling me Minnesota Fats. I got a kick out of it on account of it was just another nickname, only this one looks like it's going to be around a long, long time. I've had a lot of nicknames in my life. The old man called me Roodle and when I went down to Broadway I was Double Smart Fats and later on they graduated me up to Triple Smart Fats. When I left New York to hit the road they all called me New York Fats and after I hung around Chicago for awhile I was known as Chicago Fats. Anywhere I happened to be, sooner or later I was bound to end up being called such and such Fats. I was Kansas City Fats, Philadelphia Fats, Omaha Fats and when Georgie Jansco started his tournament in Johnston City, Illinois, right after the movie came out, they called me Johnston City Fats. But now that Zee has made a general out of me, I'm known as Minnesota Fats from here to Saudi Arabia.

Every living human went wild over the movie but nobody got as excited as Georgie Jansco. Right away he called me to get this tournament on the road and the next day he started building this fancy joint he called The Cue Club. I told Georgie there was no use talking about a high action tournament if he was going to put on a straight pool proposition on account of the big action men wouldn't go for that kind of dodge. So Georgie said he would limit the tournament to One Pocket and offer $5,000 in cash prizes. Right away I got on the telephone and lined up the best One Pocket players in the country. Georgie's tournament is a big success today but the first one back in 1961, even though it had only 14 players, got so much publicity that it really was the one that put the Jansco show in the big time.

Until that first tournament in 1961, no pool player in the country wanted any kind of publicity whatsoever, except maybe the fun players who told the reporters they grew up in the YMCA. But right away Georgie's tournament got all sorts of coverage around Southern Illinois and Southern Indiana and when the generals at *Sports Illustrated* in New York heard about the action, they sent writers and photographers to Johnston City to look over the real-live pool hustlers. Now when the top magazine writers heard me with the conversation they forgot all about the Weenie Beanies and Knoxville Bears and Tuscaloosa Squirrellies and devoted the entire article to me. They came to write about the hustlers but I ended up getting the big ovation.

When the writers first hit Johnston City, the hustlers were scared to death to tell anybody their real names. One writer asked Tuscaloosa Squirrelly his name and Squirrel said, "Who, me? Why, my name is Fred Thompson—what's yours?" That's on the square. A pool player, I mean a high stakes action player, no more wants his name, and certainly not his picture, used in a lot of publicity cons anymore than the average sucker wants somebody rattling the skeletons in his closets, understand? But I told the players in Johnston City there was nothing to worry about on account of I would act as public relations shark with the writers.

Once Georgie and all the players realized the writers weren't out to pull off any kind of skullduggery, we all got together and put on a tremendous show that would have made the movie look like *The Death of a Salesman* or one of those other dramatic jolts. The trouble with pool is that every time one of the fun players wrote a book it was so scrubbed-down and sterilized that it really wasn't about pool at all. Those fun players always took the fun out of the poolrooms, which was a brutal shame on account of pool players are a real fun-loving bunch of people. They love to laugh and crack smart and that's the kind of performance we put on in Johnston City. Everybody loved it, especially the writers.

If you've seen a lot of movies, you probably got the idea that newspaper and magazine writers run in all out of breath, ask all sorts of quick questions and run right out again to make their deadlines. That's the way it is in the flicks, only that wasn't the way it happened in Johnston City. When the writers got an earful of the back-room conversation, they came back night after night and each time they brought more people with them. Before Georgie's first tournament was over, he had to put out the SRO sign on account of the joint was packed night after night, especially when the Fat Man was performing. One night the Shriners of Evansville, Indiana, came over in a safari of chartered busses, but first they checked to make sure I was playing that evening.

Right away I told the writers I was the automatic, all-time One Pocket champion of the world on account of none of the fun champions would play me at my top game. They always demanded tremendous odds, like two balls and the break, but even when I gave them those odds they always dogged it.

"I'm the greatest money player of all time," I told 'em. "I was great back in the 20s and 30s and I'm still great in this era. I not only robbed 'em all, I've outlasted 'em all."

That kind of conversation really excited the writers and the eyeballers because they were all dying to see how a serious money match came off. So we gave them an Academy Award performance.

"You want to play me some pool?" Danny Jones wanted to know.

"Yes, I want to play you, Handsome Danny," I said, "I sure do want to play you, Danny Boy, only I want to play for some money. I sure never came to play for any bubble gum."

"Give me two balls, Fat Man, just two balls, and I'll play you One Pocket, four out of seven for $500," Mr. Tuscaloosa Squirrelly said.

"Squirrel," I said, "you sound exactly like those fun players I used to whack out. Here I am four times older than you and I've been up three days and three nights and you want two balls? You're exactly like the fun players because you don't want to shoot pool, you just want to stick somebody up."

Now it was Mr. Weenie Beanie's turn to get into the act. Beanie owns a chain of restaurants in Washington, D.C., and I've whacked him out so many times that he knows if he fools with me again I'll automatically turn him into a dish washer. But sometimes Weenie Beanie forgets and cracks smart.

"Will you play me for $500, Fat Man?" he said.

"Beanie," I said, "I've answered that question 'yes' about ten times in plain English. Don't you understand English, Beanie? You of all people ought to understand English, Beanie. You're supposed to be intelligent. The rest of these poor mooches are fugitives from the second grade but you're supposed to be a college graduate. But if you don't understand English any more, Mr. Weenie Beanie, I know several other languages— several."

Weenie Beanie, whose real handle is Bill Staton, didn't say another word on account of if he did play me he would have to play for his own money; in fact, he might have ended up playing for his whole chain of restaurants.

"Come on, Beanie," I said, "Handsome Danny wants to play me but he can't make it without a backer. You sure don't need any backer, Weenie, unless you're afraid I'll put your restaurants out of business. You know I've put a lot of restaurants out of business in my time."

Weenie Beanie didn't open his mouth after that because he really didn't want to play me in the first place.

The conversation and the propositioning went on like that for almost an hour until a half-dozen mooches formed a subsidiary and decided to finance Mr. Danny Jones against Fat Daddy. But the entire assets of the board of directors totaled only $200 so before they could get their man to the table, they had to talk my old pal Daddy Warbucks into going for three more bills. So me and Handsome Danny went to the table at last for a little One Pocket, four out of seven for a half a G.

I walked over to the table where the towel and powder and the pitcher of ice water were and I sprinkled my hands with talcum powder exactly the way Jackie Gleason had copied off of me for the movie and when I was ready to start the match I told Handsome Danny, "Daniel, you're in the lion's den."

Handsome Danny won the game; in fact, he won the first three games and was like two Gs ahead, so right away he figured he was going to put the old Fat Man on the sunset trail. Listen, Handsome Danny felt so good about winning the first three games that he started snatching dialogue right from the movie.

"You know who I am, Fat Man?" he said. "I'm Fast Eddie and I've come all the way from California to get you."

"Is that so?" I said. "Well, tell me, Mr. Fast Eddie, did you happen to bring along a beautiful doll like Mr. Paul Newman did in the flick?"

He said that was exactly right, only he had brought his doll from his hometown in Atlanta, Georgia.

"Well," I said, "somebody should warn the doll to be real careful of you, Handsome Danny. I understand you took a blood test when you went in the Army and the doctors found out your blood was made up of 90 per cent lipstick and 10 per cent Coca-Cola."

That started all the writers and eyeballers to hee-hawing, only Daddy Warbucks, who had like 60 per cent of Handsome Danny's action, could see that Danny Boy was asking for trouble. So Warbucks went over and had a talk with his boy.

"Son," Warbucks said, "I'm backing you with my cash because I think you have a chance to beat the Fat Man. But listen, son, don't make the mistake of trying to out-talk him—nobody out-talks the Fat Man. Nobody."

Warbucks told Danny exactly the way it was, only Danny didn't heed the warning and he kept giving me the needle.

"I really think you're all washed up," Danny said.

"I think so, too," Mr. Tuscaloosa Squirrelly chimed in.

"And so do I," said Mr. Cornbread Red. "I think Danny and The Squirrel are right, Fatty. You're finished."

"Is that so?" I said to Mr. Cornbread Red. "Well, I'll tell you what I'll do. When I get through with Mr. Handsome Danny, which will be very shortly, it will be your turn to come to the table with the cash, Mr. Cornbread Red. And when I get through busting you down to your last dime and paying your bus fare back to Detroit, you'll be known as No Bread Red."

That was enough to silence The Bread Man but it wasn't enough to convince Mr. Handsome Danny, on account of Handsome kept right on trying to out-talk me.

"Fatty," he said, "I really think you're washed up and if you were as intelligent as you say you are, you would know it's time for you to quit posing as a pool player."

"Intelligent?" I screamed. "Listen, Sonny Boy, I'll tell you how intelligent I am.—I could spot Einstein the ten ball."

The writers and eyeballers went into laughing hysterics and Danny Boy was enjoying the show so much that he kept right on wolfing.

"Fatty," Handsome Danny said, "you're a has-been."

"Well, well," I said, "so the assembled mooches figure the Fat Man is a has-been, is that right? Well, if I'm a has-been then I'm sure glad I'm not one of you is-beens." Then I really poured it on.

"Danny," I said, "I happen to be a businessman. Now you and I have a little business proposition going on the table and right now the stake is four C notes. That's a lot of gold, Danny Boy, so if you will kindly stop all this Who Shot John nonsense, I'd like to get back to the business at hand."

Now when I happened to mention that four grand was riding on the outcome, you could see Handsome tighten up. He knew he had beaten the poor old Fat Man three games in a row and he was thinking about the four C notes, only he knew he had to beat the Fat Man one more time for the money. He also knew that the higher the action, the deadlier I shot. Poor Danny had a lot to think about.

It didn't take long for Handsome Danny to make a drastic mistake, just one. He misplayed a safe and left me just enough room for a shot, which was all I had been waiting for. I whacked out eight straight balls quicker than Sherman marched through Handsome Danny's home state of Georgia and when Danny saw me pick up all the cash he ran out of

Jansco's Cue Club with his little tomato like a posse was after him. They all turn into sprinters when the Fat Man shoots out the lights.

The next night I happened to be paired with my old protege, Mr. Tuscaloosa Squirrelly, in a tournament match, a best three out of five pocket proposition. Naturally, I was like an 8-to-5 favorite, even though The Squirrel is one of the best One Pocket players in the whole country. Still it figured to be a real close match and with the odds in my favor, I didn't have any trouble getting down a few sizeable bets. Everybody was ready for one of those long, drawn out matches, only I broke up the ball game before the eyeballers could get to their seats.

The Squirrel made the fatal mistake of opening the rack just a little too wide on the break and the first time I went to the table I ran out the game. In fact, Mr. Tuscaloosa Squirrelly made two more crucial mistakes and I ran out three games and the match—now get this—in less than five minutes. The Squirrel managed only three shots, two breaks and a scratch, and spent the rest of the match sitting on a stool in the corner like Ned in the Primer.

You can talk about your four-minute miles all you want but running out three games of One Pocket in less than five minutes is like running a mile in two minutes. Listen, it's even better than that. It has to be a world record on account of one game of One Pocket between two top players can last for hours at a time. That's on the square.

Now you can look through all the world record books until you go blind and you won't find the results of my annihilation of Tuscaloosa Squirrelly. That's because the generals who control what they call legitimate pool have decided that One Pocket, the toughest of all pool games to play, is a gambling gimmick and therefore not worthy of mention in their records. But if running out three games of One Pocket in less than five minutes, especially against a top player like The Squirrel, isn't a world record, then my wife Eva-line, is Cleopatra's hairdresser.

There must have been 300 spectators who saw that record set in Jansco's joint so if anybody doubts my claim, there are lots of witnesses who will testify. Mr. Tuscaloosa Squirrelly says he will never forget it.

I whacked 'em all out in the backrooms in Johnston City that first year, only I didn't win the tourament. I lost four matches and ended up in a tie for third place with my old Chicago roommate, Daddy Warbucks. The winner was Johnny Vevis, who was known as Connecticut Johnny, and Cowboy Jimmy Moore was second.

Now since I'm always boasting about being the greatest One Pocket player of all time, especially for the cash, my failure to win all the marbles in Johnston City really started the mooches to giving me the Who Shot

John chatter real good. I told them the reason I didn't win the tournament was because I couldn't get a bet on my matches, which is exactly the way it was. Listen, I might lose a match to the champion of the Old Folks' Home if there's no money riding on it. They put the needle to me real good until I explained it to them in terms that they would understand.

"Listen," I said, "shooting a game of pool without some serious money riding on the outcome is like Rudolph Valentino being chased by 400 gorgeous tomatoes, only he runs to his hotel room, bolts the door and reads *Playboy* magazine." That's exactly what it's like.

That tournament in Johnston City in 1961 sure changed my life. I didn't win the title but I got the big ovations from all the writers on account of they all went crazy for my conversation. Listen, they asked every mooch in the joint to define a hustler and the mooches told the writers they should ask me, which they did.

"A hustler," I said, "is anyone who has to make a living. A golfer who plays a match for cash is a hustler just the same as the guy who plays a little friendly pool for a couple of bucks at the Elks Club or a bowling alley. Everybody's a hustler.

"Say you walk into the finest clothing store. Right away the salesman hustles you. He puts you in a size 30 suit when you really need size 50 but he tells you you look so beautiful in the outfit, that if you don't watch the guy he'll convince you it's such a bargain that you can't pass it up.

"But here's the best example of a hustler. It's a stock broker. He's not only a hustler, he's also a tout on account of he's getting inside information."

The writer said that was a tremendous definition of a hustler, only he asked me if I could give him something a little more concrete. Now this happened to be back in 1961 when President Kennedy was in the White House so I told the writer that President Kennedy was a hustler. He almost dropped his pad and pencil.

"That's exactly right," I said, "President Kennedy is a hustler. He had to out-hustle Nixon for the White House. He had to hustle a whole year to get it."

I thought about what I had said and I figured since I was just a pool player I shouldn't be calling the President of the United States a hustler. So I told the writer I would like to retract the statement.

"I take that back," I said. "I never make a practice of talking religion or politics and I have no right calling President Kennedy a hustler, even if he is one."

I thought the writer understood that I meant the quote about President Kennedy was, like the politicians say, "off the record." But the writer used it in his story and it went all over the country. Eva-line raised hell about me talking about President Kennedy that way but I never heard of any complaints from the White House.

I got so much publicity at the first tournament Georgie put on that when the word got to all the poolrooms all over the country about how I had revived the cash prize tournaments, over night the entire billiard industry was re-jived.

Today pool tournaments are held all over and the cash awards are bigger than ever. Even the fun players are having tournaments again, but the tournament that me and Georgie Jansco put on in Johnston City in 1961 was the one that really started the renaissance.

A couple months before the first tournament in Johnston City I took a trip to New York and I dropped in to see my old pal Danny Gartner at his joint in Newark. Danny was playing in the New York State tournament at the time and he invited me to take in the matches one night. They were holding the tournament in a real flea joint in Times Square and charging a whole 50 cents admission. It was brutal on account of the matches were held behind a white sheet hanging on a rope right across the middle of the room. I thought it was a Ku Klux Klan rally when I walked in. The prizes were fabulous, too—like $75 first prize, $50 second and $25 third. The players in the tournament were going broke just catching the subway to get to the matches. It was unbelievable beyond compare but that's exactly how dead pool was in 1961.

It's a lot different today. Georgie Jansco's tournament, which actually started out in the little beer shed out behind the J & J Ranch, is one of the top events in the country. Georgie puts up $20,000 in prizes and conducts divisions in One Pocket, straight pool and Nine Ball with the winners meeting in a round robin playoff to determine the All-Around Master's title. Not only that, but Georgie's tournament is an annual feature on the ABC-TV's *Wide World of Sports*. Georgie also directs a big $30,000 tournament in Las Vegas every year, too. He's one of the top men in the industry today.

Now that Georgie is such a big man in billiards, I'm always after him to buy some new ties. He's only got two and I tell him if he wants to be a real general he ought to have a couple dozen. But Georgie is real sentimental about his old ties.

Georgie had one tie which was a pretty silver and blue and the other was black and orange and I won a hundred turkey sandwiches betting on what tie Georgie would be wearing each night. I always won the propositions hands down on account of I had the cooperation of one of Georgie's waitresses, a tomato called Tombstone.

If Georgie happened to be wearing his Halloween cravat, Tombstone would give a wink with her left eye and I would bet orange and black. But if Georgie went with his silverliner, Tombstone would flick the right eye and I would take the other side of the proposition. I won a lot of calories just betting on Georgie's ties.

The first tournament in Johnston City not only re-jived the entire billiard industry but it also ended the real private life I had been living in Little Egypt. All of a sudden I was getting long distances calls from writers in every part of the country and some of them even drove all the way to Dowell to interview me.

They asked me all sorts of questions, questions you wouldn't ever imagine, like what's your neck size and your waist measurements and exactly how much cash did you win in your hustling days and a zillion other things. But the one question that always came up and always started me to telling the most unbelievable story of all time was when the writers would ask, "Fat Man, did you ever go to college?"

I went to college, all right, I told 'em, but I only lasted one day and one night on account of the day I showed up on the campus there was so much excitement and out-and-out panic you would have thought Al Capone matriculated with the freshman class.

CHAPTER 16

The Fat Man Goes to College

The way I happened to go to college was really funny because I never had a scholarship or a grant-in-aid or anything like that; in fact, I didn't even have to submit to the college boards. I just went.

One afternoon in March of 1962 I was out back playing with the dogs and cats when I got this call from a newspaperman inviting me to the National Intercollegiate Billiards Championship Tournament at Indiana University in Bloomington. He said he figured since everybody was crazy about the movie that I would add a little color to the college tournament, only he never dreamed my appearance on the campus would touch off an amazing rhubarb and to tell you the brutal truth, I didn't either.

I drove over to Bloomington, which is like 100 miles from Dowell, and I went straight to the campus and asked where they were holding the pool tournament. I was directed to this fantastic looking building called the Indiana Memorial Union and right away I could see that this tournament was being held in very high class surroundings. The Union was a fabulous looking joint; in fact, it reminded me of a church. But when the generals of the Billiard Congress of America, who gave the college tournament their blessings, found out I was on the campus, every candle in the cathedral started to melt.

To those generals, I was what the law students would call Persona Non Grata.

Now I never stormed onto the campus like a road show on account of I never even told a living human who I was. But right away a kid playing in the basement of The Union lamps me real good and says, "Hey, I know you—you're Minnesota Fats." I told him he was exactly right and the kid started asking all sorts of questions about this big ovation I had in *Sports Illustrated* a few months before. That's how it started.

The next thing I knew a curly-headed kid wearing glasses walks up and says, "Fat Man, I'm a reporter on the *Indiana Daily Student* (school newspaper) and I'd like to do a story on you." The kid's name was John Dean and he was as friendly as a politician, maybe even friendlier when you get down to it. He asked me to perform a few shots so I ran four racks of balls shooting with one hand, four racks without a miss. The kids were amazed beyond compare and they yelled for more.

Then Dean took me to a place called The Commons where we belted out a couple Coca-Colas and pretty soon a crowd gathered around our table like maybe somebody was passing out the answers to the exams. A lot of the eyeballers were beautiful little dolls, I mean gorgeous lookers, and they were all as friendly as John Dean on account of every last one of them made me feel right at home.

Dean asked me all about my life in poolrooms all over the country. He said he really liked the movie *The Hustler;* in fact, he said he liked it so much he went to see it three times. I told him the movie was exactly the way it was, all except the part where Paul Newman beat Jackie Gleason. "That was the figment of a real wild imagination," I said, "because I never lost a cash match in my life."

Now Dean asked me if I ever played Willie Mosconi and if I ever happened to beat him. I told the kid I played Mosconi many, many times and every time we played for the gold, I busted Willie flatter than a crunched cracker. Then the kid wanted to know if I thought Willie was a great pool player and I said, "Willie Mosconi is the greatest tournament player alive today."

The kid was real cute on account of he carried the interrogation a step further by saying, "Well, if Willie Mosconi is the greatest tournament player alive today, just where does that leave you, Fat Man?"

"Sonny Boy," I said, "I told you Willie Mosconi was the greatest *tournament* player alive today, but if you're talking about playing for the cash, then you're looking at the greatest pool player whoever lived on this entire earth."

John Dean, who happens to be a top-notch reporter with the *Indianapolis Star* today, almost bit his straw in half. Then he took out in a dead run for the newspaper office and banged out a tremendous feature article about how I had put Mosconi in bankruptcy every time we played. The story hit print that same afternoon and that's when the grief really started.

All of a sudden every kid on the campus was running up to me and asking if I was going to play Mosconi that night in Alumni Hall. I had no idea what they were talking about because I was absolutely unaware that Willie was giving one of his exhibitions on the tournament program that evening. I was just as surprised to hear that Mosconi was at Indiana University as Willie was later on when he found out that I happened to be around. I never dreamed Willie was active in the game again. That's on the square. The last I'd heard, Willie had been very, very sick and had been forced into retirement under doctor's orders. I thought my old Philadelphia pal, who had flunked out of dancing school when he was a kid, was taking it easy at his home in Haddon Heights, New Jersey. But now it turned out Willie had decided to be a college boy, too.

When a super star like Mosconi stages an exhibition, all of the top players go along with the act. None of them would dream of trying to muscle in. So I sure wasn't out to steal the show from Willie and I certainly hadn't come to hustle him out of his traveling expenses, but that's exactly what the college kids thought I was up to. I gave a lot of consideration to leaving because I sure didn't want to cause a beef jolt at a first class university. But when I said I was going to pack it in one of those college boys cracked smart and said, "Why, Fat Man, are you afraid of Mosconi?" It was unbelievable.

Willie hadn't arrived on the campus yet so everywhere I moved the college kids followed me around like I was the Pied Piper of Hamelin. I mean they trailed me like one of those 007 gumshoes and when I walked into Alumni Hall to look over the tournament scene the college kids gave me a tremendous ovation. That's when they really started lobbying for the big match between me and Willie and that's exactly when the generals and professors who were running the tournament became very, very upset with the development.

When they discovered that a hideous creature by the name of Minnesota Fats happened to be in the same room with all those little college boys there was so much excitement you would have thought Errol Flynn was personally staging a panty raid at the co-ed dormitories. It was amazing beyond belief.

All the college kids wanted to see was a match between me and Willie, the King of the Hustlers versus the legitimate fun champion. They wanted to see what would happen if the baddies and the goodies ever came to a showdown, only the generals said the match was out of the question. The generals even put out the word that I hadn't come to play Willie at all because my real mission was to hustle the college boys out of their allowances. They must have had me mixed up with The Kid in the NYU

Sweater, which was ridiculous because I never played a pool game for $3 in my whole life.

I was standing in the crowd when one of the top generals, the late Mr. Ben Nartzik, who happened to be the president of the Billiard Congress of America, came over and asked what brought me to Indiana University. I told him I had just come to watch the kids play, which was the brutal truth. Mr. Nartzik was real cordial and all but I don't think he believed what I said on account of a little later he asked one of the newspaper reporters what I was doing there and this reporter told him he should ask me.

"I have already asked him what he is doing here and he said he doesn't know," Nartzik said. That's on the square.

Not a living human on the Indiana campus told me I wasn't welcome and I never would have known what was going on except the students sort of kept me posted. Like this gorgeous little tomato came over and whispered real low, "Be careful, Fat Man, you're on probation." I didn't have the slightest idea what she meant until she explained that she was on probation too. "I flunked math last semester," she said.

The generals were so sure that I was part of some devious plot against higher education that they had one of the public relations sharks tell the students: "If any of you are friends of the Fat Man, please tell him he is not welcome here. His presence is bad for the image of college billiards." One of the tournament directors, a fellow from the University of Illinois, said it was even worse than that.

"This man will wreck college billiards," he said, "why, he calls the game pool."

Now that happens to be the most hideous and dastardly crime I have ever been accused of committing in my entire life. It was unbelievable beyond compare.

I could have developed a very serious inferiority complex about college only all the while the generals were burning candles that I would leave the campus, the college kids swarmed all over me asking for autographs and begging me to tell 'em stories. The whole development was a tremendous commentary on human nature.

Later on a doll named San Lynn Merrick, of Bowling Green State University of Ohio, who won the Co-Ed Pocket Billiards title, was being interviewed by a couple reporters and San Lynn happened to mention the word "hustling."

"The word 'hustling' cannot be used," said the Professor from Illinois, "oh, why doesn't The Fat Man go home?"

"Well, then," said San Lynn, "let's call it 'sandbagging,' which is the college term for 'hustling' anyway."

"No, no, you can't use 'sandbagging' either," the Illinois Professor said. "What are you trying to do, ruin college billiards?"

I tried to be as diplomatic as possible so I asked the reporters not to mention words like "hustling" and "sandbagging" in the stories but the reporters said they were all truth-seekers. That's on the square.

When the interview was over, Mr. Nartzik called me over and we had a very interesting conversation about the upward trend the movie had started in the billiard industry. He said the industry was afraid of the flick at first and all of the generals held their breath but he also said that the movie was the biggest boom the billiards industry had ever known. I remember his exact words.

"Fatty," he said, "the movie took the game and put it on a rocket and up it went. Everybody wants a table for his home. Everybody wants his own cue. They want to take it out in the billiard room and screw it together just like Paul Newman did in the movie but you just can't buy cues anywhere. Some firms are importing them from Europe so they can meet the demand."

That's exactly what Mr. Ben Nartzik said. But here I was, the person the movie happened to be about in the first place, getting the bum's rush at the college tournament. The party line was "Go Home, Fat Man, Go Home." It was a new dimension in human endeavor.

Later that night my old playmate Willie Mosconi arrived for his exhibition match and when he saw me standing in the crowd he looked at me like I was somebody who had been dead for 20 years only I was walking right out of the cemetery. I think Willie figured I had taken all the gold I won off him and had gone to live with my grandfather over in Switzerland.

Willie played San Lynn Merrick, the Co-Ed Champion, in an exhibition match and then he pulled off all the old trick shots. But when the kids asked him to play me, Willie said that was out of the question on account of my hustling background was bad for college billiards. Everybody was happy except the college kids because they were dead set on the big showdown.

After Willie's exhibition was over we had a little chat out in front of Alumni Hall. We talked about the olden days, but all Willie gave me was the same old, "Why, hello, Fatty, how are you?" conversation on account of maybe 30 students were following us like we were Hollywood stars. But finally Willie upped and asked me if I was still making serious money with my pool game.

"You still drive big Cadillacs, Fatty?" Willie asked.

"Sure," I said, "sure, Willie, I'm still wheeling a Cadillac."

Then Willie asked me if I wanted a little action.

"Fatty," he said, "you want to play some pool? You want to play pool for money?"

"Why, sure, Willie," I said, "where can we play?"

"Right over there in Alumni Hall," Willie said. "We'll go inside, just you and me, and we'll lock the door. We'll play a little One Pocket, that's your game, Fatty, and we'll play some straight pool, which is my game, and we'll play some Three Cushions and a little Rotation and some Nine Ball. We'll play a little of everything, all right, Fatty?"

I told Willie that would be just fine with me, seeing how he brought the subject up in the first place, only Willie laughed like he had said something funny and walked out of the place.

Willie really had said something funny because the 30 college kids who were tuned in to the dialogue went plumb berserk. One kid said he was going to sneak up in the balcony of Alumni Hall because he said there was no way he was going to miss seeing me and Willie take to the table. I don't know if that kid spent the night in the choir loft but the match never came off, only you couldn't tell that to the college boys and girls.

Me and Willie bumped into each other later that night in an off-campus bowling alley where I stopped in for a midnight snack. Willie was bowling when I walked in but when the kids saw I was on the scene they knew for sure that the big money match was about to come off. They begged me to play Mosconi but I told 'em Willie was a fun player and he was only kidding when he talked about playing for cash.

I shot a little AAU pool with some of the kids at the bowling joint but about one o'clock in the morning I went back to my hotel room, which happened to be in the Union Building on the campus, and had a good night's sleep. I never saw Willie Mosconi again. That's on the square.

The next morning I dropped in at Alumni Hall and signed a zillion autographs for the kids and around noon I got in my Cadillac and headed back to Dowell.

Now here comes the real funny part of the whole situation.

Three days later this young reporter John Dean went crazy chasing down a rumor that me and Willie went back to Alumni Hall after all and played all night long. The kid said the Indiana campus was buzzing about the big match, only I told him me and Willie never went near a pool table together but Dean said that wasn't the way he heard it.

"Fat Man," he said, "the story is that you and Willie went back to Alumni Hall at 2:30 in the morning and played Three Cushions until daybreak. The story says you and Willie played six games of Three Cushions for $1,000 a game and you won 'em all, Fat Man."

"Sonny boy," I said, "it's all idle rumor with only one possible semblance of truth and that's the part about me beating Willie every time. It didn't happen, but if we had played that's exactly the way it would have come out. I would have won all the cash."

The visit to Indiana University was one of the most unbelievable things that ever happened to me but the most amazing part about the whole incident was the way the college kids had me winning all the gold in a match that never even took place.

I was cast as the heavy in the Indiana University drama with Mr. Mosconi playing the role of a pink-cheeked altar boy. But when the kids got through rewriting the plot it turned out that the bad guy beat the good guy. The generals said I was a bum but the college kids made me the hero.

I guess there was something real unusual about the king of the hustlers and the king of the hot dog set crossing paths on a college campus and when it happened the college kids just let their imaginations run wild.

I told Eva-line the story and she said she didn't know what to make of it.

"Eva-line," I said, "what happened at Indiana University proved one big thing—people would a lot rather eyeball somebody they thought was Jesse James than somebody claiming to be Little Lord Fauntleroy."

CHAPTER **17**

Hustling Johnny Carson

That one day and night I spent at Indiana University was exactly all I saw of higher education after finishing P.S. 132 back in Washington Heights, but my lack of the baccalaureates and cum laudes never prevented me from starting out right at the top when I finally succumbed to the working dodge.

In the olden days my mother said if you worked like a slave from morning to night, hoarded the cash like it was uranium and layed off the tomatoes and high times, you would be a tremendous success. The only thing wrong with that kind of success is that you automatically end up dead broke and living unhappily ever after. That's the way it used to be, only I changed all that.

The Minnesota Fats success formula calls for living like a king without doing a lick of work, residing at the finest hotels, belting out the best calories, wearing the most expensive clothes, and doing exactly what you feel like doing at all times. Then if some general like Mr. Phil Zelkowitz happens to offer you a job, don't accept anything less than Executive Vice President with an unlimited expense account to take care of the food bills. That's the way it was when I let Zee make a business shark out of me.

Here I was without even a Social Security card but Zee made a real general out of me and overnight I became the biggest attraction the billiards industry ever knew. Not only that, but right now I'm getting ready to do a television series with gorgeous little playmates like Elizabeth Taylor and Kim Novak and Natalie Wood. You can't hardly beat that kind of action.

Work? Who wants that kind of grief?

People are always asking me how I happened to live like a sultan for 50 years without doing a day's work in my whole life and I always tell them

I was a hustler. They all look at me and smile like I was admitting I had done something real sinister. They're exactly like the college kids at Indiana University who thought I was Jesse James or John Dillinger. That's on account of today the word hustler doesn't mean what it did in the olden days.

Today if somebody says you're a hustler, right away everybody figures you robbed the suckers blind on the pool table. Back in the olden days, we called that kind of operator a pool shark because back then a hustler was something altogether different.

If somebody called you a hustler in the 20s or 30s, they meant it as a compliment. Mrs. O'Riley might say to Mrs. Murphy, "Sure Katie, that young blue-eyed Joe O'Dowd who married little Ruby Walsh is a real hustler—why he's been working at the bank for only three years and already he's a cashier." So Mrs. Murphy would say, "Why, bless Patty, he is a hustler."

That's exactly the kind of hustler I was, only instead of working in a bank, I worked the poolrooms and I ended up the cashier who took everybody's money.

Today there's a big romance attached to pool hustling. I figure a lot of the suckers must be thinking about taking up the trade on account of everywhere I go every living human asks me what it takes to be a pool hustler. Like last year this writer from *Life* magazine wanted me to draw a composite of all the hustlers I've known. This is how I figure the guy would come out:

He would have to be one of those nonstop chatterboxes, which might sound like me, only I'm thinking of Little Rock Skeeter who kept up a ridiculous line of conversation, most of the time when his opponent was shooting; he would have to have false teeth like Little Joe Sebastian and he would always be rattling 'em just as his opponent stroked the ball; he would have to wear real heavy shoes like Chicago Whitey and keep tromping around the table and making so much noise that you would think Mr. Shicklgruber's goose-steppers were walking in the front door; and he would have to be part Drunken Floody who not only spit on the chalk to make your cue stick slip when it hit the ball but kept nipping at a flask and pretending to be paralyzed, only the juice Drunken Floody was nipping happened to be prune juice.

Those second-rate pool sharks tried every filage known to man. Like some of them would get in the poolroom real early in the morning and stick a zillion pins in the cushions to slow down the rubber, or maybe they would put the pins under the felt right smack in front of the pockets so the balls would deflect like they were bouncing off a wall. Those mooches had all kinds of dodges going all the time but whenever they tried the skullduggery on me I shortened 'em up real quick.

Now ever since the movie, the general concept of a hustler is a real good player who goes to a strange room and plays way under his speed until the money is just right and then he shoots out the lights and runs off with all the gold. That kind of gimmick might be real effective if the hustler has found himself a real lamb but a top player wouldn't fall for that kind of filage, in fact, no top player ever did.

Now I was a hustler all right, only I never was a hustler in the bad sense of the word. I never hung out in small rooms near the bus station trying to beat the tourists and working men out of a quick deuce and unless I was playing somebody in my class, I never tried to build up the other guy and make him feel like he was better than me so he would go for the whole wad. I always told 'em exactly who I was right off so they would know they were playing the best and I never worked the sucker joints. I always walked in the biggest and best poolroom in town, the one where all the top sharks hung out, and I'd pick up a cue and say, "Here I am, boys, come on and get me." And they all died trying, I mean really died trying, because I shot 'em down in cold blood. If you want to call that hustling, then I was a hustler because that's the way it was. I robbed 'em all.

There's a zillion ways to figure the hustler gimmick on account of sometimes the lesser player might be the one who's the real hustler. Andrew St. Jean, who was called The Lowell Kid, only I always called him The Saint, was one of the greatest all-around pool players who ever lived, bar none. But he got out-hustled a jillion times by second-rate eggs who just happened to be a little sharper with the conversation.

The Saint knew he was a tremendous pool player and he knew he had to give fantastic odds in order to get the action, only most of the time he would give such ridiculous odds that there was no way he could win. So The Saint was always falling in the tapioca, which is a dreadful place to fall.

The Saint would go into the small towns and spot the yokels like 100-to-50, which meant he automatically went broke on account of 100-to-50 is a proposition that even a genuine saint can't cover. The Saint would go for all kinds of ridiculous cons. Why, he just might bet you it was Christmas Eve when it happened to be Easter Sunday.

I never went for any of those dodges because I was always a whole closetful of overcoats over those second-rate mooches in intelligence. They knew it, too, because after I whacked out every living human in every town in the country, when I'd walk into the room they would all freeze and start quivering. I didn't even have to tell 'em I was the greatest anymore

● *149*

because they already knew it. I knew they knew it on account of after awhile none of 'em would play me for a grape. I robbed 'em so many times that I put myself out of business and I had to go to work.

The good thing about the Executive Vice President proposition is the check every week. Me and Eva-line always lived like multis, in fact, better than most multis because we always wore the best clothes and drove the best cars and went first class in every way. But if Eva-line happens to want a new coat or outfit nowadays, I don't have to go out and beat somebody out of the money over a pool table anymore. I just tell her to go down to the department store and put it on the account. That's one of the advantages, but there's a lot of grief attached to the Veep gimmick on account of I'm a victim of what Zee calls future planning.

When I was free-lancing I never made any plans; in fact, I never gave four cents for plans. But as an Executive Veep, I not only have to make plans, I have to make tremendous sacrifices. Getting up real early in the morning isn't so bad but fighting the sunshine is brutal beyond compare. I always avoided sunshine at all costs on account of sunshine is one of the most dreadful things on the entire earth.

In the olden days when I woke up in the morning and looked out the window, if the sun happened to be shining a little too bright, I might jump back in bed and stay there until it looked a little more inviting outside. But things have changed since I became a Veep.

Like last year *Life* magazine flew a whole battery of writers and photographers out to Denver to interview me. Now it happened to be a real hot, sticky, sunny day and I figured we would hold the interview in the hotel ballroom on account of it was air-conditioned. But these eggs from *Life* set up the pool table right next to the swimming pool and did all the interrogating out there. It was brutal beyond compare. That sun beat down on me with such a vengeance that after 30 minutes I had to stop the show because already I was peeling like a banana with a serious sunburn. It was the first time in the history of American sports that a game had to be called on account of sun.

Sometimes the grief is a lot worse than just standing out in the sun, because more and more I'm getting robbed of sleep which was always one of my favorite hobbies. Zee won't let me get the proper rest because he has me running all over the country making more personal appearances than a Miss America. Sometimes I feel like a tourist.

Sleep never bothered me much in the olden days because back then I did exactly what I felt like doing. If I felt like sleeping, I'd sleep, but if I was getting the right kind of action, I might stay up for five days and five nights. Back then I missed so much sleep I could have kept coffee awake, but if I got drowsy I was always at liberty to take on Mr. Joe Morpheus in an extended session. But Zee stopped all that.

Zee is exactly like my mother about work because if you happen to have a little leisure time on your hands he can always find something for you to do. Last Christmas I took a two-week vacation and Zee moaned and groaned so much I thought the stock market had been whacked out again.

The reason Zee is so anxious for me to work clear around the clock is because he knows how I use the conversation on the customers in the big department stores. My side of the proposition is to convince the customers that Rozel Industries is marketing the most fabulous tables money can buy and marketing them especially for homes. I get 'em all interested and when I tell 'em how reasonable the prices are, they almost knock down the sales clerks getting in their orders.

I usually spot a prospective buyer in the crowd who looks like he's real interested and I concentrate on him and him alone.

"Now take this fantastic table for only $398," I'll tell him. "That might sound like a tremendous sum of money to a working man but nobody's talking about blowing $398 in one bundle. You can buy this fabulous table on the installment plan and take maybe two years to pay it off, which means you're thinking about $20 a month and that's less than $1 a day.

"But I can make it even cheaper than that. Say you live forever—and we at Rozel Industries certainly hope you do—then you got to figure the cost down to say four cents a day. That's exactly what I said—four cents a day. Now you compare that four cents a day to the $1.50 a hour they charge in the neighborhood rooms and there's no way you can pass up this unbelievable bargain. I'll tell you what it's like—it's like stealing."

The department store sales pitch is exactly the same kind of conversation I used in the poolrooms in the olden days to get my opponent to the table. I always had to convince them there was no way they could lose and I'm doing the same thing in the stores, only the customers are getting quality merchandise for their cash. Listen, after I give 'em the spiel they snatch those tables so quick Zee can't get 'em off the assembly line fast enough.

I make a zillion appearances in department stores all over the country every year but I've also appeared on all the top television networks and just about every local station in every town I've played in the last year or two. Everybody wants the old Fat Man on their show on account of they all like the conversation—and after they hear it they all want me back. I've got a standing invitation from Mr. Johnny Carson to appear on the *Tonight Show* any time I want, even though the last time I was on his show I hustled Johnny out of an unbelievable amount of cash smack dab in front of 30 million TV viewers.

The way the hustle came off was real funny. Johnny wanted me to perform the trick shots on his show so his crew set up the table in the studio, but instead of leveling it real good, they wheeled it in on a pair of saw horses and the table had a brutal lean. It was worse than shooting on a submarine.

I didn't have time to make adjustments so I had to alter my speed right on the show to compensate for the unevenness of the table. I got away with it on most of the shots but I really had trouble on my closing gimmick. I gave 'em the old railroad shot where you set two cue sticks on the table and shoot a ball off a couple of cushions and make it hop the cue sticks and roll down into a corner pocket like it was on a railroad track. It's not a real tough shot but on an uneven table it can be brutal, which is exactly the way it was the first time I tried the shot on the Carson show. I didn't pull it off on account I never gave the ball enough juice for it to hop up onto the track and when I missed the audience really let out a groan.

So I told Johnny I would try it again, only he said there was only 30 seconds left but I told him that was more than enough. So now I'm setting up the shot again and Johnny Carson is looking at his watch and telling me there's no way I can make the shot in that little time but I told Johnny not to worry about that. So now the time is just about run out and I'm ready to shoot when Johnny Carson says, "Fat Man, I'll bet you a dollar you miss it again."

"Mr. Carson," I said, "the bet is on."

Then I whacked the ball just right and sent it hopping the cue sticks and rolling down the tracks like it was the Night Train to Chicago. Then the house really came apart.

Johnny handed over the dollar but I told him I couldn't take it on account of I had given up the hustling dodge. But he insisted on paying off because he said it was a matter of honor. Finally I told Johnny the only way I would accept the stake was if he added it to my talent fee.

Every guest on the *Tonight Show* is paid a standard $320 talent fee. It doesn't matter if it's Frank Sinatra or Zsa Zsa Gabor or Sammy Davis, Jr., they all get $320 and not a penny more. But when Johnny Carson added the dollar to my talent fee, making it exactly $321, I became the highest paid guest in the history of the *Tonight Show*. That's on the square. I told Johnny the next time I appeared on his show he should bring along some serious money and Johnny said the next time he might even go for a deuce.

Television is a tremendous medium because every living human said he saw me take Johnny Carson to the cleaners. In fact, one fellow watching the show at a bar in Philadelphia got so carried away that he thought the hustle was the real thing.

Roy McHugh, a sports columnist for the *Pittsburgh Press,* happened to be in Philadelphia that night and watched the show in a bar. He said everybody in the place was glued to the set and when I missed the shot they all let out a groan, too. But when Carson bet the buck and I made the shot the second time, McHugh said one fellow in the bar yelled, "See how tough that fat son-of-a-bitch is when the cash is down."

I made another big television appearance on the Irv Kupcinet Show out in Chicago to debate Mr. Cassius Muhammed Ali Clay on the delicate subject of just who is "The Greatest."

Kup sat between me and Muhammed Ali and said, "Ladies and gentlemen, tonight we have as our guests two gentlemen who both claim to be 'The Greatest'—Mr. Cassius Clay, the heavyweight champion of the world, and Mr. Minnesota Fats, the all-time heavyweight champion of the pool table. The format calls for a no-holds-barred, no-decision debate. At the end each viewer can judge for himself just which gentleman is 'The Greatest.'" Then Kup rang a bell and the debate was on.

Mr. Clay was dazzling with his early boasts and poetry but when he stopped to catch a breath I shortened him up by saying, "Listen sonny boy, I was shooting out the lights when your grandpappy was drinking corn whiskey down in Kentucky."

Cassius started laughing and I never let him get a word in after that.

"Cassius," I said, "you're a helluva young man and someday you might make it real big, but right now I think you're a real sucker for a left hook."

Then I asked him, "Mr. Clay, kindly tell me if you have ever been knocked to the floor of the prize ring?" He said it was true that he had been on the floor a time or two but that was because he "wasn't looking."

"Well," I said, "that should settle it once and for all, Mr. Clay, because I've been belting 'em out for 40 years and nobody's had me on the floor yet."

After 30 minutes of nonstop braggadocio by both of us, Mr. Clay walked over and raised my hand in the air like I won the duke. "Fat Man," Cassius said, "I am convinced—you are 'The Greatest.' But I am also 'The Greatest' and this studio just isn't big enough for both of us."

"Is that so?" I said. "Well, in that case, when are you leaving, Junior?"

When it comes to the conversation, Mr. Cassius Muhammed Ali Clay is no match for The Fat Man.

Right now I'm working on a television show of my own, a gimmick

titled *Celebrity Billiards*. The show is still in the formative stage but if everything comes out according to plan it will be a weekly feature on one of the
national networks in the fall.

The gimmick is each week I play a different pool proposition with a
different celebrity or movie star. If the celebrity happens to be just a fair
player I'll spot some pretty long odds, like maybe giving one of those
movie queens the old four fronts and a back proposition. But some of those
movies stars are tremendous pool players. I've already done pilot films with
Milton Berle, Mickey Rooney and James Garner and already I've lost one
of the matches.

Garner beat me in Eight Ball and when the news got out *Sports Illustrated* wrote a real cute article about how maybe I had dumped the game
for better theater effect. The brutal truth is Garner, who happens to be an
ex-pool hustler himself, just whacked me out. He learned the game when
he was a kid in Oklahoma from an old shark named Indian Jack Jacobs,
the ex-pro football player. Listen, Garner handles that cue so well that I'm
thinking about calling him "Injun Jim" and taking him on the road.

Now when my old poolroom pals like Pots 'n Pans and Cue Ball Kelly
and Superstitious Aloysius see me hobnobbing with the stars on TV they
figure the old Fat Man really has it made. Like last winter I'm taking the
sun in Miami and who do I run into but an old hustler named Peter
Rabbit. Right away the Bunny Man starts giving me the soft con about how
fortunate I am to have such a wonderful position as Executive Vice President and how he would give anything to find a similar paying proposition
for himself. So I had to tell The Rabbit the way that it is.

"Bunny Man," I said, "let me tell you something that you don't know.
I'm already thinking about retiring."

"Retiring?" the Bunny said. "Why, Fatty, you just went to work."

"That's exactly right," I said, "but there's something else you don't
know, Mr. Bunny Rabbit. After hanging out in poolrooms for almost 45
years, I thought I knew everything there was to know about human endeavor. But I learned the greatest lesson of my whole life when I became
an Executive Vice President.

"And I'll tell you what it is: Man cannot live by work alone."

CHAPTER **18**

I'm Ready for the Rocking Chair

Thomas Wolfe, the fellow who cranked out all those novels, once wrote a book called *You Can't Go Home Again*. Now I know those novelists have all kinds of messages and meanings in their books but the way I figure this Mr. Wolfe's proposition is that he's saying, look, if you happened to grow up in New York City say 40 years ago, forget about the homecoming celebrations.

I was born and raised in New York City and if I had my way I never would go home again. In fact, whenever Zee dispatches me to my old hometown, I feel like I'm going to the electric chair.

New York isn't the same as it was back in the olden days. Back then Times Square was a real playground and the merry-go-round went round and round without ever stopping. Something exciting was happening all the time. But today Times Square is out of control with people pushing and shoving and beating each other's brains out getting in and out of subways like they're all trying to climb out of a frying pan. Most people like that kind of heat, only I never liked what most people like in the first place, which is exactly why I never went for the 8-to-5 dodge. I wouldn't give a quarter for that ritual.

I watched those poor suckers fighting just to stay alive when I was a boy and when I go back to New York nowadays instead of the situation showing some improvement, it's just gotten worse. Everybody in New York still walks around with hideous expressions on their faces like they know there's no way out and if you happen to ask one of them the time of day they're just liable to growl at you like a whole cage of lions.

I always avoided those kind of complications and that's exactly why I live in Dowell, Illinois, instead of New York City. Listen, New York City today is so out of control that even my little dog Fuzzy gets upset when she's there. She's not in New York two hours before she starts shaking and quivering like she needs a psychiatrist.

There's only one thing to do about the situation in New York and that's to turn it into a testing area for survival. Defense Secretary McNamara is always moaning and groaning about the high costs of military installations all over but if he really wants to save the taxpayers some serious cash, all he has to do is give the draftees their basic training right down on Broadway. Instead of building those high-priced camps and bases, he should check all the draftees into the Victoria Hotel and then send 'em out to Coney Island on the subway during the rush hour. They wouldn't need any 90-pound sacks on their backs because they'll have eight or nine suckers climbing all over them. That's what you call real hand-to-hand combat.

Then if Mr. McNamara wants to train the soldiers for some serious action, instead of having 'em crawl on their bellies to duck the machine gun fire, all he has to do is let 'em ride the subways around two or three o'clock in the morning on one of those night jolts. That's more dangerous than an Easter Egg Hunt in Vietnam. The way I figure it, any sucker who is brave enough to live in New York City today ought to be decorated for gallantry.

When I go to New York nowadays, which is like twice a year, I always make sure I arrive at night so I won't be part of that human bang-bang and once I'm checked into the hotel I hardly leave my room unless it's absolutely necessary.

I always stop at the City Squire Motor Lodge on account of it's on the exact spot where Greenleaf had his room back in the olden days. In fact, I always take a room on the fifth floor, which is the same floor the Greenleaf room was on in the old Roseland Building, and I'll call room service for two steaks—one for me and one for Fuzzy—and just sit around thinking about the old days.

Now I know those headshrinkers might say I'm an old man living with his memories but I'd rather sit in my hotel room and just think about the real great players like Greenleaf and Ponzi and St. Jean and Caras and Rudolph and Mosconi and Taberski and the rest of the old masters than watch the fun players masquerading as stars today. That's why I hate to go near pool tournaments on account of I get sick just looking at the hot dog set on the small tables with the fish nets for pockets. They're like somebody trying to play piano by ear. It's like Van Cliburn dropping into a cocktail lounge for a quick shot and being forced to listen to one of those barroom thumpers tickling the keys. That's exactly how I feel when I see the fun players performing.

If I had my way, it would be perfectly all right with me if I never put a foot in a tournament room again. That's on the square. But the promoters from all over the country are always propositioning me about making appearances in their joints on account of they know how I fill the rooms. Even my old pal, Georgie Jansco, whose Johnston City tournament is now an established annual event, sent me an SOS signal last year when he figured his promotion was in trouble.

I had quit playing in Georgie's spectacular after the first two years on account of the action in the back room had sunken to such hopeless depths that getting a decent bet was next to impossible. I'll tell you exactly how bad it was. In 1962, Mr. Detroit Whitey agreed to give me a game of One Pocket for $200, only he couldn't raise all the cabbage. He managed to scrounge up $180 and then tried to put the bite on me for $20. It was unbelievable. Whitey wanted me to take a piece of the action against myself. I got so heated up that I ran out of the place screaming and I never showed up at any of Georgie's affairs again.

But last year there was what you would call a revolting development among the hot dog set and right away the promoters were after the old Fat Man to get their shows on the road.

What happened to upset Georgie was the top stars who played in his tournaments the first four years, gave him the kiss-off in 1965. Instead of playing in Johnston City, they all competed in the World Tournaments Limited's National Invitational Pocket Billiards Championships in New York City. Now the two events just happened to conflict and right away both Georgie and the New York promoter grabbed for the tranquilizers. Then they both grabbed the telephone and called the Fat Man.

First, Georgie caught me out in Kansas City and said he wasn't mad at me anymore and to prove it, he said he was going to put on a "Minnesota Fats Nite" at his tournament. He said he was calling to be sure that I would be there because the whole affair was in my honor. That Georgie can be pretty cute with the soft con when he wants to be.

Now I happen to like Georgie and his wife and kids and I knew he had the big nut and the television contract and this and that to think about so I told him I would do all I could. What I did to help Georgie was brutal beyond compare because to get to his joint one night I had to drive 600 miles without a letup. I made three appearances at Georgie's tournament and the crowds were so big you would have thought he was giving away a turkey with each ticket he sold. That's on the square.

Now after I traveled all that distance to help keep the tournament alive, you would think somebody in the back room would give me a little action. But all I got was the same old Who Shot John con. Not a one of them would play me for an orange.

So I stood 'em all up against the wall and I told 'em if anyone of them would step up and play me for their own money, I would give 'em half their cash back after I beat 'em. But not one of them made a move, not a one.

"Well," I said, "I see that the grand old game has really fallen on hard times. Everybody is a fun player and that being the case, I'm going to send each one of you mooches cue sticks with mops on the end for Christmas presents."

The last night I performed for Georgie I got in my car dead tired and drove straight to Chicago to play an exhibition the next day. I swore I would never show my face at a tournament again, only when I got to my office I had a whole mailbox full of long-distance messages to call the promoter of the New York tournament. He wanted me to come to Broadway and fill his joint, too. It was unbelievable.

The New York promoter was named Emil Lence and he said he had all the top fun players in the country in his tournament right in the heart of Times Square, only they weren't drawing four people at the box office. "Fatty," he said, "you're the only man who can keep me from going broke. Please jump in a plane and fly up here and fill my joint for me." That's on the square, too.

I told Lence the same thing I told Jansco—those tournament players can't draw their breath. Everybody from here to Zanzibar knows those fun players can't beat Mother Hubbard. In fact, if they played for their own cash they couldn't beat the hairdresser at the beauty parlor.

"Mr. Lence," I said, "you have arrived at a very expensive moment of truth. You've got all the top tournament players in the country in your place but there's no way you're going to draw a crowd with them. They couldn't draw a crowd if they set themselves on fire right in the middle of Times Square."

Lence laughed real good when I told him that but he almost cried when I said there was no way I could come to New York. I told him I'd really love to come up but my schedule was so brutal at the time that I just couldn't get away.

Being a business shark is all right, only most of the time I can't be myself. I like everybody and everything but most of all I like to be myself and sometimes I have to be somebody else. I always was an individual who did exactly what I wanted to do. If I wanted to go to a Chinese restaurant, I went to a Chinese restaurant. One night about 20 years ago I woke up in the middle of the night and got to thinking about the cheesecake they had at Lindy's on Broadway. I just couldn't get that cheesecake out of my mind. So I woke up Eva-line and told her to pack up because we were going to New York to get some cheesecake. And we did. We drove 900 miles from Dowell to New York City without stopping just to whack out Lindy's cheesecake.

That's how it used to be, only Zee changed all that when he made a general out of me. Before I became a vice president, if I decided to take a little trip on the road I would gas up and drive to a big highway intersection near Dowell and say to myself, "Well, will it be north to Detroit or south to New Orleans?" Sometimes I'd start out for New Orleans and five minutes later change my mind and head back in the other direction for Detroit. That's exactly how I lived until Zee gave me the high voltage con.

What I'd really like to do is just hit the road hustling pool again like I did in the olden days. I'd like to call one of my old traveling companions, like Delmar Stanton, who is called Harrisburg Whitey on account of he's from Harrisburg, Pennsylvania, and the two of us could just take off for unknown destinations the way we used to do. But even Harrisburg Whitey has gone legitimate. He's got a Social Security card, too, and he's working as a mixologist at Hirshey's Budweiser Bar, a real old-fashioned saloon a block from City Hall in Philadelphia.

Me and Whitey did a lot of cutting up on the road years ago. Whitey was a tremendous pool player before his eyes went bad. We visited every state in the union and we won enough gold shooting pool to go in the shylock racket, only we lost all the cash on the crap tables.

Me and Whitey were a real interesting team on account of he liked to drink, although he certainly was no lush, and I liked to eat so we were always on the lookout for joints that offered the juice and the calories on the same menu. I remember one time way back we were in Macon, Georgia, and we happened to see this big sign in a restaurant window in Macon that said, "Pitch Until You Win—All You Can Eat for a Dollar."

It was a tremendous proposition, sort of like the old Swedish smorgasbord, only this was a southern style smorgasbord. They had a whole slew of tables spread out with southern fried chicken and ham and roast and veal cutlets and all sorts of fruits and salads and vegetables and pastries and for the dollar you could help yourself to all the seconds you could hold. It was a real profitable proposition on account of the average sucker wouldn't eat much more than forty cents' worth of the delicacies, but when I started belting out the calories I almost put the restaurant out of business single-handed. In fact, the first time I ate there the owner just

● *159*

looked at me like he couldn't believe what he was seeing. The second day he looked like he was trying to work up the nerve to say something. But the third day he was waiting for me at the front door.

"Sir," he said, "you are a very nice gentleman in every sense, but I have to bar you from my place if I intend to stay in business. Kindly take your business elsewhere."

Whitey's always telling the writers about another time I went on an eating kick down in Huntington, West Virginia, only that time I almost put myself out of business.

Me and Whitey went to a bar in Huntington and right away I spotted this tremendous jar of radishes on the counter and even though I was down to my last twenty dollars, I started belting out the radishes until the jar was empty. Then I asked the bartender if he had any more radishes and he went back in the kitchen and came out with another jar filled to the top and I emptied that one, too.

When the time came to leave I asked how much I owed for the radishes and he said he would call it square for fifteen dollars.

So now me and Whitey are walking down the street and who do we run smack into but a character known as Mainliner on account of he was addicted to the needle. Mainliner comes up shaking like a leaf and he tries to bite me for ten.

"Mainliner," I said, "I would gladly let you have a tenner if I had it, but I'm pretty low myself. Would a deuce help you any?"

"No, no, Fatty," he said, "a deuce wouldn't come near what I need. I have a very expensive habit."

"Well," I said, "I'm beginning to understand the situation, Mainliner, because I happen to have the same kind of problem myself. Just ask Mr. Harrisburg Whitey to tell you how much my radish habit costs me."

Now when you're down to your last twenty and you blow fifteen on radishes, that's what you call extremism, the worst kind of extremism, but that's exactly what I am—an out-and-out extremist. I never do anything halfway. I always went first class, even when I was busted.

One time about 20 years ago I happened to be so broke that I didn't even have a car but I still traveled like a general at all times. Mr. Harrisburg Whitey happened to be visiting me at the time and he just happened to be about as broke as me, so we were on the lookout for some serious action to replenish our assets. Now this day we're in DuQuoin at the St. Nicholas Hotel and we hear about some real action in Lexington, Kentucky, which is maybe 300 miles away. Whitey grabbed the telephone to call the bus station about the next departure but I told Whitey to forget about the bus station and call my cab driver, Mr. Pat Cheek, and we would take a cab to Lexington. And that's exactly what we did.

Pat Cheek is an independent cab operator in DuQuoin and in the last 25 years he's driven me all over the country. He's got a big old car with "DuQuoin Cab" printed on the door and a big red light on the top that you can see for miles. In fact, a lot of suckers think Pat is a gendarme the way he drives down the road with the red light blinking on and off.

Pat Cheek says he figures he holds the world's record for long distance fares on account of back in 1945, which was during the War, he drove me all the way from Dowell to Minneapolis, stopping only to eat. The way the Minneapolis jolt came about was my youngest sister, Jerry, died suddenly in childbirth out in Soap Lake, Washington, and when I got the call in the middle of the night there was no way for me and Eva-line to get out there on account of I was busted at the time and didn't have a car. So I called Muzz and borrowed like $700 and then I called Pat Cheek and we headed for St. Louis to catch a plane, only when we got to St. Louis there was no way to get a reservation because the soldiers had the planes all tied up.

They told me and Eva-line that if we could get to Minneapolis in the next 24 hours we might be able to get reservations there, so I told Pat Cheek to head for Minneapolis. The whole trip was like 771 miles and even though I can't remember the meter reading, I remember I put a $50 tip on Pat Cheek and he was the happiest guy you ever saw.

Me and Pat Cheek don't travel around the country the way we used to because now that I'm wheeling a new Lincoln Continental I don't have to make those long hauls by taxi anymore. But every now and then when I'm home in Dowell, I'll call Pat and have him drive out to the house and take me into town just for old time's sake.

I'm happiest when I'm in Dowell belting out the conversation with Pat Cheek and Muzz and Scoffie and another pal of mine, Bill Such. This Bill Such was the toughest hombre in all of Little Egypt when I came to Dowell 25 years ago. He got a pretty high rating in the Marine Corps during the war; in fact, he was with the Marines who ran up the flag on Mount Suribachi on Iwo Jima, and when he marched home from the war he had so many medals he looked like General Patton. Bill was so crazy about the rough stuff that when he came home he organized a pack of tush hogs who called themselves The Night Riders and they went all over Little Egypt looking for fights. They wrecked more joints than a bulldozer but one day I got Bill off to the side and told him he never would get anywhere being a tush hog. I told him a lot of times until he finally got the word and settled down to be a real first class gentleman.

Now if you run into a kid with a wild streak like Bill Such in a place like New York there would be no way you could talk a little sense to him on account of New York is such a frantic place nowadays that a kid doesn't have time to sit down and think things out. But Dowell is different on account of it's more peaceful and easygoing and the people are real friendly, which means you can get to know 'em better. Now when people are friendly, you not only get to know 'em better but you get to know more about them and the good qualities they possess. That's why it was no problem whatsoever talking Bill Such out of the tush hog jolts. I just got to know him and when I gave him the conversation about all the good qualities he had, he was so impressed that he even started going to church. That's on the square.

I love every living human in Dowell and DuQuoin and everyone of them is wild about me. The bankers and preachers and business sharks and even the nuns at the Catholic school are all crazy about me. In fact, about the only person in all of Little Egypt who ever has a bad word for me every now and then happens to be my wife, Eva-line. My mother-in-law, Orbie, gives me a little trouble sometimes on account of she's always after me to go to church. I tell her I go to church more than she does. "Orbie," I say, "you know I always go to church when they have those chicken fries."

The thing I like most about Dowell is coming home. A lot of people think a home is a place to go away from, but the way I see it, it's a place to come back to. So no matter where I roam, I always come back to Dowell.

When I get back from a long trip, I can't wait to pull my big Lincoln in the drive on account of I know my dogs and cats are going to give me an ovation like I'm Lyndon Johnson or somebody. Sometimes I'll be so tired I can hardly unbend but no matter how cranked down I happen to be, I get out the bone meal and the dog food and decorate the banquet boards and me and Eva-line just stand around and watch 'em belt out the menu. Listen, I can be so tired that I can hardly stand up, but those dogs and cats refresh me like a Turkish bath.

After I get a little sleep my first stop in DuQuoin is always The Perfection Club to pay a social call on my old pal Muzz. Me and Muzz still keep about the same weight and when he sees me walk in he pulls off his belt and I pull off mine and we compare the holes to see who's the biggest around the middle. If Muzz happens to have an inch on me, he's the happiest fellow in the whole state of Illinois.

Muzz's joint is a real tremendous place nowadays. He's gone legitimate, too, and everything about his club is first class. The decor is exactly the same as Toots Shor's and the food is just as good; in fact, I figure Muzz's steaks are even a little better. He puts out a steak a foot long and two inches thick and the suckers like 'em so much they wait in line to get tables. The joint is not only the favorite stop for tourists going through Southern Illinois but during the big DuQuoin State Fair every August, all the top bananas in show business eat at Muzz's.

Muzz has what he calls an Honor Roll of Celebrities who ate at his joint with my name heading the list. He's put on spreads for Milton Berle, Lawrence Welk, Carol Channing, Bob Hope, Julius LaRosa, Sammy Davis, Jr., and a zillion others. Muzz claims he's served the calories to every top star except Sarah Bernhardt and The Beatles.

Of course, I still reign as the all-time calorie champion at The Perfection Club but here lately I've been out on the road so much that a lot of people in Little Egypt are forgetting the way I handle the knife and fork. The last few times I've been home I hear 'em whispering about how Mr. Andy Williams, the singer, came in a few times and whacked out two steaks at one sitting; in fact, a lot of them figure this Mr. Andy Williams has replaced the Fat Man as the king of the festive boards. But Muzz says the title should be decided in head-to-head combat and he wants me and Andy Williams to have an eat-out for the championship.

I've been home so little since Zee turned me into a business shark that when the time comes to hit the road again, I really don't want to go. When I used to drive out to the big highway intersection near Dowell in the olden days, my only problem was whether I would head north or south. But when I get out there nowadays, I always feel like turning around and going back home on account of I'm happiest at home.

When I'm on the road nowadays I'm not exactly what you would call unhappy, but since I've become an Executive Vice President, Eva-line says I don't smile the way I used to. That's because I've got lots of things on my mind. In the olden days, I was automatically unhappy if someone mentioned the word work so I avoided it at all times. But now I'm not only working but I've become a worrier. I worry about business problems. Now when a man has worries he can't ever be completely happy. But who is ever completely happy? In fact, who knows what complete happiness is in the first place?

My friend Johnny Carson wrote this little book called *Happiness Is a Dry Martini* and it's full of cute little sayings about happiness. Like: "Happiness is seeing a teen-ager mug the man who just held you up"; and "Happiness is having the finance company burn down with all your records." But Mr. Johnny Carson never said anything about what happiness is not.

I'll tell you exactly what happiness is not. Happiness is not a job.

Of course you can derive a lot of pleasure out of a job, but only so long as it provides you with a sense of satisfaction. Being satisfied on a job is one of the most important things in life. Now in my particular case, even though

I never went to work until I was 51 years old, for better than 30 years I got a tremendous satisfaction out of knowing I was the best top action pool player in the whole country. It wasn't so much the amount of gelt I won on the pool table as it was knowing I was the best when the cash was up for grabs and then proving it to all comers.

Pool players are a funny bunch. They all derive great satisfaction from their game and when they reach a certain proficiency, they all think they're the greatest. That's why it was so gratifying for me to whack 'em out one after the other, especially when the stakes were big. I knew I was the best there was and they were certain they were the greatest so the real payoff was proving to them that I was the top banana. They all knew me and they knew my reputation for being a deadly killer when there was serious money riding on the outcome so you would think that if they had their right minds they never would want to play me for the gold. But none of the pool players I ever knew would ever take my word that I was the best there was. Every last one of them had to be convinced, so I convinced 'em. I convinced 'em all.

It took me 30 years and a jillion miles of bumping and bouncing all over the country, but I convinced every mooch in every poolroom from here to Zanzibar that I was untouchable for the cash. I did such a tremendous job of convincing 'em that today there's not a living human who will play me for a pineapple. Like last spring I was in New York City on business during the 1966 World's Pocket Billiards Championships at the Hotel Commodore and one night I dropped in to take in the matches. When those fun players saw me walk in the tournament room they looked at me like I was the Boston Strangler, but not a one of them would play me for a pineapple. They just stood around in their form-fitting tuxedos giving the suckers the YMCA con. It was ridiculous beyond compare because dressing a pool player in a tuxedo is like putting whipped cream on a hot dog.

Now I not only convinced all the fun players and the mooches that I was the deadliest of all killers, but I did such a fantastic job that I ruined every fat pool player in the entire country. If a fat man walks into a strange room today, he can't get a game for two dollars on account of all the mooches are scared to death because they're afraid the fat guy might be me.

Now that I'm an Executive Vice President, my satisfaction is knowing that I'm playing a part in the tremendous comeback pool is enjoying all over the country. Every living human is plum crazy about pool nowadays. Today pool is a family game in every sense of the word.

The old, drab, dimly lit, smoke-filled poolrooms of the 30s have been replaced by air-conditioned, plush-carpeted and gaily decorated and lighted neighborhood establishments that look like exclusive clubs. You can walk in any of the modern rooms almost any time of the day or night and see couples, fathers and sons, mothers and daughters, sisters and brothers all hunched over the tables and having the time of their lives. Listen, these modern rooms are such fabulous joints you could hold wedding receptions in some of them. The Mamas and Papas of the Great Society don't have to worry about the poolroom being a bad influence on Junior anymore.

I think the greatest satisfaction I get out of being a Good Will Ambassador for pool is the pleasure of meeting people who want to buy tables for their homes. They crowd around me in the department stores and ask all sorts of questions about what size table is the most practical and which color cloth would blend best with the decor of their recreation room and a zillion other questions about the game and the equipment. It's a real genuine pleasure to see so many people interested in pool.

Of course, sometimes I meet extraordinary individuals, like the little 14-year-old boy I spent a whole afternoon with when I played an exhibition in a shopping center in one of the Chicago suburbs last summer. The boy was unbelievable.

He was waiting for me when I pulled up into a parking spot in the shopping center and right away he got all excited about my car.

"Gee," he said, "my mother will never believe that Minnesota Fats drives a Lincoln Continental."

Then the next thing he was asking about was how much I paid for my suit and if I was married and what kind of hotels I stopped in. The kid even begged to carry my cue stick.

So when my exhibitions were all over, the kid asked if I would meet his mother, only he said he would have to telephone her so she could drive to the shopping center. So I told him I would be real happy to meet his mother and while we waited for her, we went over to the lunch counter and belted out a couple of turkey sandwiches.

When his mother finally arrived, the kid went out of control.

"Mother," he said, "I want you to meet Mr. Minnesota Fats and I want you to admit that you're wrong about a poolroom being a hangout for bums, too. See? Minnesota Fats isn't a bum. Look at how nice he's dressed and come on outside and see the car he's driving. He's no bum, Mama, he's no bum. He's a very nice man. He even bought me a turkey sandwich."

The mother was what you would call nonplussed on account of she blushed something awful. She said she had been very worried about her son being so crazy about pool and wasn't so sure that a poolroom was the proper place for a growing boy.

"I remember my father would never allow my brothers around a poolroom," she said.

So I told her the way it was.

"Lady," I said, "you don't have to worry about your son frequenting poolrooms anymore. Pool is different nowadays. Everything is clean and antiseptic looking, I mean real clean and antiseptic.

"Look, even an old hustler like me has been laundered."

Part Two

CHAPTER 19

The Blocks and Sandpile of Billiards

Before I break the rack on the basic fundamentals of billiards, I want to make a very important point—especially with the beginners. My point is this: Learn to play the game properly; get a good foundation in the proper techniques, such as grip, stance, bridge, stroke and follow-through, cueing the ball and hitting the object ball.

These are the basic fundamentals, the blocks and sandpile of all forms of billiards. And you don't learn them by grabbing a cue and trying to run 50 balls the first time you're on the table. Nobody runs 50 balls the first time on the table. Nobody. Let me give you an example:

Back in the olden days in my old neighborhood in Washington Heights in New York City, there's this doll who needs a job badly. She applies for a recreation director's job at a Settlement House over on the East Side. They ask her if she knows how to play piano and she says, sure, no sweat, although she didn't know a note of music and she had never sat down at a piano in her life. So she gets the job, believe it or not, but the first time she sits at the keyboard, well you should have heard it. It sounded like somebody was tickling a gorilla. It was unbelievable. The doll, she busts out crying and says she thought all you had to do was sit down at the piano and play. It's a true story. Now I'm not going to tell you everybody believes you just sit down to a piano and play Rachmaninoff's "Prelude," just like that. But the point I'm making is that a lot of people have an idea you shoot pool that way—you just pick up a cue and run the table. Well, I've got news for you, junior.

Say you want to play the trumpet like Al Hirt. I mention Al Hirt because I am very partial to fat men. Now you don't think that Big Al just picked up a horn one day and started to blow, just like that. Not a chance. First you learn to hold the horn and after you learn to pucker the lips they hit you with the scales and after a while they teach you to read music. And maybe after a few months you're blowing "John Brown's Body Lies Amould'ring in the Grave," or something like that. By then you know the fundamentals and you're ready—you're ready to practice, practice, practice. But if you just pick up the horn and start blowing with the wrong techniques, I mean a hit-and-miss proposition, well, you might end up tooting the calls at the race track.

It's the very same thing with billiards. You've got to learn the proper techniques from the start because pool is a game of good habits. Unfortunately, a lot of promising young players get off on the wrong foot because they learn all the bad habits. They pick up the cue and attack the balls without having the slightest idea of what they're doing. Nobody tells them what they're supposed to do, I mean the right things to do. So they develop all sorts of bad habits because their game is fundamentally bad and their techniques are all wrong. Sometimes these bad habits become part of your game and they can never be corrected. You're just stuck with them. I've seen it a jillion times.

Of course, there are the exceptions, like Stan Musial's peekaboo batting stance. This is a baseball example, but I think it's a good one because Musial was an exception. His technique was all wrong, standing up there all screwed up like a pretzel. But Musial felt comfortable in that stance and he's one of the greatest hitters of all time. How can you argue with that kind of success? But how many big league hitters use the Musial stance? I never saw one outside of Stan. He was the exception.

There are several exceptions among the top billiard players. My own stance at the table is unorthodox, which I'll explain later on. But most of the top players—Willie Mosconi and Jimmy Caras and Irving Crane, and before them the legendary Ralph Greenleaf—all employed the basic fundamentals and techniques. That's why they were so great.

So let's call the class to order with these words: Get a good foundation in fundamentals. Stick to the accepted techniques, all things being equal, and you'll avoid the pitfalls that could plague your game as it progresses. Remember, there's only one way to play the game and that's the right way. So develop the good habits, the right habits, from the very start.

You want to play a trumpet, the first thing you do is buy a horn. Well, in billiards you pick out a cue that you feel comfortable using. Most of the good rooms offer a wide selection of cues, so you won't have a cue problem if you're a sometime player. But there's a trend on nowadays for personalized cues. It's a status thing to walk into the neighborhood room with your own cue. You can buy a personalized cue in most of the bigger rooms and many firms market a large assortment of cues with a wide price range, including cue cases or bags. Some outfits specialize in the super-personalized cues with the owner's name and a lot of gingerbread on the butt end. You can pay up to a hundred dollars, sometimes more, for these cues but it's not necessary to invest that kind of money. The important thing about a cue is its weight and its feel.

A cue should be selected according to individual requirements of weight and feel. It's all relative. Myself, I use a 20-ounce cue and always have. I feel comfortable with 20 ounces. And the cue must be straight. You can check it by sighting down the length of the cue. This is very important because there's no way you can play the game if the cue is crooked. You might pocket a ball in the chandelier.

I remember I was playing an exhibition at a college out in Indiana and a student came up and said there was something wrong with his cue. I said I'd try it but I couldn't make a ball. So I sighted down the stick. It was unbelievable. That stick had a crib in it like a walking cane. It was like trying to shoot with a frankfurter. When you have a cue like that, get rid of it. Right away.

Now we're ready to talk about the grip. The first step is to locate what is called the fulcrum point, which is simply the point where the butt end and the shaft balance. To find this point, you lay the cue across your fingers (see Figure 1) and slide it along until both ends balance.

Figure 1

Grip your cue about four inches back of the fulcrum point. Never exceed that distance, unless, of course, a shot requires a very long reach (Figure 2). This is extremely important because if the distance between your bridge hand and your right hand (assuming you're right-handed) is great, it can throw you off balance.

GO LIGHTLY WITH HOLLY

Once you're familiar with the point at which to grip your cue, be sure to grip it lightly. Don't grab it like it's a shovel. I'm out in Omaha playing in a big department store and a young girl asks me about the grip. I tell her to go lightly and she said, "Oh, that will be easy to remember— Holly Golightly, the girl in *Breakfast at Tiffany's*." That's a doll for you, but it's a very good way to remember a very important factor about the grip: Holly Golightly.

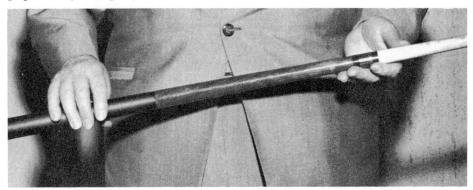

Figure 2

One final word on the grip. Use your thumb and three fingers. Nothing else. Never let the butt of the cue touch the palm of your hand. The cue isn't a baseball bat or a hockey stick. So grip it gently. The light grip is the right grip. It makes for a fluid motion and a spring action, and the cue is much easier to control

Stance at the table is the next key. Just as balance in the cue is important, so is body balance. Different players use different stances at the table, but the top-notch players are balanced and comfortable, with their heads over the cue and in the line of aim. The tip of your nose should be in a straight line with the cue and the cue ball. This means you can see the cue ball perfectly with both eyes.

My stance at the table differs from most because I stand almost erect, almost straight up. Most people figure I stand that way because I'm so fat and I can't bend over, but my 52-inch waistline doesn't have a thing to do with it. I've always used the erect stance, even when I was 80 pounds lighter. Why? Because I feel comfortable this way. No other reason. If you find a stance that is comfortable and doesn't interfere with your stroke or your line of aim, by all means use it.

The next step is lining up the body with the cue ball. Face the direction of your shot and stand back about one foot with your right foot in line with the cue ball (Figure 3). Turn your left foot slightly to the right. Move your right foot back until the toe of your right foot is opposite the middle of your left foot. You don't have to hop around like you're at one of those discotheque joints, but practice the footwork until it becomes second nature to you.

As you bend forward, be certain that your weight is distributed evenly on both feet (Figure 4). It's all right to move the body slightly forward as you stroke. The bridge arm is extended straight to the bridge position. bending very slightly.

Your position may vary according to the distance of the shot, but at all times take the same relative position with your head in the line of aim. Position is one of the most important essentials of the game. It's the secret to skillful performance. Good habits in position are a must.

The next fundamental is the bridge. Most beginners confuse the bridge with the grip and that's because of the mechanical bridge which is used when shots cannot be reached while keeping one foot on the floor. But the term bridge is the term for what I call a cylinder formed by the thumb and index finger through which the cue shaft slides (see Figure 5).

Figure 3

Figure 4

Forming the bridge is one of the paramount techniques of the game. It must be comparatively short, firm and closed, yet the shaft must have a little room through which to slide. It's like the pistons in an automobile. The movement must be easy and free.

Figure 5

Most of the top players use the conventional tripod bridge (Figure 6) because it provides firmness and thus good control. The bridge hand practically becomes an integral part of the table. No matter how proper your grip and stance and position might be, poor execution of the bridge can wreck your game.

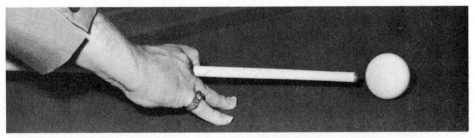

Figure 6

Some players, especially beginners and women players, lean to the open bridge—the V bridge. The V bridge is formed by placing the palm of the hand on the table and sliding the cue over the fat part of the hand between the thumb and the index finger. It is more difficult to control the cue from the V bridge. You lose something in accuracy. The tripod gives you much better control. But all the leading players go to the V bridge if they have to reach for a long shot.

JOE BALSIS AND THE ONE-ARMED BANDIT

However, younger players and some women players may be limited to the open bridge because of their small hands and fingers. If you have small hands or small fingers, don't get discouraged. Take heart from Joe Balsis, the 1965 pocket billiard World Champion, from Minersville, Pennsylvania. Here's a World Champion who can't use the conventional tripod bridge because he has small fingers. So he had to adjust. What he does is place the last three fingers flat on the table and presses the thumb against the middle finger. Then he forms a bridge by bending the index finger, letting it press against the middle finger with the end of the index finger barely touching the thumb. It's not quite the same as the tripod. If I had to have a name for it, I might call it a fish-hook bridge because of the way the index finger is bent. Balsis simply says it's an unorthodox bridge. But no matter what it's called, Joe was a World Champion. Like Musial, Balsis was an exception.

Listen, I know a pool hustler from down in Rutherfordton, North Carolina, by the name of Ernest Morgan. Now here was a guy with a real handicap. When he was a kid he lost three fingers on his left hand, so there's no way he can come near the orthodox bridge techniques. So he slides the cue over the nub of his left hand. The pool players call him Nubby but Morgan calls himself The One-Armed Bandit. He's always coming up with propositions to even up his handicap. He's got all kinds of of angles—one-handed, jacked-up, underhanded, overhanded. When he's shooting overhanded, you'd think he was spearfishing or maybe throwing a javelin. And I'll tell you something: If you don't watch that One-Armed Bandit, he's liable to steal your socks.

Then there used to be this fellow around New York in the olden days by the name of Tom Clark. He didn't have any arms, so he had a special mechanical bridge made that he strapped around his chest and controlled the cue with his neck muscles. He held the cue between his chin and the neck and he could run a rack sometimes. It was marvelous to watch. He made his living painting houses—but don't ask me how he did that.

There are several other factors concerning the bridge, such as the cue level, the short bridge, rail bridge and the mechanical bridge.

The bridge may be raised or lowered as required for draw or follow shots. However, do not raise or lower the butt end of the cue. Make your adjustments by raising or lowering the bridge hand. There are a few exceptions to this general rule, say, if the cue ball is too close to the rail, or in situations where you have to stroke over an object ball that is too close to the cue ball. Then you make adjustments by raising or lowering the cue itself.

Unless you're reaching to make a long shot, the distance between the tip of your cue and your bridge should never exceed eight inches. You're sure to have better control of your shot when you use the short bridge.

In every match a situation arises wherein the cue ball is too close to the rail to use ordinary bridge. To overcome this, slide the cue between the

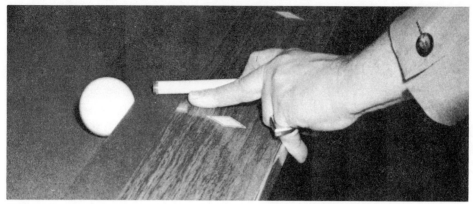

Figure 7

index and middle fingers (Figure 7), using the rail for support. To assure accurate aim, press the fingers snugly against the cue shaft.

CROSSING A BRIDGE WITH THE LADIES' AID

Now, let's talk about the mechanical bridge. Some guys call it the Ladies' Aid. It is the saver when shots cannot be reached by keeping one foot on the floor, but to be effective it must be used accurately. This requires lots of practice.

Be sure to place the mechanical bridge on the table in such a way that it does not disturb the cue ball or any of the object balls. If you disturb any of the balls, you will commit a foul and be penalized. On occasion you may have to hold the bridge in your normal shooting hand, because of the arrangement of the balls, and make your shot with the other. This can be as tough as tightrope walking and requires a lot of skill. Look before you make a move in a situation like this.

When employing the mechanical bridge, grip the butt end of the cue the same as you do for conventional shooting (Figure 8). My best advice on the use of the mechanical bridge is to practice with it regularly, as there will be many occasions for its use.

For our finale on fundamentals, let's cross over the bridge to the strokes and the follow-through. The stroke is so important that it can be the difference between mediocrity or being a very good player. Personally, I think great players are born, although you can develop a sound game by concentration and lots of practice. But no matter how you cut it, the stroke is the meat of the coconut. Some players are blessed with a natural stroke while others can never seem to acquire it.

Figure 8

The proper stroke is the culmination of the key fundamentals, like gripping the cue properly and executing a good, sound bridge. Both must be consistent or your whole game will fall into the rabbit hole. Be sure to grip the cue lightly and you'll be able to control the cue after it contacts the cue ball. The more you play, the more you will realize how important the stroke is. Without a sound stroke, you're just another thumper.

I suggest you practice warm-up stroking before striking the cue ball. Take careful aim, letting your shooting arm swing easily and freely. It's like the calisthenics before the football game. You've got to get loose and stay loose. And remember, your head must always be over the cue and in the line of aim.

Of course, the follow-through is just as important as the stroke itself. I'd have to call them the Daily Double of billiards. It is just as important as the follow-through in baseball or golf, and the motion must be definite, casual and rhythmic. This is a good example of natural aptitude, because it is difficult to teach the follow-through. Some develop it instinctively while others never acquire it. But even if it's natural, constant practice has top priority. All players can improve their follow-through by constant practice and endless determination.

A LESSON FROM LADY ASTOR

Before we start running balls, I want to tell you a story. And this story is one that I would say has a moral, billiardwise, that is.

The story is about Lady Astor, the first woman to sit in the British Parliament. Lady Nancy (that was her first name) Astor died a couple of years ago, at the age of 84, and I remember reading about her approach to her golf game. It made a lot of sense, and the same thinking can apply to a beginner's approach to billiards.

Lady Astor was advised to take up golf for her health. So she went to a top golf pro over in England for lessons. Now here's the important part. Lady Astor took lessons for six weeks without hitting a ball. She went out to the club and just watched her friends play. She was very critical of their form because she was a perfectionist. She studied stance and grip and swing and she tried to develop each of these fundamental techniques herself before she so much as drove a ball. This way she learned the important phases of the game the right way. Right from the start she developed the good habits.

Now when Lady Astor figures she's ready to start playing, which is six weeks after she starts taking lessons, she goes out and tours the course in the low 80s. It was amazing. You know what that's like in billiards? I'd have to say it's the equivalent of running maybe 50 balls the first time on the table.

Of course, I don't want to discourage anybody from getting to the table, because that's where the fun starts. But before you start attacking the balls, be sure you're grounded in the fundamentals. Watch the good players, watch how they handle themselves. And if you're doubtful about anything, ask the good players for their advice. They'll be glad to help, because 99 out of 100 pool players are easygoing people, like violin players, maybe.

And one more thing. Never be satisfied. If you ever reach the point in this game that you think you've got it made, well, you're liable to find yourself shooting out of the hole more and more. And by shooting out of the hole I mean finding yourself in trouble on the table because of your carelessness.

Lady Astor was never satisfied with her game. In fact, she was seldom satisfied with other people's game. One day she was playing in a foursome with the Grand Duke Michael of Russia and she didn't like the way the

Grand Duke was holding his club. Instead of gripping the club according to fundamental techniques, the Grand Duke gripped it entirely with his fingers.

So you know what Lady Nancy Astor said? She said, "Your trouble, Duke Michael, is that you are holding the club as if it were a piccolo." Now there was a doll for you, that Lady Nancy.

Now I think we can break the rack. So here we go—with lots of English, on the ball, that is.

CHAPTER 20

A Chalk Talk
with Lipstick Jack

There's an old saying you'll hear in a poolroom when two players are trying to set up a proposition. You're liable to hear almost anything when a proposition is being discussed, but sooner or later you're bound to hear one of the players crow about as how he's willing to play anybody "for money, marbles or chalk." Now this line always gets a big laugh from the eyeballers, because the eyeballers never know the score. But any time a player who wants to bet on his game talks about chalk he's got to be serious, because without chalk a top-notch player might get beat by a girl. Just as money is important to every living soul, chalk is a must essential to a good pool player.

Now all good players know this, but it's amazing how a lot of them are careless about the way they chalk the cue tip. Some of them go so heavy with the chalk you'd think they're drilling for oil. And others apply the chalk as an outlet for their nervous energy; you know, it gives them something to do with their hands. Most of the time this is a subconscious gesture and they no more realize what they're doing than somebody who might be walking in his sleep. You've got to be very careful about this, because the improper application of chalk can ruin your game. I mean, it can turn your game into a disaster area.

Anybody who has ever seen me play ought to remember how much detail I give to chalking the cue. I chalk up after every single shot. I always apply several light strokes of chalk, making certain that the chalk is spread lightly and evenly on the tip. This is the best insurance against miscues, especially when your game progresses to the point where you're able to use

English. You might get away without the right amount of chalk as long as you're hitting the cue ball dead center, but when you move into English, the chalk is the difference between night and day.

Now the reason the chalk is so important is because you're striking the cue ball, which is a round object with no flat surfaces, with the cue tip, which is leather. What the chalk does is increase the friction between the leather tip and the slick surface of the cue ball. This increased friction is more important today than it was when I was just starting to play because the balls they're making nowadays are plastic. They're of very light composition, so the least bit of a slip in any manner will throw the ball off. It's liable to look like a flying object that's gone berserk. In the olden days, when I was a beginner, the balls were heavier. Some were made of ivory and some were made of Belgium clay, but they were much easier to control. The manufacturers use the plastics today because the price of the old ivory or clay balls would be prohibitive.

So the things to remember about chalking the cue are: (1) don't put too much chalk on the tip because your tip will wear away so quick you'll think somebody heisted it; (2) don't put too little chalk on the tip because, without the exact amount of chalk, you're not going to get the increased friction and you'll miscue something awful and (3) be sure to chalk the tip lightly after each stroke. Like the doll in Omaha said about the grip—Holly Golightly. I'll tell you what it's like—it's like Goldilocks when she got into the bear's porridge. Too hot, too cold and just right. That's how your chalk must be applied—just right.

It's like a beautiful doll applying lipstick. If she applies too much she's gonna look like a siren and if she applies too little she might look like a ghost. I remember I'm in Houston one time and there's this guy named Jack Terry of Buffalo, and he's a real fine pool player. But he didn't have any nickname like the others, and he said to me, "Fat Man, give me a nickname." Well, one day I'm at the table and in walks this guy Jack and he's got lipstick all over his lips and chin and cheeks and even some on the collar. So I said, "Well, well, if it ain't Lipstick Jack." He was crazy about this nickname but he got me over on the side and whispered, "Fat Man, how come you call me Lipstick Jack?" So I said, "My boy, I call you Lipstick Jack because your tomato doesn't know how to chalk." It's a true story.

CHAPTER 21

A Lecture in *Proper* English

Now that we're ready to hit the ball, once again remember that the cue ball is a round object with no flat surfaces. So for beginners it is best to emphasize center-ball stroking at the start. I'd have to say that eight out of every ten shots in pocket billiards can be made with the center-ball stroke. The other two shots would probably require some form of English, which is the most important part of this chapter.

By center-ball stroking I mean stroking the cue ball in the very center of its vertical axis (see Figure 9). With a center-ball stroke you use no English at all. The value of center-ball stroking will become more apparent once the player realizes the influences of English. English influences the path of the cue ball to the object ball. It also influences the path of the object ball from cue ball to pocket. The player must understand these influences of English; otherwise he can fritz up an easy shot by using English improperly or, perhaps, when English is not required. So a very good rule of thumb for the beginner might be this: Stick to the center-ball stroke on every shot unless English is absolutely necessary. English should be used only if (1) you want to throw the object ball or (2) in playing for position, you want the cue ball to take English off a rail.

English, of course, is necessary for position play and without position play you'll never become a top banana on the table. But before you start using English like you were some kind of university professor, the important thing to master is the pocketing of balls. I will discuss the pocketing of balls at length in a chapter on hitting the object ball, but the point I want to make here is that before you begin using English make sure you've developed a knack for pocketing balls by center-ball stroking. This will help you develop your stroke and a good, consistent, springlike stroke is a must when you get to applying English.

If you're able to run, say, a dozen or so balls using center-ball stroking I'd say you're ready for promotion to English. English in billiards is like a post-graduate course. If you tackle English without the proper foundation in stroke and follow-through and the ability to hit the cue ball properly, well, you're liable to flunk out before the midterm exams and end up majoring in basket weaving.

Most of the top players will tell you English is a necessary evil in pocket billiards. It's evil because it's difficult to pull off, especially for beginners. But it's necessary if you want to bring the cue ball to where you want it for the following shot. This is called position, and position play is the heart and soul of all billiards. Without position, you'll always look like a shoemaker on the table.

When I was a schoolboy at P.S. 132 in Washington Heights in New York City, my teacher, Miss Katie Bockenstedt, always made us define our terms. She said that was the only way we would know for sure what we were

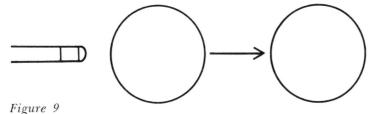

Figure 9

talking about. She always had us defining terms. One day she asks this flaky kid to define a cow and he said, "A cow has four legs." So after that we all knew what a cow was. Well, English in billiards would have more in common with an octopus than a cow because it's very complicated. So let's start defining the term.

The dictionary defines English as "a spinning or rotary motion round the vertical axis given to a ball by striking it to the left or the right of its center. Such a spin influences the direction it will take after striking a cushion or another ball." That's what Mr. Webster says. But right here, let me point out that spin, or English, can also be imparted by striking the cue ball above or below its horizontal axis (see Figure 10). This spin, or English, will determine the forward or backward movement of the cue ball after it strikes the object ball. It's called Follow (forward motion) English and Draw (backward motion) English. You might call it Uptown English and Downtown English.

There are several degrees of English you can impart to the cue ball, depending on where you hit it. I've already said that when you hit the cue ball dead center you're not using any English at all. But whenever you vary your hit—to the left, or the right, or the top or the bottom—you're using English (see Figures 11 and 12 for English areas). Then there's the question of how much English you might use. Normal English would

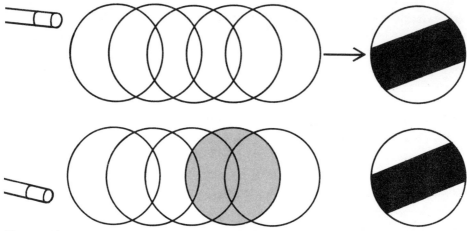

Figure 10

be just a touch to the right or left, bottom or top; Higher English is the next step, like when you move further right or left, or up or down: and the third degree would be what I call Extreme English, which is way-out English—like the Far Right or the Far Left, or the Bargain Basement or the Penthouse. We'll discuss these degrees in detail as we progress.

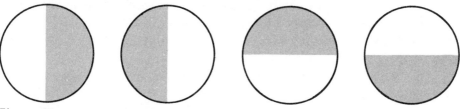

Figure 11

Generally, English can be divided into two classes—Natural English and Reverse English.

Natural English adds speed to the cue ball after it comes off a cushion or hits another ball. It also widens the angle (see Figure 13) after it strikes a cushion and will throw the object ball to one side or the other from its original course. Of course, Reverse English means just what it says. Reverse. It will have the opposite effect of Natural English. It will slow the speed of the cue ball after striking a cushion or another ball and, therefore, will narrow the angle.

REVERSE ENGLISH FOR SCHOOL ZONES

Natural English is used primarily in caroms and three-cushion billiards, but it is also employed on the break shot in 14.1 pocket billiards. With Natural English, the cue ball spins around in its natural form. I mean

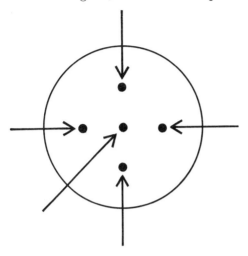

Figure 12

it spins in the direction it is going. When it hits the rail or another ball, it just glides around in its natural direction. It'll go without any trouble—like it's walking. When it hits the rail it'll juice off and look like it's breaking out in a run. It'll widen the angle and just drive around the table. It's the kind of English you need if you're shooting at one end of the table and you want to get into position for a following shot at, say, the other end (see Figure 14).

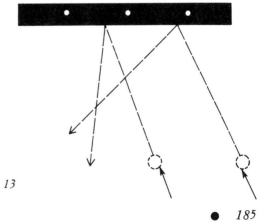

Figure 13

● *185*

Now Reverse English, of course, will have the opposite effect. The cue ball will spin against its natural direction, so that when it strikes a cushion its speed will decrease, like maybe you're putting on the brakes. It will also

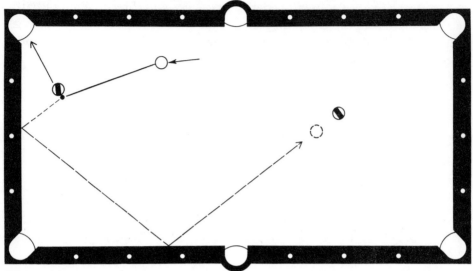

Figure 14

distort the angle (see Figure 15). With Reverse English you can slow the cue ball down maybe 50 per cent, like you're driving through a school zone. It just depends on where you want to the cue ball to go.

The big thing to keep in mind about Reverse English is that it will not take effect until the cue ball hits a rail or another ball. For example, if you want to throw an object ball and you use Right English, this English is Natural when it hits the object ball. But if the cue ball is going into a cushion after hitting the object ball, you must determine whether the English remains Natural. When playing for position, you might want the English to become Reverse.

So here's the way you break it down. To apply Natural English, hit the cue ball on the side that you want the cue ball to travel after it hits an object ball or a cushion. If you want it to juice off to the right, hit it to the right side. On the other hand, if you want the cue ball to take off to the left, you hit it on the left side, where else?

Now the principle of Reverse English is that it will force the cue ball to reverse its natural course after hitting a cushion. In other words, you slow it down. You frustrate it, in a way. This is all right, because if you don't frustrate that cue ball by giving it the proper stroke on Reverse English, it's sure going to frustrate you.

DON'T STRIKE OUT ON THE CURVE

There's one more effect of English that must be understood and that's the dangers English imparts to the cue ball. For example, let's say you're faced with a shot almost the length of the table and you decide to use English. A shot almost the length of the table could be four, five, six, even seven feet in a given situation. So, remembering that English will definitely influence the path of the cue ball to the object ball, you must allow for this influence over the long haul, in this case a shot nearly the length of the table. With English, that cue ball will curve as it approaches the object ball —if you give it Left English, it will curve left, while Right English will cause it to curve right. So you must allow for this curve or you're flirting with disaster. The allowance is in the radius of the curve, which must be in direct proportion to the length of the shot. This is done by adjusting your aim on the object ball to allow for the expected curve. If your judgment is wrong, you'll strike out, I mean miss the object ball altogether. This is especially true if you're aiming for, say, a thin hit to the left or the right of the object ball. The way out of such a predicament is to anticipate the curve of the cue ball, that is, how much it will curve away from the object ball, and then adjust your point of aim by aiming to hit more of the object ball. The best advice I can give is to get on the table and put this theory to test. The logic of the proposition will hit you right between the eyes.

Thus far we've discussed the effects of Natural and Reverse English. Now let's look into the cause, that is, how the cue ball must be hit to bring

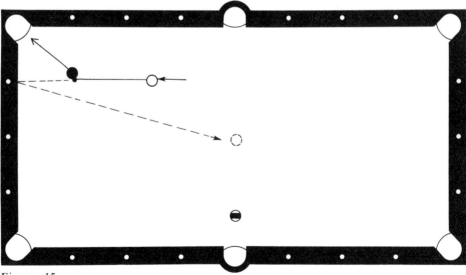

Figure 15

about these desired effects. If you hit the cue ball to the right of its vertical axis, the cue ball will spin to its left, or counter-clockwise. If you hit the cue ball to the left of the vertical axis, it's going to spin to the right, or clockwise. Understanding these effects, you must be very careful how you apply English. As a rule of thumb, I've always felt that a cue tip's width to the right—or left, or bottom, or top—is about as far as you ought to go if you're a beginner. Anything further is inviting miscues, and miscues in pocket billiards spell trouble, with a capital T. Sometimes one miscue can provide your opponent the break he's waiting for to run the table and he'll grab all the cabbage.

So for beginners I suggest just Normal English at the start, moving into the more complicated aspects as your skills develop.

Now let's talk about Follow English and Draw English. Your ability to draw and follow will determine the strength of your position play, and without a sound position game you have only two chances in pocket billiards: none and absolutely none. There's no substitute for good position. If you're a good shotmaker, I mean a tremendous shotmaker, you might make up for a lacking in cue ball control, but that's doing it the hard way. If you're not a particularly good shotmaker, cue ball control has to be your strong suit. But if I had my druthers, I'd druther have good cue ball control than shotmaking every time. Except for the speed of your stroke, which we'll get into later on, I'd have to say that the ability to execute the Draw and Follow—especially Draw English—is the most important factor in pocket billiards.

To impart Follow English, stroke the cue ball above its horizontal axis, and use a good follow-through stroke. For Draw English, do the opposite; stroke the cue ball below the center and snap your cue to draw it back. That's why it's called Draw English. Again, assuming your stroke is solid, don't go more than a cue tip's width above or below the horizontal axis.

THE DRAW SHOT: TO THE REAR, MARCH

The encouraging sign to look for as you apply Follow English is that the cue ball is following—moving forward. A Draw will make the ball move backward after striking the object ball, a sorta to the rear march gizmo. If you can pull that cue ball back like it's walking, the eyeballers will be impressed. They'll figure you're a shark for sure, because even eyeballers know that the Draw is the most difficult of all English shots.

The Draw is about the only situation I would recommend using more than a cue tip's width of English, especially if you have to pull off a real deep Draw shot. Here you have to drop the cue down farther below the center than you usually do for a light Draw. So you would be using Extreme English. On a Draw shot you not only lower your bridge, but you must lower the butt of the cue so it will be as near to level with the tip as possible. This is only common sense, because if the butt is elevated in the back, you're not going to get the proper balance and push on a Draw shot that you will if the butt is lower. Going to baseball again, with the butt up in the back, the player would be like a batter swinging down on the ball. You're a cinch to ground out to the pitcher.

There's another common-sense factor in lowering your Draw hit on the cue ball. Most of the weight of the cue ball is above the spot where you strike it, so, naturally, the lower you strike the cue ball, the better you compensate for the uneven distribution of the weight. Even my mother-in-law would understand that kind of logic.

I want to be sure that you understand the perils involved in the Draw. I think the late Ralph Greenleaf, the greatest World Tournament champion of all time, could execute the Draw better than anybody I've ever seen. I'll tell you what, Greenleaf miscued on the Draw once every 19,000 times. I was never around when he miscued once. If he saw he had to go for a Draw, a deep Draw, he called time out and walked over to the table where they had the water and the powder and the towels. He would pick up a file and rub the cue tip against the file ever so gently to make sure the tip was loose. Then he would chalk the tip, light and even. Then he would shoot out the lights. Your cue tip has to be loose to get perfect execution on the Draw. You'll realize this as your game improves.

There's one more pitfall involved in Draws. Usually you don't run into trouble if you can level your cue stick, but if you're shooting a Draw when the cue ball is near a rail, or if you're forced to stroke over an object ball, that's something else. You compensate for the difficult angle by elevating the butt end of the cue in order to draw on the cue ball. Here the horizontal axis of the cue ball is parallel to the angle of the elevation of the cue. Draw an imaginary line between the angle of the cue as it bisects the cue ball. If you stroke down on the cue ball, that is, if you hit it below its horizontal axis, you will draw the ball. You will run into this kind of shot a zillion times in any game. The situation is almost identical where you have to stroke over an object ball. The difference, however, is in the type of bridge. When the ball is near the rail, the conventional rail bridge is used, whereas in shooting over another ball a firmer bridge is required. The secret to this bridge is in the fingers. They must be planted firmly on the table to give your stroke a foundation. If the fingers aren't firm and steady, you won't get a good even hit on the cue ball and it will stagger like a drunk. These types of shots and bridges call for lots and lots of practice.

SPLITTING HAIRS ON THE SHORT DRAW

One more important phase of English is the Stop Shot (see Figure 16). It's the shot you go to when you want to stop the ball dead on a dime after striking an object ball for position. It's a tough shot to pull off because everything depends on your stroke. The cue must be level, as level as possible; the aim on the cue ball must be dead center; and the stroke must be a definite snap stroke. A good Stop Shot can be a tremendous asset. One time I won a bundle on a Stop Shot proposition. Some mooch bet me a zillion I couldn't stop the cue ball on a hair. He gave me three shots but I made it in two. I split that hair so nice I could have combed it.

Well, scholars, that's English—poolroom style. In the poolroom, English is just about another language. If you know English, you can really make those balls talk. At the start English can be as puzzling as Latin, or Greek or even Swahili, which is what they talk in Zanzibar. But once you master billiards English, controlling the cue ball for position will be as easy as ABC.

You know a couple of years ago *Esquire*, the big magazine, got ahold of me in New York and asked me to do an article on the variations of English. They sent a jillion editors and writers with me to Bob McGirr's poolroom on Eighth Avenue and they all took notes while I talked. You never saw anything like it. If the fuzz comes in during the lecture, they got to figure it's a bookie operation with all those Square Johns writing in those little notebooks.

Well, they call the article "Proper English," by Professor Minnesota Fats. They even dressed me up in one of those tuxedos—the monkey suit the fun players wear in the big tournaments—and they ran a picture of me in the tux with the article. When my mother-in-law saw it, she said, "Oh, thank the Lord, Rudolf has joined the church." It was unbelievable beyond compare. But when the lecture was over, the head mahah of *Esquire* came over and told me, "Fat Man, I think we will have to print your instructions just the way you gave them—in your own words. I didn't know pool could be so technical but the way you explained it you made it sound simple." So I said to this big mahah, "Listen, the only thing I would have to do to teach in the colleges and universities would be to brush up on the conversation."

The only way in the world you will understand my kind of English is if you have a natural talent or aptitude for pool. If you have it, you'll know after a while because the tough shots will come easier. If you don't have a natural bent for the game, you'll never have it. You can teach some suckers the works and they can't sink a ball in an ocean. It's like the Cherry Sisters from back in the olden days. They called the Cherry Sisters singers, which

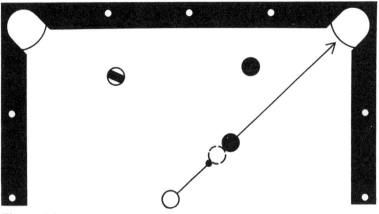

Figure 16a

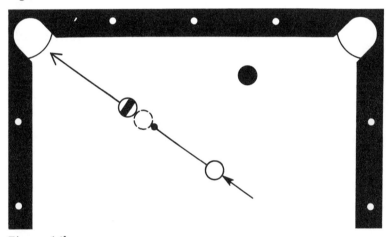

Figure 16b

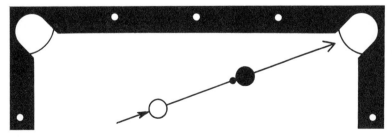

Figure 16c

was all right except they couldn't sing. No matter how they cut it, the dolls couldn't sing. It's the same thing with pool. If you can't master the table, you can't master the table.

Which reminds me, there's one very important form of English which I haven't discussed. It's called Masse, which is a French word. Literally it means to maul—and when you pull off a Masse shot that's exactly what you do to the ball. You maul it, like you were hitting it with a sledgehammer. You can also miscue and maul the table, which many an ambitious beginner has been known to do. So, since I have a lot of friends making a living running poolrooms, I'm not going to give any How To instructions on the Masse. If I did, there would be so many demolished tables the industry might go into a spin. If you reach the point where you figure you're ready to tackle the Masse, ask a top-notch player how it's done. If your game develops to the stage where you can even think about a Masse, you're a candidate for a Ph.D. in pool. It's a shot that even the masters avoid.

To close out the chapter, let's have a refresher course in what has been covered. Read over the following breakdown on the various forms of English and study the illustrations.

NORMAL ENGLISH: Just a touch of English—to the left, right, top or bottom. Master Normal English before you try the more complicated steps.

HIGHER ENGLISH: This means you hit the cue ball a little higher, or a little lower, or more to the left or the right, than you would in Normal English. It's a matter of degree, like finishing grade school and going to high school.

EXTREME ENGLISH: This means just what it says—extreme. Be careful. Be sure that your cue is down in the back when you're using Draw English on a deep draw and hit the cue ball as low as you can. Now if you want Extreme High English, do exactly the opposite. Hit the cue ball as high as you can without missing it completely. Extreme English is a many splendored thing, but if the execution isn't just right you'll blow yourself out of the tub. Tread slowly and carefully.

FOLLOW ENGLISH: This is the opposite of Draw, so your stroke must be the opposite of the Draw stroke. It must have a definite follow-through. If you want the ball to follow just a little, hit it a little high with a follow-through.

TOP HIGH ENGLISH: This is the kind of English you use if you want the ball to follow a great distance, like drive around the table. Hit the cue ball as high as you can.

HIGH RIGHT ENGLISH: You use this English when you want to drive the ball around the table fast and to the right. You hit it high and right. The secret is in the speed of your stroke, which we will discuss in a following chapter.

HIGH LEFT ENGLISH: The very opposite of High Right. Everything's the same except you hit the ball high and left.

DRAW RIGHT ENGLISH: This is what I sometimes call Downtown English. Cue the ball near the bottom on the right side, using Natural English in the direction of your shot. You would go to this shot if you wanted to draw the ball around the table. Actually, this is a combination of Natural and Extreme English. Remember, the key is in the snap of your stroke. Make it snappy.

DRAW LEFT ENGLISH: The opposite of Draw Right. Cue the ball low and left with a good snap to make the ball draw.

SHORT DRAW ENGLISH (or Stop Shot) : You split the medium on this one. If you hit the cue ball high, it would follow; but if you hit it low, it would draw. So you hit it dead center with a level cue and a definite follow-through.

End of refresher.

CANNONBALL AND BBs

The most important thing about English is knowing when to use it (or when not to use it). You can kill your game by using English unnecessarily and sometimes you can ruin yourself by using too much English.

There's a player down in Houston by the name of Cannonball. He's one of the finest Negro players in the game, but his weakness is that he puts too much English on the ball, which is why they call him Cannonball. When he's shooting with that assault-and-battery stroke of his, you would think somebody was setting off firecrackers. He hits the balls like he wants to hurt them. He's a Fancy Dan with the stick, and that's a crying shame because it takes away from his game.

One night a few years ago I was in Houston and he came up and introduced himself. "I'm Cannonball," he said. "I'd like to play you for a stake, Fat Man." I watched him run a few and he was using enough English to be in Parliament or maybe on television. So we went to the table and just before the break I said to Cannonball, I said, "My boy, I understand they call you Cannonball." And he said that was what they called him. So I said, "Well, Mr. Cannonball, when I get through with you tonight, they'll call you BB." Then I beat him 15 straight for the gelt.

Take a lesson from my pal, Cannonball. Don't use too much English. It's murder. And don't be discouraged if it comes slow. English is something you've always got to work on. Even the top pros run into trouble with their English sometimes. I know. Some nights I put a million dollars' worth of English on a ball and only a nickel's worth takes. That's when I know I need practice.

CHAPTER 22

The Object of the Game: Pocketing Balls

One of the cardinal rules of baseball is that you've got to keep your eye on the ball at all times. It's one of baseball's Ten Commandments. It's really a very simple proposition because if you take your eye off the ball, you're not going to see it and if you can't see the ball, there's no way on earth you're going to hit it. It would be like playing Blind Man's Buff or Pin the Tail on the Donkey.

The secret of success with all the great hitters in baseball is that they all had great eyes. Ted Williams had such tremendous eyes that one time they brought this fantastic scientific machine out to Fenway Park in Boston and they put Williams through a lot of eye tests. They found out that his eyes were so strong that he could almost count the stitches on the ball when the pitcher came in with it. No wonder he whacked so many out of the park.

Now while this book has nothing to do with baseball, the importance of the eyes is just as crucial in billiards, especially pocket billiards. In carom or cushion billiards, the most important factor is controlling the cue ball; therefore, you look at the cue ball last before you shoot. However, in pocket billiards, the object of the game is to pocket the object ball, so the last ball you look at before you stroke is the object ball. But at the same time you must control that cue ball for position. This is what I call splitting the medium. It's the meat and potatoes of pocket billiards. This splitting of the medium is just one more reason why pocket billiards is one of the most difficult games to master and why there is more margin for error in pockets than there is in carom or cushion billiards.

The secret is in the eyes. First, take careful aim at the spot where

194 ●

you want to hit the cue ball. Then, as you take the warm-up strokes, shift your vision from the cue ball to the object ball, concentrating on the spot where you want to hit the object ball. Thus you are aiming at two points, the cue ball and the object ball, and to pull off the shot you've got to have good eyes, tremendous power of concentration and lots of tranquilizers. That's what I call the warm-up shots—the tranquilizers. After taking dead aim on the spot where you want to hit the cue ball, you go for the tranquilizers. Take as many warm-up strokes as you need to feel sure that your aim on the cue ball is correct and, assuming that your stance and your bridge are right on all counts, shift your vision to the object ball and where you want to hit it. The warm-up stroke will steady your stroke, and as you shift your vision back and forth between the two points of aim, the cue ball and object ball, these two objects become trained in your line of sight.

Stroke your cue stick back and forth, back and forth, without actually hitting the ball. It will steady you and sorta serve as a narcotic for your concentration. If you've ever seen a top player at the table, you'll know what I mean. Some of the champions take so many warm-ups they look like just another beginner at the table. Some are so methodical they might take as many as a dozen warm-ups. Myself, I usually take two or three, sometimes four. That's all I need because I'm a fast thinker and a very fast shooter. But the actual number of warm-ups you take won't make or break your game because it's a relative factor. Some players just happen to need more warm-ups than others. It might be a psychological factor. Some of them use the warm-ups as a crutch to settle their nerves and some do it from habit. Take Tuscaloosa Squirrelly (Marshall Carpenter, of Tuscaloosa, Alabama). He's one of my top proteges and one of the best One Pocket players around today. But you should see him on those warm-ups. He might take 15 before he strokes the ball. Squirrelly shifts his eyes from the cue ball to the object ball, back and forth, back and forth, dozens of times. And when he's shifting his vision like that he wrinkles his forehead up and down, up and down, like a neon sign going off and on. It drives me crazy, but that's not the reason I gave him the nickname Squirrelly. This is how he concentrates to make sure of his shot.

What Squirrelly does at the very last second before he shoots, I mean when he's confident of his stroke and his aim on the cue ball, is shift his vision and his concentration to his point of aim on the object ball. This adjustment must be mastered if you want to be a solid stick at the table, and the only advice I can give on this point is that old cliche: PRACTICE. Practice this adjustment of vision and concentration again and again, because by doing so you become more aware of the relation between your two points of aim, cue ball and object ball. And the more you practice it, the more the logic of the game becomes obvious. Just as you make sure that these two points of aim are trained in your line of sight, so, too, will you train your eye and your mind to recognize the relation between the two points and, more important, the many angles involved.

HIT 'EM SOFT—LIKE THEY WERE EGGS

So now you're ready to run some balls. But first a final warning about two dangers. Watch how you hit the balls. Don't whack 'em like you're trying to put them in orbit. Hit them real gentle, like they were babies. I'd say that 99 out of 100 shots can be pulled off with a soft, gentle stroke, like a surgeon's touch. Never wham, bam the balls. Hit 'em sure and soft, like you were handling eggs.

The second danger is English. Remember I said eight out of ten shots in pocket billiards can be made without using English. So, as a rule of thumb for beginners, I suggest staying away from English altogether until your game and your confidence warrant it.

The most basic shot in pocket billiards is a situation where you have a dead aim on the pocket, I mean straightaway. The thing to remember here is that old geometric proposition—the shortest distance between two points is a straight line. When there's a straight path to the pocket, hit the cue ball in the center, unless you're playing for position on the following shot.

The next proposition is the angle on a shot. A lot of beginners fritz up easy shots because they don't take time to study the angle. Always take your time and look before you shoot. The best insurance on an angle shot is to draw an imaginary line in your mind from the pocket to the object ball and then to hit the object ball at the point where the imaginary line bisects the object ball. If you execute this theory, you'll drive the ball right into the pocket.

Of course, your judgment is necessary on just how hard or soft your stroke must be. Sometimes you can hit the ball too hard and knock it out of line with the pocket. This is why I encourage the soft, gentle stroke. On the other hand, you can shoot too soft and not give the object ball enough juice to make it to the pocket. These are factors that require a little skull work. You've got to think out each shot. Some days you might shoot a hundred times and never see the same shot twice, while other days you might run into the same type of shot a zillion times. That's why pool is the thinking man's game. The thinking aspects might appear difficult for the beginner, just as algebra does the first week in high school, but as your game progresses and your knowledge of it increases, you'll find that experience will provide the answers to angles and speed of stroke. We'll talk about the speed of stroke factor later on, but now let's get the right angle on angles.

In Figure 17 we illustrate the most basic example fo hitting the object ball. Since the line of aim from the cue ball to the pocket bisects the object

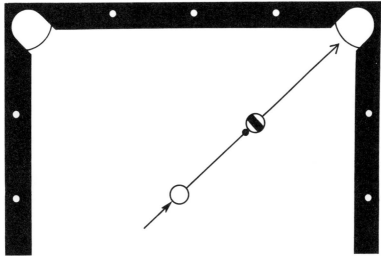

Figure 17

ball, there is no angle. The shot is straight and direct. Use center-ball stroking for a full hit on the object ball to drive it straight ahead for a split of the pocket. Simple. But there's more to the game than that. If it was that simple, John-John Kennedy might be the world champion.

Moving to Figure 18, we find the object ball in the same spot on the

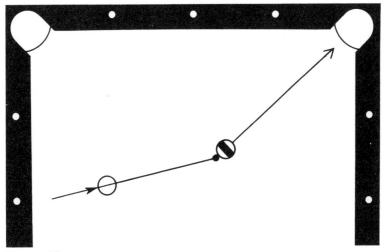

Figure 18

table but the cue ball off to the left. Therefore, the angle shot is "on." To determine the angle, draw that imaginary line from pocket to object ball and another imaginary line from the object ball to the cue ball. The point of aim on the object ball must be at that spot where the imaginary lines bisect the object ball. To pull off this shot, the secret is in the "hit" on the object ball.

To illustrate the different "hits," in Figure 19 we demonstrate the degrees of these hits on the object ball. The illustrations run from a full-hit

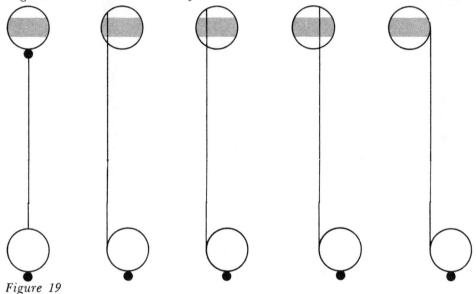

Figure 19

(some call it full-ball) to three-quarters, one-half, one-quarter and, the most difficult of all angle shots, the feathered or thin hit. The important thing for beginners to note is that the cue ball is hit with a center-ball stroke each time.

Now in Figure 18, the angle illustrated here requires a three-quarter right "hit" on the object ball, and if you can pull off the third-quarter contact, you'll pocket that ball as easy as breathing. The rub is scoring your "hit" just right. If you're off on your "hit," you'll drive the ball away from the pocket and lose your turn at the table. Again, the answer is practice.

An example of a narrowing angle is found in Figure 20, where the object ball remains in the same position but the cue ball is farther left. Again, draw those imaginary lines and, sticking to the center-ball stroke, aim for a one-half right "hit" on the object ball.

In Figure 21, the angle is more pronounced but the procedure is the same; only the "hit" on the object ball lessens. This shot calls for a one-quarter right "hit." The most extreme illustration of the angle shot is shown in Figure 22. This one calls for a feather touch on the object ball, hitting it razor thin to the right. If your "hit" is on target, the ball will ease

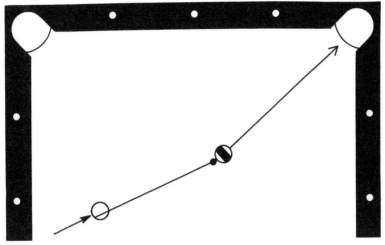

Figure 20

into the pocket. This is the toughest of all angle shots and requires a real soft stroke and a thin "hit." I mention this to stress. the importance of the soft stroke. Never assault the balls if you want to master the table.

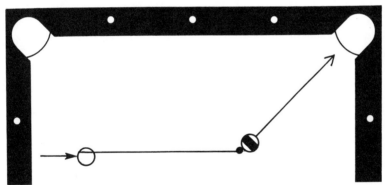

Figure 21

The angle shot, of course, is "on" at any angle up to 180 degrees, which would be a straight line.

The one simple rule to remember on angle shots is that center-ball stroking remains constant, whereas the "hit" on the object ball varies according to the angle. There is an exception and that would be where English is involved.

● 199

THE MARGIN OF ERROR

Now let's reverse the approach. In Figure 23, the cue ball remains in the same spot on the table while the location of the object ball varies. In this case, the distance between the object ball and the pocket becomes the

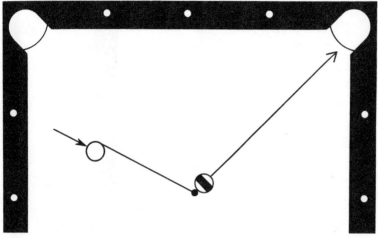

Figure 22

prime factor. If the ball is close to the pocket, a margin of error is permissible. However, the farther the object ball from the pocket, the less the permissible margin of error. This is only logical because the longer the roll of the object ball, the greater the chance for it to roll out of line.

The answer to this one is getting the right "hit" on the object ball. The best way to perfect your "hit" is to practice the various degrees of contact with the object ball. And practice them again and again. That's what this game is all about. Practice to make perfect.

In Figure 23, for example, the first ball could be pocketed, despite a too full hit. This is because it is close to the pocket and a margin of error is permissible. However, too full a hit on the second and third balls would drive them away from the pocket and into the rail. Spot object balls in the different spots as shown in Figure 23 and practice your "hits." As a beginner, you'll hardly score the right "hit" two in a row, but the experience will teach you a lesson in the advantages of scoring the right "hit" in the right spot. And practice will perfect your "hits" on the object ball.

Two other factors in hitting the object ball are the influence of English on the object ball and the proper techniques for hitting an object ball on the rail.

There are two rules to remember in employing English. First, you use English when you want to throw the ball. Second, use English when you're playing for position and you want to make the cue ball take Natural English, or Reverse English, off a cushion. Stick to center-ball stroking otherwise.

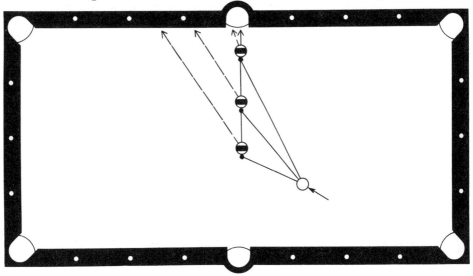

Figure 23

The thing to remember about English is that English applied to the left will throw the object ball right and, conversely, Right English will throw the object ball left. So if you want to use English, you must allow for it on your point of aim. And don't forget that the throw of the object ball increases in proportion to the distance to the pocket.

Diagram 24 is a good example of how the throw of the object ball increases in proportion to the length of the shot. Here the distance is relatively long so the throw of the object ball would be greater. Actually, the proper execution of this shot requires no English, no English at all. If you hit the object ball with the proper "hit," you'll drive it right into the pocket. However, if you hit the ball at the same spot with Left English, the ball will be thrown into the rail on the right; and Right English will throw it into the rail on the left. Here we illustrate the danger of ill-applied English. It can wreck your game. So again I say, stay away from English until you learn to pocket balls. Then, as your game progresses and your understanding of the theory of pocket billiards increases, the advantages and disadvantages of English will become as obvious as a pretty doll, as plain as two and two equals four.

Now let's take to the rail, which is a place you'll find yourself time and time again on a pool table. One of the worst feelings is to have your opponent put the cue ball on the rail and say, "Your shot." One time I'm playing Handsome Danny (Danny Jones, of Atlanta, Georgia) for a jillion

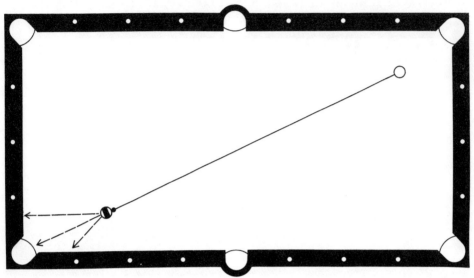

Figure 24

and he keeps leaving me on the rail. So finally he cracks smart and wants to know, "How do you like it on the rail, Fat Man?" So I said, "My boy, I was born on the rail." And I was.

AN UPTOWN WORD—"SIMULTANEOUSLY"

This lecture has to do with the proper techniques for pocketing object balls left on the rail. The average shot on the rail looks impossible unless you understand the procedure. It's really very simple. In the situation shown in Figure 25, employ a center-ball stroke while aiming to hit the object ball and the cushion simultaneously. That's an uptown word one of the college deans taught me when I played an exhibition at a university in Ohio. It means at the same time. So aim to hit the object ball and the cushion at the same time.

The pitfall on this shot would be getting too full a hit on the object ball. The results would be disastrous, because a too full hit would bounce the ball away from the rail and, therefore, out of line with the pocket. But the right "hit" will send the ball hugging the rail and down into the corner pocket.

Stepping the theory up a level, we illustrate the use of English to pocket a ball on the rail. In Figure 26, the cue ball and object ball are almost in a straight line, so English is necessary to throw the object ball. Therefore, aim for the cushion with a razor-thin hit on the object ball and

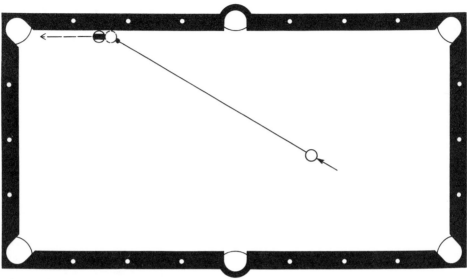

Figure 25

use Right English to throw the object ball to the left. If your "hit" is right and your English proper, the ball will snuggle up to the cushion and travel down to the corner pocket like it was a yo-yo.

Funny thing about those rail shots. They puzzle a lot of people. I was

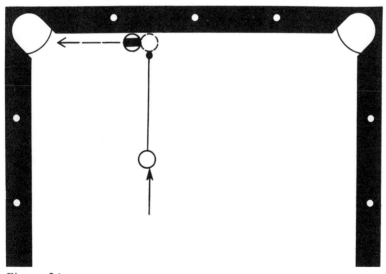

Figure 26

● *203*

playing a two-day exhibition at Kaufman's Department Store, a fabulous place in Pittsburgh, and after my first show a business tycoon came up and asked me to show him how to pull off a shot with the ball frozen on the rail, as in Figure 25. I showed him how simple it was and then he tried it. He caught on right away and made the shot three out of five times.

The next day he was back in the store and smiling like he knew who was going to win the Irish Sweepstakes. He told me, "Fat Man, I played at my club last night and thanks to that rail shot you showed me, I won five martinis." Then he asked me to show him a few other shots but I said, "Hold on, my boy, if I show you too much you're liable to become an alcoholic."

CHAPTER 23

The Speed of the Stroke Is Secret of Success

Before we hold graduation exercises, we must discuss one more factor in pocket billiards—the speed of the stroke. It's the meat of the coconut.

No one can teach you the speed of the stroke. It's something you must learn yourself. You can get all kinds of instruction and advice and know-how from the greatest pool player who ever lived, but when you get to the table you have to do it yourself. It's like the poem—I am the master of my fate, I am the captain of my soul. That might be dramatizing the point, but the naked truth is that you and only you can master your speed of stroke. And how well you master it will determine how well you play this game.

What it boils down to is *feel*. You've got to have a *feel* of the situation to know what you're doing when you stroke the ball. All the great players had it. I guess you would call it a sixth sense. If you have it, you'll know it. If you don't have it, maybe you should try ping-pong. Without it you're never going to win a grape playing this game.

Of course, it's not something you develop overnight. It's something that will come as your game progresses, but the progress of your game will depend on how natural your pool sense is.

Let me give you another baseball example. Sandy Koufax is the greatest pitcher in the game today. No doubt about it. He has all the natural ability, the fast ball, the good curve, the change-up, the slider and, of course, the heart. But five or six years ago, Sandy Koufax was just another journeyman left-hander in the National League. He won his share and he lost his share and nobody foresaw greatness in his future.

But one day in 1959, the guy who was catching Koufax said, in the smallest kind of small talk, "Sandy, why don't you take a little off your curve?" Koufax thought it was worth a try so he began "taking a little off the curve ball." The result is that Koufax skyrocketed from just an average pitcher to the greatest pitcher the game has seen since Bob Feller, I guess.

Koufax is a good example of the advantages of taking something off a pitch, but the kid who quarterbacked Notre Dame in 1965 needed to put a little something "on" his passes. He didn't do it and Notre Dame lost a couple of games, especially that crucial game to Michigan State.

Everybody raved how the Michigan State line held Notre Dame to almost nothing in yardage. But in the post-mortem, the Michigan State secondary let the cat out of the bag. They said they were able to play the Notre Dame passer loose because game films had shown that the Notre Dame quarterback lobbed the ball. He was lofting the ball instead of firing it, and that one factor allowed the secondary to play him loose. The result was a calamity for Notre Dame. Michigan State intercepted passes all afternoon, a crucial one in the end zone.

I cite these two examples to push home a major point in developing your speed of stroke. Sometimes you've got to put on a little more speed and sometimes you've got to take something off. This is where pool sense comes in. The *feel* is actually your judgment, your knowing when to do it. Until you develop this *feel* you're never going to master this game, especially position play which is the heart of pocket billiards.

While the speed of stroke cannot be taught, we can, however, offer some rules for the road that should help in developing your judgment of speed. If you can understand the theory of everything we've discussed thus far—the value of center-ball stroking, the execution of the Follow and Draw shots and the Stop Ball, you are prepared, theoretically at least, to judge the degree of juice to give the cue ball in a given situation.

THE JUICE MUST BE JUST RIGHT

The most crucial aspect of the speed of stroke is the application of English. So let's discuss English. We know that (1) English influences the path of the cue ball to the object ball; (2) English will throw the object ball; (3) English increases the speed of the cue ball when it caroms off a cushion and (4) English has a better chance to work on a soft stroke. Conclusion: The effectiveness of English depends on how much juice you give to your stroke. The secret is, again, knowing how much juice to use. The answer should come with practice. You can't get enough practice in this game. Like the apple and the doctor, practice will keep old man trouble away from your pool game. I guess the best advice I can offer on practice is that you become addicted to it.

I think a good practice routine might be to set up an angle shot near a pocket and, as you pocket the ball, move the cue ball back further from the object ball. Try pocketing the object ball by three methods: (1) with a center-ball stroke, (2) with Left English and (3) with Right English. By such a process of elimination you will discover not only the proper way to stroke the cue ball, but, more important, the proper speed to use in a given situation. Try this theory again and again, moving the object ball and cue ball all over the table. The possibilities are unlimited. And so is the experience.

Such a practice routine would enable you to develop a skill in pocketing balls—but gaining desired position for a following shot would be something else. Here a more advanced use of English is necessary, involving, sooner or later, the use of the cushions.

The Draw, Follow and Stop Ball shots are keys to position, but the cushions can be a port in a storm when you want to move the cue ball into the proper spot for a subsequent shot. But, again, the speed of the stroke is the big thing.

For example: A cue ball with Natural English imparted is going to step up speed coming off a cushion, so the amount of juice you give the cue ball will have a say as to just how much speed that cue ball will add. If you whack it too hard, you're going to roll too far, maybe three or four feet farther from the desired position. Some guys whack the cue ball so hard that it is liable to roll clean off the table and over to the lunch counter.

Another thing to remember about a ball hit into a cushion with Natural English is that the English will widen the angle where the cue ball leaves the cushion. So the speed of your stroke has to be adjusted for the desired difference. The big fact to keep in mind is that English works best on a soft stroke, so therefore the softer the stroke, the wider the angle. But the shoe would be on the other foot, so to speak, if you wanted to narrow the angle coming off the cushion. In that case you would go to Reverse English, but the speed of the stroke would remain the major factor. No matter what the shot, the speed of your stroke is always the meat of the coconut.

I'll tell you what it's like. It's like Goldilocks and the Three Bears and the porridge proposition: too hot, too cold and just right. Well, on a table, your speed of stroke will depend on how well you know how to heat up the porridge. Nobody can do it for you. You're on your own.

I've recommended practice before but I'll recommend it again: Practice. You can't get enough of it. Then there's concentration. Keep your mind on what you're doing and your mind will tell you when you can let go on a shot, like a prize fighter throwing a punch. A good fighter knows when to throw the bomb and he knows when to duck the bomb. They call it instinct. In this game we call it pool sense or a *feel* of the situation.

● 207

It's like Daniel Boone in the woods; he knows what to do. Or a cab driver in New York; he can spin through that traffic like he's threading a needle. You take a country boy from a place like Dowell, Illinois (my home town) and put him in Chicago and he can't find his way to the bus station. But you take somebody off Broadway and drop him in Dry Prong, Louisiana (yeah, there's a town by that name) and he'll end up a lost ball in high weeds.

In pool, instinct is hard to define in exact terms. You can call it what you want—*feel,* savvy, pool sense, the smarts or the noodle. But if you don't have it, you can play this game forever and never master it.

There's one more piece of advice I'd like to pass on: Develop confidence in your game. Believe in yourself because it helps you keep your nerve. That's the most important single thing a pool player needs: nerve. You need it at the table when you've got to come up with the "big" shot. And you need it when the other fellow is off on a high run. Don't panic. Keep your head and wait until his luck runs out. Then you get up and shoot out the lights.

Lastly, play the game for the fun you get out of it. Don't get too good or you might end up like I did—a top money player. In the olden days everybody wanted a piece of the Fat Man, like I was the fastest gun in town or something. But over the years I whacked out so many of them that after a while I couldn't get a nickel's worth of action.

CHAPTER 24

Key to Long Runs: Combinations, Kisses and Bank Shots

The most important thing to remember about combination shots is that they're in order only when a better shot is not available. The good thing about combination shots is that they can be the way out when you're in trouble at the table. No matter how skillful a player might be, he's sure to find himself in trouble during a run in Pocket Billiards and often the combination shot is the only way out.

Therefore, you should understand combination shots and be able to recognize almost immediately if the combination is "on." If it isn't "on," forget it and look for something else, or, as a last resort, play a safety. Sometimes a player, determined to pull off a combination that is not "on," will miss and in so doing spread the balls all over the table—and probably open the door for his opponent to launch a good run. A bungled combination shot can be costly. So beware.

To understand combination shots a player must understand the "throw" of the balls. This is the same principle as the effect of English, in that Left English will throw the object ball right and vice versa. Likewise, on a combination shot, if the key ball (see Figure 27) is hit left, the called, or object, ball is thrown right, or if the key ball is hit right, the called, or object, ball will be thrown left.

In Figure 28, the balls are frozen and, although the object ball appears headed for the rail, it can be driven into the pocket by hitting the key ball, or first ball in the combination, to the right of center. This will

The Bank Shot and Other Great Robberies

throw the called ball (second ball) to the left and into the pocket. It's simple logic when you get down to it. This combination is possible even if the balls were not frozen. If the balls are separated, but by no more than a quarter of an inch, the only adjustment is that the first ball, or key ball, must be hit a little closer to the center. Practice on this type of shot will improve your judgment for such situations.

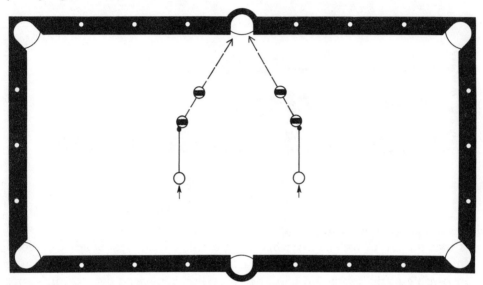

Figure 27

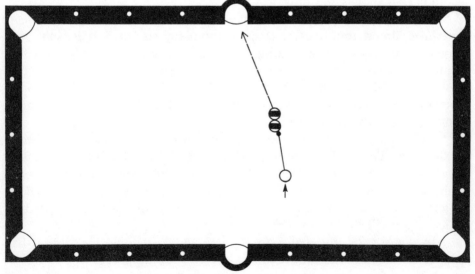

Figure 28

210 ●

To illustrate a similar yet different combination, in Figure 29 the called, or object, ball seems headed for the rail. Yet, by hitting the key ball on the left, the called ball is thrown right and into the pocket. Again, practice will make perfect on these types of combination shots.

In Figure 30, the combination is somewhat removed from the pocket, so therefore we must allow for the distance involved. In this shot, with the

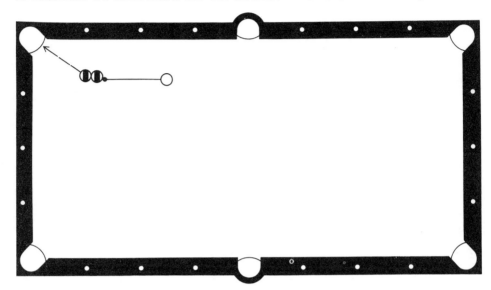

Figure 29

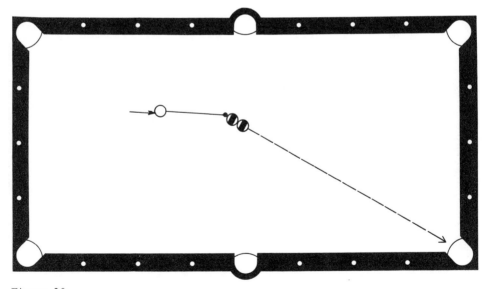

Figure 30

balls frozen, use Right English and a slow speed for a one-quarter left hit on the key ball. This will throw the called, or object, ball to the right and into the pocket.

The next logical step would be to illustrate the application of a combination shot with more than two balls. This is shown in Figure 31 with three balls. This shot is "on" because the key ball (nearest cue ball) is in the right position. The key ball hits the middle ball on the right, throwing the called ball to the left and into the pocket.

Moving ahead to a five-ball shot, in Figure 32 the key ball is the third, or middle, ball and it is lying in the proper position. The shot is definitely "on." When the chain reaction gets down to the key, or middle, ball, the middle ball will hit the next ball on the left, throwing the called ball to the right and into the pocket. The key to this shot being "on" is that the key (middle) ball is in the proper position.

A TRICK SHOT WORTH NOTING

I think the best example of how far combinations can go, theoretically anyway, is to illustrate a trick shot involving ten balls. See Figure 33. A player would of course never find this type of shot in a match, but the principle involved here is worth noting.

Notice that the nine balls in the semicircle are all frozen and in proper position for a combination in the corner pocket. Also note that the one other object ball in the foreground makes it impossible for a shot into

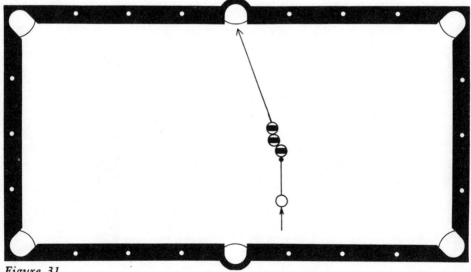

Figure 31

the circle. Again, this situation would never come up in a match, but with a center-ball stroke and good speed, the first ball, driven into the first ball in the semicircle with a full-ball hit, will trigger a chain reaction that will end up driving the last ball in the semicircle straight ahead into the corner pocket. Try it. It'll be a great trick shot to show your friends at the neighborhood room and it will give you an idea of the possibilities of combination shots.

However, combination shots will never be learned from a book. The

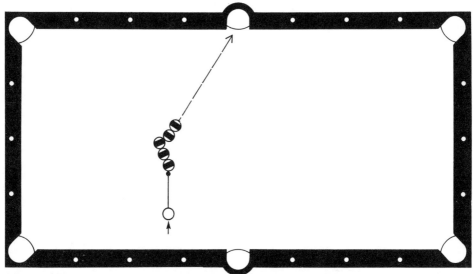

Figure 32

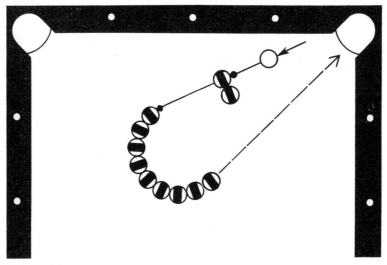

Figure 33

surest way to master this phase of the game is practice. Go to the table and set up the shots yourself and practice, practice, practice until you've learned all the combinations. There are zillions of them.

A kiss shot is actually a carom, meaning the ball may kiss from one object ball to another. It's the opposite of a combination shot because on combinations you drive one ball into another to pocket a called ball. On a kiss shot, the object is to make the called ball carom off an object ball. Sometimes the carom can be so light that it's like kissing your wife on the run. That's where the name comes from. The hit can be so light it's just a kiss.

The most basic theory in kiss shots is called line measurement. If a line drawn from the middle of a pocket runs between two balls (Figure 34), the shot is "on." If the line doesn't run between the two balls, the shot is "off." To pocket this shot, hit the cue ball with a center-ball stroke, driving the first ball into the second ball, from which it will kiss off and into the corner pocket. The line measurement theory can serve as a compass, providing an accurate estimate of the possibilities of pulling off successful kiss shots, no matter where the balls are located. Remember, if that line from the middle of the pocket passes between the two balls, you're in business.

In Figure 35, the ball nearest the cue ball can be pocketed with a kiss off the second ball. A three-quarter full hit on the pocket side of the second ball will send the object ball down the table and into the corner pocket. For the umpteenth time, the proving grounds of these theories are practice sessions. Get on the table and try it.

A more extreme application of the kiss shot is illustrated in Figure 36. Here the cue ball is relatively removed from the two object balls, but the kiss shot is "on." Using a center-ball stroke with fast speed, aim for a full

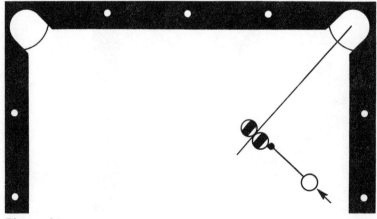

Figure 34

hit on the object ball and a thin kiss off the second ball. Result: the object ball caroms off to the left and into the corner pocket.

For an illustration of a three-ball kiss shot, see Figure 37. The first ball, nearest to cue ball, is the called ball. Drive it into the middle ball, kissing off the second ball and into the corner pocket.

Although it may sound repetitious, I must urge you to practice these theories and suggestions on the table. Set up every possible kiss shot and then see how many times you can successfully execute the shot. By trial and error the principles involved in this phase of the game will come through

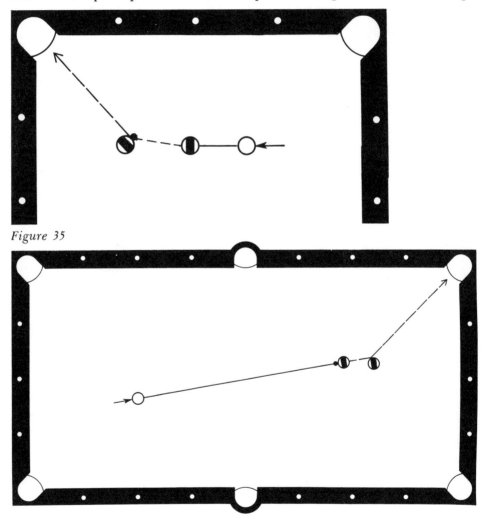

Figure 35

Figure 36

to you like a full moon, provided the Russians haven't gotten up there first.

YOU CAN ALWAYS BANK ON A BANK

This brings us to the final section of this chapter—bank shots. Although bank shots are seldom employed in a game like 14.1 Continuous, I've leaned to the bank shot in my game, One Pocket. This is just one of the many reasons why I contend One Pocket is a more difficult game to play and master.

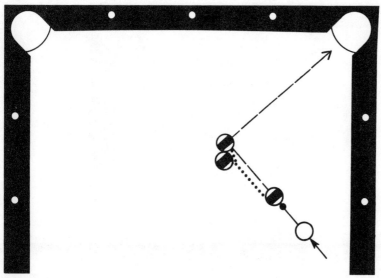

Figure 37

There are two types of bank shots—those without English and bank shots using English. The shot without English, of course, is the easiest to pull off.

To pull off this shot (see Figure 38), draw an imaginary angle from object ball to the far side pocket and the first diamond, which we will call Point A. Draw another imaginary line from Point A to the cross side pocket. From the point where these two lines intersect, draw another imaginary line to the far rail. This spot we will call Point B. Now you're ready. Using a center-ball stroke with medium hard speed, aim the object ball to hit Point B. If you do everything right, the ball will drop in the cross side pocket like it had eyes.

The big factor in bank shots is the stroke. As the angle widens, the stroke must become harder, because a ball approaching the rail at a wide angle will drift off the rail at still a wider angle if the stroke is too soft.

English is used on bank shots with various speeds of stroke on the cue ball to alter the angles, that is, widen or narrow the angles. For example, Natural English on one side of the cue ball will open the natural angle, while Reverse English will narrow the angle. However, the use of this advanced aspect of the game is something a beginner should avoid until, as I've said in previous chapters, he's mastered the art of pocketing balls. Unless you're a Three-Cushion player, the use of English on bank shots is something you should study in postgraduate school.

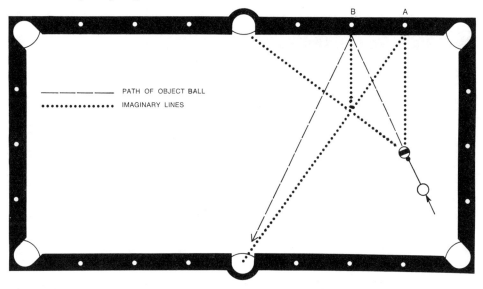

Figure 38

217

CHAPTER 25

The Games

When I was six years old and already hanging around the neighborhood pool hall in Washington Heights in New York City, my mother began to worry about my becoming a juvenile delinquent. "Roodle," she asked, "is that all you're going to do with your life, hang around poolrooms?" I told her, "Yes, ma'am, that's exactly what I'm going to do all my life, hang around poolrooms." And that's all I've done for the past 45 years. I've played in every top room and all the flea joints in my time. If there's a poolroom in this country that I haven't played in, you can bet your next mortgage note that it's just been built. I've played them all.

During that near half century of haunting poolrooms from Bangor to Burbank, I've seen and played every game in the book, plus a few that you won't find in the book. There are a zillion different games with a zillion different variations, but in this chapter on The Games, I'll limit my discussion to pocket billiards.

Billiards, of course, is divided into two general categories, pocket billiards, which is universally referred to as pool, and carom billiards, which is always called billiards. Pocket billiards gets its name from the pockets on the table, while carom billiards is played on a table that has no pockets.

I remember when I was a kid in Washington Heights there was this pal of mine who used to look at the billiards tables and shake his head. "Man," he'd say, "the only guy stupider than the man who built a pool table without pockets has to be the man who would buy one." He was an incurable pocket billiards man who wouldn't acknowledge the game of carom billiards. It's a game that requires great skill and if you start out playing Three Cushions or Bank Cushions, you'll have a tremendous foundation for pocket billiards because you'll know how to control that cue ball.

Unfortunately, carom billiards is a thing of the past. Today so few people play Three Cushions, for example, that there's nobody coming up to replace the old masters as they die off. It's what baseball would be like without the minor leagues. It's as dead as Kelsey. Willie Hoppe, the all-time king of Three Cushions, is gone and there'll never be another player his equal; nor are there any players the match of Hoppe's contemporaries, Johnny Layton and the great Mexican champion Joe Chamaco. Arthur Rubin, of Brooklyn, is the current Three-Cushions champion but nobody's knocking down doors to see Rubin play.

Actually, back in the olden days there was a time when Three Cushions was my best game, but it's been a long time since I had any real action. They still play cushions in the top men's clubs, like the Detroit A.C. and the New York A.C., but it's not like it was 30 years ago and I don't think it's ever going to be.

Another form of caroms that has seen its day is Balkline. It's a tremendous game but it's not for the fast-paced Great Society. Balkline is like grand opera: nobody understands it. Jake Schaefer and after him his son, Jake, Jr., were the best ever at Balkline but Jake, Jr., gave it up because he couldn't make a living at it. Last time I saw Jake, Jr., he wasn't playing Balkline. He was playing the horses.

14.1 TOO SLOW FOR FAST-PACED TIMES

So it's obvious that the most popular side of billiards today is pocket billiards. The traditional championship game of 14.1 Continuous pocket billiards remains the game by which world title honors are decided, but, like Three Cushions and Balkline, 14.1 is on the sunset trail. It's another victim of what the sociologists call the Social Revolution of America.

You read and hear a lot about the Social Revolution every time there's a demonstration in the streets or a big labor strike. These things don't just happen. They're a reflection of the Mass Man's desire for change and, although it's not apparent to the average pool buff or even to the championship caliber players of today, the game of 14.1 Continuous is already a victim of the changing times. The reason? It's too slow and drawn out for today's nonstop society.

They started playing 14.1 when the dolls were wearing babushkas and although everything else has changed with the times (pro football is a good example), 14.1 is still the same old 14.1. In fact, they've made the game longer by increasing the winning total to 150 balls and it just takes too much time to run 150 balls on modern time tables. I don't want to put the rap on the game. I'm just telling you the way it is. It's dead and the body's getting cold. I haven't had any real action in 14.1 in more than 25 years because the game went out when they had cranks on cars. The only section where it is still played in is the East, where a small group manages to keep it alive.

People like to do things in a hurry today; in fact, people *have* to do things in a rush nowadays. It's a compulsive thing. Take the housewives. They don't do things the way their grandmas did. Look at those TV dinners and the instant coffee and the new gimmick, instant potatoes. You just heat it up and the hash is on. Everything today is quick. My wife, Eva-line, comes home from a shopping spree in St. Louis a while back and she takes out this wig. That's another new twist. Wigs. So she puts it on and says, "Rudolf, how do I look?" I said, "Well, to tell you the truth, Eva-line, you look like Martha Washington." She got sore. She claimed the wig would save her a lot of time because she wouldn't have to be running to the beauty parlor two, three times a week. That's all people think about today—saving time. Everything is rush, rush, rush. It's a disease.

It's the very same thing with pool, especially since more dolls are playing the game than ever before. The women love to get out of the kitchen and drive to one of those carpeted rooms in suburbia and get on the table. But they don't want to play long, drawn-out games that take the whole morning or all afternoon because they've got to hurry home to heat up that TV dinner for the old man who has been driving through all that traffic from downtown.

They play Eight Ball, which is the most popular game on earth today, and they play a lot of Nine Ball. The next time you're in a poolroom, see for yourself. That's all the young people play today, Eight Ball and Nine Ball, with the expert players, the top pros, going for my game, One Pocket. So is it any wonder why those fun players who play in the 14.1 tournament in New York can't draw flies? It's not that they're not tremendous players. It's just that 14.1 is too slow for the times. It's been on the way out for 30 years.

Now when I say that Eight Ball (sometimes they call it Black Ball) and Nine Ball are the most popular games, I speak from firsthand, eye-witness experience. I travel 40,000 miles a year for my company. I play in the big department stores and the fabulous new shopping centers in suburbia. I play at dozens of colleges and universities and the big athletic clubs in all the major cities. I even played in a church one time. And everywhere the quickest games are the thing.

When I complete an exhibition, I always invite anyone in the house to play me. There are always lots of comers and 99 out of 100 say they want to play Eight Ball or Nine Ball. It never fails. Once in a jillion times somebody will want to play 14.1. Eight Ball and Nine Ball are what I call The People's Choice. That's the way it is.

Eight Ball is a pretty interesting game for beginners, although it takes some skill to play it well. The skill is required in controlling the cue ball and knowing where your object ball is going. If a player accidentally pockets the eight ball before pocketing the balls of his numerical group he automatically loses the game. The shooter must also call the pocket when shooting the eight ball. These factors take the element of luck out of the game but also enable beginners and novices to see just how well their game is progressing. There's no greater feeling for a beginner when he calls a ball and pockets it, especially on a shot that might be a little tough.

If I'm playing a kid, a young boy or girl, in one of the stores, I like to play Eight Ball because I can fix it so the kid wins. I call the Eight Ball in one pocket and then deliberately bring it off two or three cushions and pocket it at maybe the other end of the table. That means I lose because I failed to pocket my call. Sometimes I purposely sink the eight ball on a combination, which also means I lose. You should see those kids' faces light up. "Gee, Mama," they say, "I beat Minnesota Fats." And Mama gets to feeling so proud that she just might tell the salesman to deliver a table to her rumpus room.

"HEY, GRAMPS, I BEAT THE BUM"

I remember playing an exhibition in a store down in Houston and this friend of mine, a city detective, brought his grandson. The kid was only ten or so, but his grandfather had taught him how to handle a cue stick and the kid was a tremendous shot for his age. So I played him Eight Ball and after he ran three or four, I ran a few and then purposely pocketed the eight on a combination shot. "You win, sonny boy," I told the kid and he yells to his grandpa, "Hey, gramps, I beat the bum, I beat the bum." I got a Christmas card from the grandfather. There was a note saying that the boy kept asking him, "When is that fat bum coming back to town? This time I'm going to hustle him good." I sent the kid Cannonball's address.

If you're looking for suggestions on strategy in Eight Ball, the best advice I can give is to work everything about the key ball, which is the eight. If your opponent breaks and doesn't pocket anything, that means you have a choice of the solids or the stripes. Before you make a choice, study the way the balls are lying and look for a ball near the eight. Then work your run around that ball nearest the eight, making sure to get in position for a shot at the last ball. If everything works, you'll be in a good position to pocket the eight and win the game. If you don't have the choice, you can make the best of the situation by doing the very same thing—picking out a ball near the eight for your last shot to get position on the eight.

Of course, this theory is sound only as long as the balls remain in the same spots. If the eight ball happens to get whacked to the other end of the table, well, you've just got to take another look at the table and pick another ball near the eight. The big thing to keep in mind at all times in Eight Ball is position on the eight.

Nine Ball is a different proposition because there's a lot of luck involved. For example, the nine ball can be, and often is, pocketed on the break and there's no skill to making a ball on the break. This means the lesser player can win, so it's not the kind of game to bet your eating money on. Every year in Johnston City, Illinois, there's a Nine Ball division in the All-Around World Championship, with the best 11 out of 21 deciding the winner. I've seen two tremendous players go to the table and on many an occasion I've seen the lesser player pocket the nine on the break four or five times. That means the better player has to win four or five, just to get even. You get better odds than that playing the horses, and I never played the horses in my life because I didn't think I was getting the best of the odds. Just like you can't win playing the horses, you can't win playing Nine Ball. I know a former world champion who was headed south for a jamboree in Georgia and when he got there he was busted out. What happened? Well, he got talked into a little Nine Ball action with a 17-year-old kid somewhere in the Carolinas or Virginia and the kid thumped him out. The kid didn't belong on the same table with this fellow but the kid won all the money. Why? Because the lesser player is liable to win in Nine Ball.

On a more positive note, the best advice I can give on Nine Ball strategy is to look for combinations on the nine. If you develop a good touch on combination shots, you can win a lot of Nine Ball games. The other advice is advice that holds for all forms of pocket billiards: good position play. Play for position on the nine in Nine Ball the same way you play for position on the eight in Eight Ball.

Another game that's played frequently today (although not as frequently as it was once played) is Rotation. Some of the old-timers call it Chicago because there was a time when Rotation was about all they played in Chicago. Rotation actually went out when they made the tables smaller and the balls got jammed up. This is a good game for beginners because you can combine the principles of Three Cushions, Banks and Caroms with a position game to get to your object ball. I say it's a good game for beginners, but at the same time let me warn you to be careful who you take to the table in Rotation. You're liable to meet a fellow wearing a gas station attendant's uniform who says he works in the next town 17 miles away. Well, that might be true but if he suggests "a friendly little game of Rotation," be careful. He's sure to be a hustler. In Rotation a good player can tell you he's shooting at one pocket and bring that cue ball off a rail or two and sink the object ball on a combination or a kiss. Then he'll say, "Boy, am I lucky today." Well, there's no luck involved in this kind of situation because the gas jockey knows just what he's doing and if you're not careful he'll take your socks.

There are a zillion other games of pocket billiards but Eight Ball, Nine Ball, Rotation and 14.1 (which I'll get to) are the games most played. Games like Baseball Pocket Billiards, Golf Pocket Billiards, Bottle Pocket Billiards, Cowboy Pocket Billiards, Mr. and Mrs., Boy and Girl, Poker, Forty-one and Cribbage are what I call gimmick games. They're like the appetizers at a big cocktail party in, say, Washington or New York. They're something for the Sociables to pass the time playing before the main course is served, so to speak. But you'll hardly find these games played in the average room unless it's a recreation center or a boys' club, and to tell you the truth nowadays you will hardly find them played there. Another game that went out with high-button shoes is Line-Up. I haven't seen it played in years.

SNOOKER BIG IN ENGLAND AND CANADA

American Snooker is another part of pocket billiards, although it's played with more balls, 21 (15 red, 6 colored), and usually on larger tables. But it's seen its day, too. You might find one Snooker table in one of the old-time rooms, but in the average modern room most people won't know what you're talking about if you ask to play Snooker.

In Snooker, the shooter must pocket one of the red balls before he can select a colored number-ball. If a player doesn't pocket a red, he can't shoot at a numbered ball. When a player is in a position where he can't shoot in a straight line at a ball he is on, because other balls are in the way, the player is said to be "snookered." In the olden days the term "snookered" held the same meaning as the modern term "hustled." Many a time I've heard a loser wail, "I've been snookered." Today the guy would say, "I've been hustled."

All things being equal, I suggest that the beginner player stay away from Snooker. The balls are smaller and there are more of them, and the game will only get you "off" your pocket billiards game. Anyway, it's an English game. The British have always excelled at it and the best Snooker player alive today is Joe Davis, of London, the undefeated World Champion. Snooker is big in Canada, too. No American has ever been in the top pro class in Snooker simply because the game isn't played very much in this country.

I've heard lots of stories about Americans visiting Canada and getting taken in a little Snooker action. But only one time I heard of a Canadian coming to this country and getting cleaned. I didn't see it, but they talk about this Canadian kid from Toronto going to Broadway and getting into some action at the 7-11, a walk-up joint in the heart of Times Square. I understand the kids up there cleaned the Canadian, but the gimmick was the table. They've got an old 6-by-12 Snooker table up there with pockets the size of an eye dropper, and the New York kids had an overcoat (one size better) on the Canadian. They "knew" the table. They took him so bad they had to pass a collection to raise the kid's bus fare to the border.

The game of 14.1 Continuous pocket billiards, although I think it's on the way out in popularity, is a contest where they separate the men from the boys. The only other game that I think requires more skill to play is my favorite game, One Pocket, which I will discuss in the following chapter.

The basic difference between the two games—14.1 and One Pocket— is that in 14.1 the object is to pocket balls, whereas in One Pocket the situation might dictate preventing your opponent from pocketing a ball. So you play safety, that is, you place the balls in a position so that the opponent doesn't have a shot at his pocket. This is the very same principle involved in the safety shot in 14.1: don't leave the other fellow anything to shoot at.

The traditional game of 14.1 requires great skill, a sense of generalship, a complete command of position play and a thorough knowledge of billiards.

The most challenging aspect of 14.1 is to score a high run, say, 75, without making an error. What makes such a run not only a challenge but actually difficult is the very nature of the game. The name 14.1 Continuous is derived from the game's object: pocketing 14 balls and leaving the 15th ball on the table for a run on the next rack of 14 balls. This type of game, naturally, requires a thorough and complete knowledge of cue ball control and position play, the effect of English, the advantage of using the rails (especially for safety play), the value of the Stop Ball, a good foundation in combination and kiss shots (sometimes a combination or a kiss is the only answer to continuing a good run when you're in trouble on the table) and, of course, the ability to open the rack, ever so slightly, to assure yourself of a shot after you've pocketed the called ball on the break.

The game of 14.1 was never my game, and I think one reason for this is that the bank shot is seldom used in 14.1. That's because bank shots are never regarded as easy. Ask any of the top players and they'll tell you the same thing. You could watch a zillion 14.1 championship matches and never see a bank shot.

There was a time when bank pool was my strong suit. I won zillions playing banks because I had a tremendous foundation in Three Cushions. Banks is a beautiful game because it requires a great understanding of angles, and if you understand the angles you can run off banks till you get tired. I used to play the game from morning till night back in the olden days.

"I DON'T WANT TO HEAR NO STORIES"

I remember one time I was playing a fellow by the name of Louie Russo in a little town outside of Perth Amboy, New Jersey. Louie Russo was from Port Reading, N.J. He's dead now, died in his 20s of leukemia. It was a tragedy because he would have been a great player had he lived. This had to be 20 years ago because I remember I weighed in around 280, heaviest I've ever been in my life. In those days I gained weight every time I took a breath.

Well, Louie and I are playing bank pool for about two jillion and I'm moving around the table like a floorwalker. And every time I move, the floor creaks, like on that old radio show, "Inner Sanctum," you know, when the guy said, "Goodnight, Raymond," and everything creaked like a haunted house. So I'm moving around and the floor is making this creaky noise and Louie Russo is shooting out the lights. He's missing nothing.

Finally, Louie Russo misses, needing one ball. He's in the one hole, which is what they call it when a fellow needs one ball to win. In my day I left a lot of top players stone cold dead in the one hole. So Louie Russo's in the one hole and I need six to win it all. Now I'm not missing a thing and now I've run five and I need one more to win it.

So I walk around the table to study the shot and I see I can't miss the last bank in the side pocket. I couldn't have missed it in a hundred years. So I called the ball on a bank in the side and as I came into contact with the ball I said "One ball, cross side." And at that very moment, the floor caved in and down I went into the basement, like somebody sprung a trap door. Down I went, just like somebody in a parachute.

But as I was going down, I followed the ball with my eyes and just as I dropped past eye level with the table I saw the ball drop in the cross side pocket. There were hundreds of people in the room and they all rushed over to this big hole in the floor and yelled down, "Fatty, Fatty, you all right?" I looked up and said, "Yeah, I'm all right, but when I come up out of this basement, I don't want to hear no stories about that one ball. I saw it go in and I heard it drop."

To sum up the popularity of the games today, I'd have to say that Eight Ball and Nine Ball are the most played games on earth today, straight pool (14.1) is the least played and One Pocket is the most difficult.

That's the way it is.

CHAPTER 26

One Pocket

The game of One Pocket is the most difficult of all games played on a pockets table because it combines all of the intricacies of both billiards and pocket billiards. It is played properly only by experts. Next to One Pocket, the so-called championship game of 14.1 Continuous Pocket Billiards is an amateur's game.

The object of One Pocket, sometimes called A Pocket Apiece, is, as the name of the game implies, to sink eight balls in one pocket. This means that One Pocket is automatically six times tougher to master than any other form of pocket billiards. That's just plain common sense.

One of the most important requirements for One Pocket is the ability to control the cue ball. Cue ball control is necessary in all forms of billiards, but in One Pocket you have to control the cue ball to a point where you can stop it on a dime. Sometimes a hair's width can be the difference between surrendering your turn at the table by playing a safe or running out the game. That's how important cue ball control is in One Pocket. But that's only one reason why it's such a difficult game to master.

To strike a contrast on this very important point, let's say you get out of line in 14.1 Continuous pocket billiards. You still have an out, in fact, five outs, because you can look for a shot in one of the other five pockets. If you happen to get out of line in One Pocket, then you can really end up out of pocket because you're deader than a dinosaur, which is about as dead as you can get. The importance of cue ball control will hit home time and time again when playing One Pocket.

The ability to pull off kiss shots and combination shots are two other *musts* for the ambitious One Pocket player. More often than not, you will find yourself facing the seemingly impossible task of pocketing a ball from a cluster of object balls grouped so closely together that they appear they've just been racked. In this kind of situation (and it turns up time and time again), the ability to size up the way the balls are lying and come up with a kiss or combination shot can start you off on a run to win the match. Properly executed, a kiss or combination shot in a given situation can open the cluster of balls just enough to launch a run. Take several long looks for combination and kiss shots. This is one of the keys to mastering One Pocket.

Still another important requirement, possibly the most important of all, is the ability to execute the bank shot. Many, many times you will find yourself hemmed in with no way out except by banking a ball off a cushion or even two or more cushions. This is the reason why good three cushion and bank pool players have very little trouble adapting to One Pocket. The late Harold Worst, of Grand Rapids, Michigan, in my opinion the best all-around pool player in the world at the time of his death in the summer of 1965, at age 37, was the World Three Cushion Champion in the early 50s but when his best game died, he had to adapt to pocket billiards. Worst not only made a successful switch, but he whacked out the top One Pocket and straight pool players all over the country.

Worst won the overall title in both the $30,000 Stardust Open in Las Vegas and the Jansco Brothers' $20,000 All-Around Masters Tournament in Johnston City, Illinois, in 1965, and he came out of many a tight spot in both One Pocket and straight pool with remarkable executions of the bank shot. What made Worst's achievements so remarkable was that he only entered two tournaments, yet he won both of them. He won out over a star-studded field, too. One of his playoff victims in Las Vegas happened to be Irving Crane, who is not only a three-time former world pocket billiards champion but one of the all-time greats of straight pool.

If you can pull off the bank shot, you'll have a tremendous advantage in One Pocket. The one big reason why I was such a good One Pocket player was because I could bank balls almost at will. This was because I had mastered the art of banking years earlier as a Three Cushions player long before I ever heard of One Pocket.

Of course, the stroke is another essential in One Pocket, especially an understanding of the proper speed of the stroke in various situations. The speed of stroke is one of the most crucial aspects of One Pocket. Nine out of ten times, a soft, delicate, precise stroke will do the job, particularly when you want to keep the cue ball in relatively the same area for position on a following shot. Yet, there are situations that will call for a real hard stroke to get you out of a hole. The secret is knowing when to turn on the speed and when to turn it off. This is something you will learn and develop with experience.

So far I have given a rundown of the basic essentials a player must possess to master One Pocket. But the real secret to the game is understanding the strategy.

THE NAME OF THE GAME IS DEFENSE

The single most important aspect of strategy is knowing when to pocket a ball and when not to pocket a ball. Sometimes it might be the smart thing to pocket a ball and yet sometimes it might be even smarter *not* to pocket a ball. There might be a situation where you'll have a shot dead on the pocket but no follow-up shot. If you pocket the easy shot and then find yourself without a second shot you just might give your opponent the position he's looking for to run out the match. In a situation such as this, usually the best thing to do is play a safety, so as not to give your opponent a shot. This is the key to the strategy of One Pocket.

Then too, you might find yourself in a spot where your opponent will have a real easy shot if he gets to the table. Say, for example, there's a ball almost on the lip of his pocket. In such a situation, the smart thing to do is knock that ball away from his pocket and to do this you must be able to make that cue ball (and the object ball, too) almost walk a tightrope. You not only have to knock the object ball away from his pocket, but you have to master the cue ball's movement in order to bring it off a cushion for a safety.

So as you can readily see, the defensive aspects of One Pocket are unlimited. This is what makes it such a difficult game to master. It's natural for a pockets player to instinctively strive to pocket balls, but in One Pocket, more often than not, a decision not to pocket a ball is often the wisest. This, of course, is the point on which the 14.1 players and the traditionalists of straight pool harp when they criticize One Pocket by calling it "the hustler's game." Their contention is that One Pocket is not a game of pocketing balls, but a game of dodging and finessing, which is ridiculous beyond compare. The way I see it, it's just as much a challenge to tie up your opponent by not letting him have a shot as it is to overpower him with a very high run.

The reason why most straight pool players put the rap on One Pocket is because very, very few of them have the all-around ability to play the game of One Pocket the way it should be played.

Actually, the defensive principles of One Pocket are almost identical to the safety principles of 14.1 Continuous pocket billiards. When a straight pool player doesn't have a shot, he resorts to safety play in order to tie up his opponent by not giving him a shot. It's the very same thing in One

Pocket, but since each player has only one pocket in which to sink his object balls and since a total of only eight balls wins the match, the permissible margin of error is almost nil. That's exactly why defense is such an intricate part of One Pocket. You can make a mistake or two in a 150-point game of straight pool and still manage to win the match. But in One Pocket, one mistake is frequently disastrous.

To drive home my point, let's draw a parallel with football. When the ball is at, say, midfield, the defense has a lot of weak spots. For example, it is more vulnerable to passes for the simple reason that half the playing field is a sort of no-man's-land. The defense is also more vulnerable to ground plays because the secondary defenders must be on the alert for passes.

Now let's move the ball down inside, say, the ten-yard line. At this spot, the defense is actually in a stronger position simply because there is not as much ground to cover. True, the pass is still a potent weapon, even on the ten-yard line, and a good ball-carrier with lots of power can be just as effective as he would be at midfield. But on the ten-yard line the passer and receiver don't have the area in which to spread out to execute pass patterns and the ground yards come a lot tougher.

The reason for this is because the perimeter has been narrowed and the defense is able to play a lot tighter.

It's the exact same thing in One Pocket. The pocketing of balls is tougher because you have only one pocket. The perimeter is narrowed down to one-sixth of the boundary covered in straight pool. The straight pool player is like the quarterback at midfield. He can do almost anything he wants. But when he gets down to the ten-yard line he has to be pretty choosy about what plays he calls. Of course, the defense has to play it real tight in the shadows of its goal, which is the way the One Pocket player must approach the defensive aspects of the game of One Pocket. He is literally on the defense at all times and almost any slip could be disastrous.

With the defensive aspects of One Pocket in mind, the manner in which the rack is broken is very important. Say you're shooting at the rack from the left side of the table. According to the rules of One Pocket, this automatically means you must pocket all of your balls in the right corner pocket at the other end of the table. So it's only common sense to realize that the smart thing to do is to drive the balls in the direction of your pocket while moving the cue ball to the left, or near your opponent's pocket. To do this use Right English on the cue ball and aim for a light hit on the first ball at the point of the rack and a pretty good hit on the second ball on the left side. This kind of hit will send the balls to the right. Applying Right English to the cue ball and then hitting it into the rack will throw the ball to the left and onto the cushion on the left side of the table. (Note: If you open the rack from the right side of the table, use Left English.)

If you're able to pull off this type of opening shot, you might sink a ball on the break. If so, with all of the balls over to the right nearer your pocket, you will be in a good position to pocket additional balls, enough, perhaps, to run out the match. If you don't make a ball on the break, you're still in a good position because your opponent will face the task of playing the cue ball from his side of the table with the object balls on your side. If you break the rack just right, your opponent is automatically in trouble.

But let me give you a word of warning. Don't smack into the rack like you're setting off a charge of dynamite. You might open the rack a little too wide and send some of the object balls over to the left side of the table. Then you're the one in trouble because you've given an advantage to your opponent by putting object balls in a good position for him. The speed of stroke on the break shot determines the spread of the object balls. This is something you must develop and this can only be done by practicing the break shot. The more you try it, the more obvious the logic becomes.

Once the rack is opened and you're at the table, the important thing is to keep everything in the direction of your pocket and, conversely, away from your opponent's pocket. And, more important, maintain complete control of the cue ball to insure proper position for your following shots. This may sound simple in print but it's very, very difficult, especially for beginners. But lots and lots of practice will do wonders. Try it.

APPROACH THE GAME WITH CAUTION

Now let's put the shoe on the other foot. Say your opponent opens the rack and leaves you on the rail with the object balls on his side of the table. The smart thing to do in a spot like this is to look for a bank shot that you can juice off the rail and into your pocket. If you can pull a bank shot off with proper control of the cue ball, you can get in position behind several object balls and start a run of your own. This is just one example of the advantages of the bank shot in One Pocket. As your game steps up and improves, you will be able to spot bank shots more quickly and, as your stroke and ability to impart English with a degree of finesse develops, you might be brave enough to attempt bank shots off more than one cushion. But another word of warning. Be very careful with bank shots and extreme use of English until your game has reached the point where you have control of the cue ball (and the object ball, too) because if you fritz up the difficult shots, you just might open the door for your opponent to shoot out the lights.

Remember, in One Pocket the name of the game is defense. The best way for beginners to approach One Pocket is with caution. Approach it like a Republican: conservatively. Only the masters can be daring in One Pocket, but even the masters play it close to the vest, all things being equal.

Inasmuch as none of the official rule books of billiards and pocket billiards include the rules of One Pocket, a section of this text includes the rules for the game, the toughest of all forms of pocket billiards to master.

OFFICIAL ONE POCKET RULES

The game may be played on a rectangular table twice as long as it is wide. The table may be 4-by-8 feet, 4½-by-9 feet or 5-by-10 feet. (Note: Professor Minnesota Fats says One Pocket is more difficult to play on smaller tables.)

One Pocket is played with 15 object balls, numbered from 1 to 15, and a white cue ball. Although One Pocket is usually played individual against individual, it is possible for teams of two or more to compete. (Note: Professor Minnesota Fats does not recommend team play, however. He contends One Pocket is primarily a game for individuals and not teams.)

OBJECT OF THE GAME

To put eight balls into the one pocket at the foot of the table designated as the player's pocket. The choice of pockets is usually left to the winner of the break. Alternate breaks can determine a change in pockets or choice of remaining the same.

HOW TO PLAY

1. Balls are racked at the foot spot. There is no order in which the balls are racked, nor is the numerical value of the object balls a consideration.

2. Conventional methods are used to choose the player who breaks. Lagging or flipping a coin can determine the player who is first.

3. There are two advantages to being first in this game. A ball may be scored on the break by going into the pocket designated as the player's. The first player can choose his pocket, leaving the other to his opponent.

4. On the break the object ball or cue ball must touch a rail for a safety, unless a ball is pocketed on the break.

5. A ball which falls into the player's pocket or his opponent's pocket is a score. The score is made no matter which player is responsible for putting the ball into the pocket.

6. There is no order by which the balls are to be dropped into the pocket. Any ball in a player's pocket is a score, providing there is no scratch.

7. Three consecutive scratches by a player forfeits the game to his opponent.

8. First player to pocket eight balls in his designated pocket is the winner.

9. Safety play is suggested for the player without a shot to score a ball in his pocket. The general rule should be: if you can't pocket a ball, try to prevent your opponent from scoring when he gets to the table.

10. After each ball is pocketed in the player's pocket, the player continues to shoot.

11. If player and opponent need only one ball to win, and player accidentally drops his winning ball and the opponent's winning ball on the same shot, the player or shooter making his game ball is the winner.

12. If player scores a ball in opponent's pocket in error and continues to score in opponent's pocket, opponent must call player's attention to the error and player loses turn at table. However, the balls pocketed are credited to the opponent.

13. If all eight balls are scored in error in opponent's pocket, player pocketing the balls is the winner. Opponent must call attention to the error before the winning ball is scored improperly in order to continue the game.